ARTHUR SCHWARTZ'S
Jewish Home Cooking

ARTHUR SCHWARTZ'S
Jewish Home Cooking

Yiddish Recipes Revisited

Photography by Ben Fink

TEN SPEED PRESS
Berkeley | Toronto

*For my sister, Andrea, and her children,
Rachel and Brian. A little legacy.*

Ten Speed Press
PO Box 7123
Berkeley, California 94707
www.tenspeed.com

Distributed in Australia by Simon and Schuster Australia, in Canada by
Ten Speed Press Canada, in New Zealand by Southern Publishers Group,
in South Africa by Real Books, and in the United Kingdom and Europe
by Publishers Group UK.

Jacket design by Nancy Austin and Chloe Rawlins
Interior design by Chloe Rawlins
Food styling by Megan Fawn Schlow
Photograph page vi used by permission of New York Public Library.
Photograph page xii © Time-Life Pictures/Getty Images.

Library of Congress Cataloging-in-Publication Data on file with the publisher.

Printed in China
2 3 4 5 6 7 8 9 10 — 12 11 10 09 08

CONTENTS

❧ Introduction ❧

On Ariel Sharon's 78th birthday ... those closest to him joined his two sons around the bedside where he lies, silent and comatose, in a hospital on a hill high above Jerusalem. They chatted and ate cake, made by a friend of his late wife, Lily, using her recipe.

—Steven Erlanger, *New York Times*, March 25, 2006

Food can connect us to our past. In fact, food is often our very last and only connection to our pasts, enduring long after the old language has been forgotten and other traditions have died. There's many a Jew, for instance, who identifies as a Jew mainly through his or her love of pastrami, or potted brisket, or chicken soup with matzo balls.

Still, if a kosher martian landed in New York City today and observed what Jews were actually eating, he would think pizza is the most Jewish food on earth. And although he would have trouble finding a good piece of gefilte fish, he could get very good kosher sushi. Then, to confuse matters more, he'd discover that Jewish people eat a lot of falafel and hummus, even though these are Arab foods. He'd even find that "modern Orthodox" Jews in Brooklyn dote on *penne alla vodka* (Italian-style macaroni with spicy vodka-tomato-cream sauce), and that in the Williamsburg section of Brooklyn, the Satmar Hasidim, who pride themselves on their isolation from the culture at large, eat salade niçoise.

Listen, you can still get a great pastrami sandwich in New York City. And, if you look hard, you can get an excellent and restorative bowl of chicken soup with matzo balls. But by and large the foods that everyone thinks of as Jewish—the foods that connect us to our past—have almost disappeared from public eating places. There was a time when New York was so Jewish that mainstream restaurant menus listed, among their appetizers, gefilte fish next to shrimp cocktail. Boiled flanken followed broiled ham steak among the main courses. Today, the

Kosher chicken store on Manhattan's Lower East Side, about 1900

traditional foods of Eastern European Jews are served mainly in the homes of the Orthodox. They appear on the tables of Reform and Conservative Jews solely on the major Jewish holidays of Passover, Rosh Hashanah, Yom Kippur, and, in the case of latkes, on Chanukah. Then, unfortunately, to maintain traditions and contact with our past, every dish the family associates with grandma and grandpa is put on the table. Is it any wonder everyone goes home groaning and blaming the heavy Jewish food?

Laden with animal fats and, admittedly, often poorly cooked by women who thought eating a juicy, medium-rare steak was sinful, against the laws of kashruth, the dishes of Eastern Europe as interpreted by immigrant home cooks could certainly cause indigestion. The Jewish comic Buddy Hackett used to tell the story of his Army experience: suddenly, as soon as he started eating military food, as bad as that can be, the burning in his chest stopped. The fire was out. He had lived to age eighteen with constant heartburn. He thought he was dying.

Until the flight of middle-class Jews from the city to the suburbs in the 1950s and 1960s, New York City was a very Jewish town. One in four New Yorkers identified as Jewish. Most of them had Central and Eastern European roots. They were Ashkenazim. Yiddish was their mother tongue, and they ate the foods of Poland, Russia, Lithuania, Latvia, Germany, Austria, Hungary, and Romania.

The historic tendency is for Jews to assimilate culturally, including gastronomically. That's why Polish Jews eat the same pierogi as Polish Catholics, why Russian Jews love buckwheat groats (kasha) as much as their Russian Orthodox neighbors, and why Italian Jews imitate prosciutto by curing goose thighs. Today, in New York City as elsewhere in the country, pizza and sushi are popular mainstream foods, so Jews eat kosher versions of them. Jewish food is, really, any food that follows the kosher dietary laws.

One problem with old-time Eastern European Jewish food, Ashkenazic food—let's call it Yiddish cooking, as it is the food of the people who spoke and speak Yiddish—is that the recipes are dated. They come from a time when few people related what they ate to their health and well-being. They come from a time before elliptical machines and treadmills. However, Yiddish cooking can be prepared in a more healthful manner, and more to today's tastes, than the way great-grandma cooked it, while still retaining its old-time flavor, its *tam*, as one calls a soulful taste in Yiddish. This book tells you how. It also gives the recipes with precise measurements, as cooks expect these days. Great-Grandma called her measuring *shiterein*, meaning a handful of this, a glassful of that, a pinch of the other. A cup of something meant a Yartzeit-glassful, the amount held by the glass left behind after the burning of a memorial candle on the anniversary of a death. Frances Blum remembers her mother getting nervous when she heard a rumor that Yartzeit glasses might be discontinued. What would she measure with? She sent Frances to the supermarket to buy all she could. Indeed, Yartzeit candles and their glasses are now half the size they were only ten years ago.

The traditional food of the Ashkenazim has a good place at the contemporary table—with a lessening of the schmaltz here, a tweak there: a little makeover never hurt anyone. With a green vegetable or two alongside the braised brisket or the sweet-and-sour flanken or the potted meatballs, plus a piece of potato kugel, it all of a sudden looks pretty modern, a contemporary meal. If short ribs can be trendy at fancy restaurants, flanken, the same meat cut in the opposite direction, is just as stylish at home.

Then there are the almost-forgotten dishes, classics that suit contemporary taste as much as they did the palates of our great-grandparents: the various types of vegetarian "chopped liver" are also called "poor man's caviar." Fancy pastry chefs stew dried fruits. They just don't call it "compote," as your *bubbe* did. Cakes with oil as shortening are considered healthful today. In my grandmother's time, they were merely pareve, cakes that could be served after a meat meal because they didn't contain butter or milk. Beef cheeks? There's a TV chef who stuffs them into ravioli and has made them into a trendy sensation. He's got nothing on a Lubavitcher Hasidic homemaker in Brooklyn. She'd laugh. She's been braising beef cheeks with beans and potatoes all her life. She calls it cholent, the ages-old Sabbath casserole. The list of old Yiddish dishes that look modern again could go on and on.

ແລ ແລ ແລ

Until recently, when anyone in the U.S. spoke of Jewish food, they meant Ashkenazic food, as most Jewish-Americans were of Ashkenazic heritage. And when "out-of-towners," which is what New Yorkers call tourists from anywhere, spoke of New York City food, they spoke mainly of Yiddish Jewish food.

In the past five decades, however, the population shift from New York City to the suburbs has been monumental. From nearly two million Jews in the 1950s, there are less than a million in the five boroughs now—about 12 percent of the city's population. Still, New York City metro, which encompasses Nassau and Suffolk counties on Long Island to the east of the city; New York State's West-chester, Rockland, and Orange counties to the north; and northern and central New Jersey to the west and south, has 1.97 million Jews, the largest concentration of Jews outside of Israel.

Interestingly, as the number of Reform and Conservative Jews across the country is decreasing because of intermarriage and other sociocultural phenomena, the Orthodox community, meaning the kosher and Sabbath observant, is increasing. Brooklyn is home to twenty Hasidic groups, and is the world head-quarters of three—Chabad Lubavitch, Bobover, and Satmar. They have many children and, along with other ultra-Orthodox communities and the so-called modern Orthodox, those highly observant but not Hasidic, have a rate of inter-marriage estimated at less than 1 percent.

Even given the increased rate of assimilation in recent years, one can still say that the influence of Jews on New York City's food culture cannot be over-estimated. To start, some of the most quintessential New York City foods are of Central and Eastern European Jewish origin: bagels, pastrami on rye, corned beef, pickles, cheesecake, matzo balls, knishes, and egg cream. The hot dog is not a Jewish concept. It's German. But one can argue that it was Eastern European Jewish entrepreneurs who made it the food of the people. With a nod to this kosher heritage, a real New York hot dog is all beef and well spiced.

Ironically, the first Jews in New York were Sephardim of Spanish origin. When the Jews were expelled from the Iberian Peninsula by the Spanish Inquisition in 1492, they left for many different, more welcoming places. One of these was Holland, including its outposts like Recife in Brazil. The group of twenty-three Spanish-Portuguese Jews that arrived in New Amsterdam in 1654 was from Brazil. The Dutch were, and still are, a relatively tolerant people, and like the Jews, were of a mercantile mind. But Brazil's new Portuguese colonists brought the Inquisition with them, so the Jews of Recife sailed for New Amsterdam, again seeking refuge among the tolerant Dutch.

Peter Stuyvesant, the governor of New Amsterdam, refused to accept them. He thought the introduction of Jews would be unsettling to his largely Protestant town, which was owned, in effect, by the Dutch West India Company. However, the company's board back home included a Jew and it differed with Stuyvesant. The board ordered him to accept the Jews of Recife. Stuyvesant notwithstanding, New Amsterdam was already religiously and racially diverse. In 1638, when the first census was taken, there were 440 residents and they spoke eighteen different languages, setting the stage for New York's continuing diversity.

Throughout the next two centuries, Jews continued to come to New York City. In the eighteenth century, when New York was one of England's thirteen colonies, Polish and Russian Jews arrived from England, where they had emigrated to nearly a century earlier. But the first major wave of Jewish immigration was not until the 1840s, when the Germans arrived, both Christians and Jews.

During the last quarter of the nineteenth century and until 1924, when the immigration laws were changed, two million Jews emigrated to America, mostly from Eastern Europe. They mainly spoke Yiddish. Most of them remained in New York, the main port of entry, if only temporarily, changing the city's culture forever. Unlike the Italians, for example, who intended to earn money in America and then return home, the Eastern European Jews came to America to stay. They were not escaping mere poverty, but also persecution. America was to be their new permanent home, their country. Consequently, they learned English quickly, encouraged their children to become educated Americans, and immediately set up institutions that would foster their assimilation and their attainment of the American Dream. By 1910, there were about one million Jews in New York. By 1957, the Jewish population had risen to more than two million.

Not least of the Jewish influences on New York's food culture is the peculiar Jewish openness and taste for the exotic. For instance, kosher Jews adopted sushi as soon as they realized it could be made without shellfish, and there was nothing intrinsically unkosher about the other ingredients. Peculiar because, after all, after generations in small villages in Russia, Poland, Romania, and other nearby countries, the most exotic food the Jews might have eaten was the occasional orange. Perhaps we allowed ourselves to be adventurous because there was always the thought that we'd have to move along once again.

ℭℒℴ ℭℒℴ ℭℒℴ

Sabbath Eve dinner in New York City, 1938

In Judaism, food is sacred. The purpose of eating and drinking is to give courage and strength to better serve G-d by using this energy to study, pray, and practice the teachings and lessons of the Torah.

Eating at the Sabbath table is said to be akin to partaking of the sacrificial lamb at the ancient Temple in Jerusalem. Therefore, there is symbolism, ritual, and many regulations built around its production, its purchase, its preparation, and its consumption. That New York is a food-obsessed city is in part due to the Jewish obsession with food, and in eating well, which is a sign that you are blessed.

In New York, kosher Jewish foodways continued for a time, but not for long. At first, "Jews lived primarily where they could buy Jewish food," says Hasia R. Diner in *Hungering for America*, which is one good reason that so many stayed in New York, and not many became pioneer farmers in Iowa. Notably, however, there were Jewish farmers in the rural areas just north of the city.

Jews did become traveling peddlers, though. These men either carried kosher food with them or abandoned kashruth as they gave up their wagons to found America's department stores in places with no sources of kosher food. Even in urban areas it was often difficult, if not impossible, to obtain kosher meats and poultry. New York City, however, had such a concentration of Jews that kosher butchers, fish markets, bakeries, and groceries soon supported the community. If you spoke only Yiddish when you arrived, opening a store in the Jewish enclave was a good way to earn a living.

In 1899, a survey of the Lower East Side counted 631 Jewish food purveyors. Among them were 140 groceries, 131 butchers, 36 bakeries, 14 butter-and-egg stores, 62 candy stores, 21 produce stands, and 10 delicatessens. In 1910, there were 60 delicatessens. During the early years of the century, the streets of Lower Manhattan, as well as Brownsville and East New York in Brooklyn, became congested with peddlers and carts. Even as late as the 1960s, Orchard and Essex Streets in Manhattan boasted both stores and street carts bursting with Jewish foods. Until the late 1950s, it was the same in the Jewish commercial centers of Blake and Belmont Avenues in Brooklyn. These streets were veritable food festivals. The few remnants of this world include The Pickle Guys on Essex Street, an offshoot of the original Guss's Pickles, now in Cedarhurst, Long Island; Gertel's Bakery, only recently moved from Hester Street to a wholesale plant in Brooklyn; Economy Candy on Rivington Street; Streit's matzo factory on Rivington Street; Yonah Schimmel's knishes on Houston Street; Katz's Delicatessen on the corner of Ludlow and East Houston Streets; Russ & Daughters appetizing store on the next block of Houston, between Orchard and Allen Streets; and Kossar's Bialys on Grand Street.

As Katz's, founded in 1888, once exemplified (it hasn't been kosher for years), Jews could also eat away from home and keep their dietary laws. In 1903, the Yiddish word *oyesessen* (eating out) first appeared in the *Forverts, The Jewish Daily Forward*, the most important Yiddish-language newspaper—then and now. According to Diner, "The newspaper considered the growing interest in eating outside the home a positive step in immigrants' education and part of a larger process of social evolution."

But eating out could hardly have been a new concept for Jews in New York. By the time that Russians, Poles, and Romanians began arriving at the end of the nineteenth century, German and Austrian Jews had already established themselves in New York. Many of them had reached the pinnacles of economic success. They had their own coffee houses and delicatessens. Indeed, Diner credits Berlin-born Isaac Gellis, a Jewish sausage manufacturer on Essex Street, for popularizing the typical German-Jewish delicatessen meats. Already in 1872, she says, he was producing "mountains of kosher sausages, frankfurters and other cold cuts" that, along with the pastrami of Eastern Europe (namely Romania), became the hallmarks of the New York Jewish delicatessen.

As a young man, sometime in the early 1900s, the legendary Jewish entertainer Eddie Cantor was for a brief time a delivery boy for Isaac Gellis's company. Cantor's family came from Russia, where frankfurters did not exist, so, Cantor remarked with glee in his autobiography, he became "the world's supreme delicatessen eater, absorbing more salami, pastrami, bologna, and frankfurters in that short span than most families do in a lifetime."

Although Eastern European Jews "had not eaten these foods before migration, as American Jews they learned to think of them as traditional," says Diner. This would explain the popular belief among New York Jews that the first Jewish delicatessens were opened by and for immigrant men who came to America without women (much like the Chinese did a half century before them), calling for their wives and young children only after they had found work and a place to live. But this would not fit the pattern of German Jewish immigration. It fits only the later Eastern European immigration, which came after Jewish delicatessens already existed. What is true is that the delicatessen became a home-away-from-home for many new immigrant men. They were a simple, nonintimidating kind of restaurant that provided familiar foods, as well as the kosher but unfamiliar foods of Jews from other European Jewish communities.

When Jews started doing business away from the immigrant ghettos, they faced the enticement and convenience of non-Jewish food stores and restaurants. Upwardly mobile Jews found it difficult to keep the kosher laws. This, as well as a whole spectrum of food-related problems, became a subject of much contention in the Jewish community. It wasn't just the divisive question of whether to keep kosher or not, but also the politics of supervision, of regulating food production, and of the observance of Sabbath by some stores and not others. The end result was that most New York Jews gradually started abandoning their religious foodways. I saw how this happened in my own family.

My maternal grandmother was the American-born daughter of a Russian-born Orthodox rabbi. While her parents were alive, my grandmother kept a

Clockwise from upper left: pickles at The Pickle Guys on Essex Street in Manhattan; pastrami on rye at Katz's on Houston Street; a vat at The Pickle Guys; Avrumi Weiss with poppyseed cake at Weiss's Bakery in Brooklyn

kosher house for their sake so they could eat in her home, and out of respect. Out of habit, not conviction, she continued to follow the kosher laws for several years after they died, until, as she told the tale, an illness prevented her from getting out of bed and a Christian neighbor cooked for her family. Not knowing about such things as keeping separate pots and dishes for dairy and meat, the neighbor destroyed the kosher order of my grandmother's kitchen. From then on, Mamma (as we called my grandmother) wasn't so strict. In the beginning, her transgressions were relatively minor. Besides having the pots and dishes mixed, she would serve ice cream or a pastry made with butter for dessert after a meat meal, which the kosher laws forbid. But she would never put butter on the table for a meat meal, or pour milk for the children at a meat meal. Milk drunk with meat was repugnant to her aesthetically. In her final years, it was like she had never been kosher. She would cook shrimp and lobster, although she never cooked pork. She only ate that outside the house, mainly in Chinese restaurants or at mainstream restaurants that served liver with forbidden bacon. I once asked her why she never cooked bacon or ham, but would broil lobster tails. "I can eat bacon in your house," she answered.

In America, the individual Jew's acceptance of nonkosher foods and foodways came to symbolize—even measure—his climb up the socioeconomic ladder, the distance he had traveled on the road to assimilation, and his attainment of the American Dream. This is one of several reasons that New York's Jews are famously in love with Chinese food (see page 134).

At the same time that Jews were moving away from their dietary laws, mainstream America started catering to them. In New York, in 1936, the Maxwell House coffee company courted Jewish customers by publishing a Passover Haggadah, the book that outlines the order of the seder and is read at the ritual meal of the holiday. More than 20 million were distributed free. A big move on a national level was Procter and Gamble's introduction of Crisco in 1911. The fat was neither dairy nor meat and so foods made with it, particularly baked goods, could be pareve, a word that means suitable for meals of either kind. Crisco allowed Jews to eat some all-American dishes with their traditional foods. In 1930, Crisco published a cookbook in both Yiddish and English.

After the delicatessens, Jews opened full-service restaurants to feed each other. By the 1920s, the area between Delancey and Houston Streets was filled with Jewish eateries that catered to the better-off area residents, but even more to the

Jews who had moved out, mainly to the Bronx and Brooklyn, but came back to eat their soul food. The era of the "Romanian steakhouse" began (see page 120). The flip side of the steakhouses were restaurants that served only dairy and vegetarian dishes—from blintzes to fish entrees—among them the fairly recently demised Ratner's and Garden Cafeteria and the long-gone Rappaport's.

Then, as their clientele continued to move uptown and to the boroughs, and eventually to the suburbs, mingling with the city's non-Jewish citizens (mainly the Italians and Irish), so did the restaurants. Now they were not necessarily kosher, although some were "kosher-style," a phrase that came to denote the service of traditional Jewish foods, still keeping the separation of dairy and meat, but not officially kosher. For instance, the meat and poultry might not be slaughtered in accordance with Jewish law.

Arnold Reuben opened a simple Jewish delicatessen in 1908, but by 1918 Reuben's was a full-scale restaurant on Madison Avenue, where it would eventually offer ham on its famous sandwiches. It was a Jewish delicatessen, but it wasn't.

Jack Kriendler and his cousin, Charlie Burns, two Lower East Side Jewish boys needing to pay for their college educations (which they never completed), opened their first speakeasy in Greenwich Village in 1920. It eventually became known as "21," after their final address on West 52nd Street. At first, Kriendler's mother, by all accounts a traditional Jewish woman, actually distilled the booze for their speakeasy in her tenement kitchen, but her son apparently never even thought of serving kosher food. In fact, "21" became famous as a bastion of fine dining during the rough years of Prohibition, which turned out to be good for drinking but bad for eating well.

By the 1940s and 1950s, mainstream menus such as those at Soloweys' across the street from Penn Station, and late-night hot spots like Leon and Eddie's (a former speakeasy), listed blintzes and chicken soup with matzo balls alongside such blatantly nonkosher food as grilled ham steak. These restaurants, although Jewish owned, and giving a culinary nod to their nouveau riche Jewish customers, were meant for and appealed to all New Yorkers. They offered newly assimilated Jews their first taste of ham or Lobster Newburg, and also provided non-Jews with their first taste of gefilte fish.

CHAPTER 1

⊰ Appetizers ⊱

An appetizer is called a *forshpeiz* in Yiddish. But a *forshpeiz* to an *alter kocker* (old-timer, in Yiddish) might be so copiously portioned that it could be a whole meal to a Gentile, or to a buff *boychik* of today.

After generations in poverty, Jews from the little villages of Eastern Europe, the shtetls, came to New York to live the American Dream. They viewed their ability to eat as much as they wanted as a sign of their affluence and of their particular zest for the good life in America. New York Jews would even make jokes about how little food Gentiles ate (except Italians), or how they didn't know how to eat.

> *How do you know who the WASPs are at a Chinese restaurant?*
> *They're the ones not sharing their food.*

After World War II, at Jewish wedding and bar mitzvah receptions in New York, guests would first encounter a smorgasbord of "appetizers," meaning a buffet with cold foods, hot foods in chafing dishes, and special food stations serving roasts carved to order and even crêpes made on the spot. Then came a five- to seven-course sit-down dinner. It's not much different now, except a sushi station has replaced the crêpes, and at bar or bat mitzvahs, pizza is a requirement for the guest of honor and friends.

Sometimes Jewish appetizers are actually main courses, only in slightly smaller portions. Stuffed Cabbage (page 118) goes either way, as does sweet-and-sour tongue, brown-sauced sweetbreads and mushrooms (page 36), and chicken-giblet fricassee with tiny meatballs (page 29). All of them are, in truth, more appropriate *after* something else than before, but so it goes at the Yiddish table.

Chopped liver

1

Arbes
Seasoned Chickpeas

Long before American Jews knew about hummus, the Arab chickpea puree that, ironically, has become one of the national dishes of Israel, chickpeas were a "Jewish" food, even among the Ashkenazim of Central and Eastern Europe. The legume is mentioned in the Bible (Daniel 1:12), and it is a symbol of regeneration, which is why chickpeas are served at a *sholom zachar*. That's a festive gathering held in some Jewish communities on the first Friday night after a boy is born. Friends and family toast the parents and child, and no matter whatever else is served, they nosh on *arbes* and salute life (*l'chaim*) with beer.

Chickpeas are also traditionally served at Purim, the holiday that commemorates the rescue of the Jews from genocide by the Persian Jewish queen, Esther. Queen Esther became a vegetarian so she could live at court and remain kosher, and not divulge that she was Jewish. Chickpeas were among the foods she ate, along with seeds and nuts, hence the custom of eating poppyseed-filled Hamantaschen (page 237) on Purim.

I remember *arbes* (in Polish Yiddish, *nahit* in Russian Yiddish) from Ratner's and Rappaport's, the most important dairy restaurants on the Lower East Side. A bowl of chickpeas bursting from their skins, salted and well peppered, was on the table when you sat down, like the pickle bowl at the deli. You ate them with your hands, like nuts.

At Purim and birth celebrations, chickpeas are often tossed or drizzled with honey instead of a savory seasoning. For variety beyond just salt and pepper, you can season *arbes* lightly with ground cumin or flakes of red Aleppo (Syrian or Turkish) pepper, which combines sweet and fiery flavors, or both.

Canned chickpeas, drained, rinsed, and dried with a paper towel, make excellent *arbes*. To cook dried chickpeas, first soak them in water—start with hot—for at least 8 hours, then boil them, uncovered, in fresh water for at least $1^1/_2$ hours, until they are very tender and their skins begin to burst. They may seem overcooked when the skins burst, but they will firm up again when cooled.

Chopped Eggs and Onions

The usual name for this egg salad is deceptive. Much of its appeal comes from the unmentioned ingredient, schmaltz. You must have good schmaltz to elevate what would otherwise be an ordinary egg salad. Even better, if you add some *griebenes* (chicken cracklings, see page 10) it becomes divine and very dangerous stuff that you won't be able to stop eating. As an appetizer, serve this dish as a spread with crackers. As a first course at the table, or for a light meal, pair it with cut up raw vegetables like sliced cucumbers and tomatoes (or cherry tomatoes), whole scallions, and red radishes. It is particularly good with black bread or pumpernickel, but challah or matzo is excellent, too. In fact, in some households, this salad is the first course of Shabbos dinner, served with the braided challah, over which a blessing has been made giving recognition to G-d for providing us with food.

Instead of onion, you can use minced scallions. Some cooks prefer to sauté the raw onion before adding it to the eggs. That's delicious, too, but another dish entirely. Speaking of another dish entirely, the salad is, of course, delicious with mayonnaise, too.

The texture of this salad is best when the eggs are chopped by hand with a large, sharp knife on a board, or in a wooden chopping bowl using a *hochtmesser*, a curve-bladed chopper, like an Italian mezzaluna. For egg salad, a pastry blender in a wooden bowl also works well because the eggs are soft.

Serves 2

4 hard-cooked eggs, peeled
1 very small onion, finely chopped
  (about ⅓ cup)

1 rounded tablespoon Schmaltz
  (page 9)
Salt and freshly ground black pepper

Place the whole eggs and chopped onion on a board or in a chopping bowl. Chop the eggs and onions together until the eggs are the desired consistency. If you have been using a chopping board, transfer the mixture to a bowl.

Add the schmaltz, and season with salt and freshly ground black pepper. With a fork, gently combine with the egg mixture, being careful not to mash the eggs too much.

Serve at room temperature. The salad can be refrigerated, tightly covered, for 1 day, but should be eaten at room temperature.

Chopped Herring Salad

Here's an example of the famous Litvak-Galitzianer gastronomic divide (see page 32): the Russ family, which owns Russ & Daughters, the landmark appetizing store, are proud Galitzianers, Jews who were originally from Galicia, a region in East Central Europe now divided between Poland and Ukraine. They make their chopped herring salad with the sole addition of tart green apple and nothing more. My maternal grandmother, whose parents (not she) hailed from a shtetl near Minsk, was a proud Litvak (a Jew of Lithuanian or Russian descent). She prepared her chopped herring with chopped hard-cooked egg as the only addition and nothing more.

Chopped herring was always among my grandmother's appetizers for her annual Chanukah party, as well as other festive occasions. Chopped herring, actually any herring, was considered the perfect accompaniment to schnapps, a word that covers all strong alcoholic spirits. In reality, however, to middle class New York Jews of those days, it meant only Scotch or rye whiskey, or maybe Canadian whisky, plus Cherry Heering for the ladies. Vodka hardly existed

then; bourbon was, at least to my grandfather Louis Sonkin, "country club whiskey," which meant for Gentiles only. And no one we knew drank martinis, based on gin as they always used to be, although herring and gin are a natural combination.

Chopped herring also appeared frequently on our Sunday breakfast table along with bagels, lox, cream cheese, and the other pickled and smoked fish from the appetizing store (see page 1). I still like to spread cold herring salad on a warm bagel, and this combo remains an option at most New York City bagel bakeries that make sandwiches and provide a schmear of this or that.

As a formal first course, serve a scoop of herring salad on a plate lined with lettuce and garnished with the usual raw vegetables—cucumber, radish, tomato, scallions. Pumpernickel and black bread are traditional and excellent accompaniments. Seeded rye and Corn Bread (page 205), even matzo or crackers, are great, too.

Makes about 2¹/₂ cups, enough for 6 to 8 as a snack with drinks

2 cups well-drained jarred herring fillets in "wine sauce" or snacks (smaller pieces of herring) in "wine sauce," including the pickled onion

3 or 4 hard-cooked eggs, peeled
Bread or crackers, as accompaniment

In the bowl of a food processor fitted with the metal blade, combine the herring with the bits of onion (from the jar) and the whole, hard-cooked eggs. (Use 3 eggs for a stronger herring taste, 4 eggs for a slightly milder flavor.) Pulse until the ingredients are finely chopped and hold together as a paste.

Chill well before serving with bread or crackers. The chopped herring should keep well in the refrigerator for at least several days.

Smothered Onions

 ———————————————————————————————————

It is written that the manna from heaven that sustained the Jews during their forty years of wandering in the desert could have any flavor one imagined it to have, except for onions and garlic. Does this have something to do with why onions and garlic play such an important role in all Jewish cuisines?

In any case, onions apparently grew well in the shtetls of cold-climate Poland and Russia. Grated, chopped, and sliced; raw or fried anywhere from lightly golden to a deep caramel brown; cooked in schmaltz, in butter, in peanut, corn, or canola oil, and, unfortunately (in the modern American kitchen), in margarine and solid white shortening, onions are an important ingredient in the Yiddish pantry.

You could say onions are a defining flavor, in the sense that some dishes rely so heavily on onions that they wouldn't taste Jewish without them.

Chopped liver immediately comes to mind. In fact, I'd say mock chopped liver, the vegetarian version, relies mainly on fried onions to resemble the real thing. And there's mushrooms and egg barley, kasha varnishkes, and knish and blintz fillings, as well as lox, eggs, and *onions*, to name a few more. Potato kugel and potato latkes would be insipid without onions.

At many of the old-time Jewish meat restaurants, you could order fried onions à la carte, a bowlful to strew wherever you pleased.

When I was boy, my mother always ordered her hamburgers and my father his steaks with smothered onions. Nowadays, if you ask for smothered onions the waiter will be bewildered. You could request fried onions, but caramelized is the fashionable name. It's all the same: they are onions that are wilted and cooked until golden, deeply browned, or even almost burnt.

Many of the recipes in this book start with this process. Sometimes you will want to make them specifically for a recipe, in which case it's good to, for example, fry the mushrooms in the same pan—don't clean it yet—used to cook the onions. The flavor the onions leave on the bottom of the pan should not be wasted. Somehow, incorporate it into your dish. In some cases, you can pour in a little liquid (deglazing, to a professional chef) and scrape up this glaze into the liquid used in the recipe.

To smother (fry) onions, first either chop or slice the onions according to the recipe instructions. Add enough schmaltz, butter, or peanut, corn, or canola oil to cover the bottom of a covered skillet or sauté pan large enough to comfortably hold the onions. (A 10-inch pan will usually hold up to 2 pounds of onions—about 6 cups—and will require about 3 tablespoons of fat.) Heat the fat over medium-high heat.

Add the onions and toss in the hot fat; cover the skillet, decrease the heat to medium, and let the onions sweat for 10 minutes, tossing them once after 5 or 6 minutes. Uncover the pan and stir the onions; they will have begun to brown.

Increase the heat to medium-high and continue to fry the onions, uncovered, for at least 20 minutes more for browned onions, about 30 minutes more for dark-brown onions. Stir the onions every 3 to 4 minutes as they cook, scraping up the residue on the bottom of the pan. (I like to use a straight-edged wooden spatula for this.) The onions may need more frequent stirring as they brown. If the underside of the onions aren't browning after 4 minutes, increase the heat.

The fried onions can be stored in the refrigerator, tightly covered, for a couple of weeks, so it pays to do a lot at once.

Schmaltz

Rendered Chicken Fat

The smell of schmaltz always reminds me of my early childhood in Brooklyn. My mother and grandmother started saving schmaltz for Pesach weeks before, probably right after Purim. Since it was still cold outside, they stored it in a bag that hung near the electric lines outside my bedroom. Sometimes, of course, it got a little warmer and the fat began to melt. For years after, there remained a large black stain under that section of the window from the melting schmaltz!

—A memory of Martha Usdin

My grandparents and other relatives all lived in Brooklyn, though my parents relocated to Kingston, New York, where I grew up. I remember taking the Trailways bus from Kingston to my grandmother's apartment in Bensonhurst. When it was time to take the bus home, she would prepare a meal for me. She'd take a hard roll, remove almost all of the bread from the inside, and fill it with chicken schmaltz and chicken. What a thing that was!

—A memory of Greta Ginzburg

The aroma of chicken fat rendering on the stove, or anything being cooked in chicken fat, is one of those sensory cues that brings back memories of cuddly Jewish grandmas. It was the most important cooking fat in old-time Jewish kitchens, and it is another defining flavor in the Yiddish kitchen. Although we rarely fry with it today, preferring less saturated vegetable oils, it is still a necessity for flavor. What are Knaidlach (page 43) without it? Just any old dumplings. Chopped Liver (page 11) has to have it (at least a little). Kasha Varnishkes (page 85) and Mushrooms and Egg Barley (page 87) are so much better with it. In the old days, it was even used as a spread—on matzo during Passover, on challah on the Sabbath, and on rye bread any other day of the week.

The word for rendered chicken fat in Yiddish is "schmaltz," but the word is also used figuratively to mean something that is overly sentimental or overblown in a less than tasteful way. You might say cloying, as in an orchestral arrangement with an excess of strings (like those by Mantovani) or a melodramatic, tearjerker movie (*I'll Cry Tomorrow*).

Few chickens these days have the big clumps of fat they used to, but even in my grandmother's day it was always necessary to collect fat from quite a few chickens to have enough to render. For use at Passover these days, starting the fat collection a month earlier at Purim, as in Marsha Usdin's memory, would no longer be time enough. I collect fat in a plastic bag that I keep in the freezer for up to three months. I pull off the clumps of fat, and trim off and save the excess fatty skin from the whole chickens I cook.

Use the *griebenes* (cracklings) and darkly caramelized onions that you have strained out to season Chopped Liver (page 11), Kasha Varnishkes (page 85), mashed potatoes, the mashed potato filling for Knishes (page 90), Mushrooms and Egg Barley (page 87), Potato Kugel (page 76), or *fleishig lukshen* kugel or Matzo Farfel Kugel (page 174). Or, salt the *griebenes* and eat it for its own sake as a treat.

When I have saved about 2 cups of fat in my freezer, I render it. You can render the fat and turn the skin into *griebenes* while still frozen.

Makes about 2 cups schmaltz

2 cups chicken fat
1 medium onion, thinly sliced

Chop the frozen pieces of fat coarsely, then put them in a skillet with enough water to barely cover. Place over low heat. The fat will start liquefying when the water begins to simmer.

When the fat appears about half rendered and the water has evaporated, add the onion. Continue to cook over low heat until the cracklings and onion are well browned.

Pour the fat through a strainer into a jar. It will keep in the refrigerator, tightly covered, for several months. Save the onions and *griebenes* to flavor dishes, or, if you dare, eat them as is, sprinkled with salt.

Chopped Liver

Gehochte Leber

Chopped liver is a treat, a godsend, a delicacy, an emblem of the Eastern European Jewish heritage, another defining food. Ironically, because the dish is also so common and humble, the words "chopped liver" can also be used sarcastically to mean something that is worthless. For instance, when you are being ignored, taken for granted, in general, disrespected, you might say, "What am I, chopped liver?"

Chopped liver is usually served as a first course or as an appetizer spread for crackers. It also makes its way into delicatessen sandwiches, on its own or paired with corned beef, roast beef, tongue, or turkey. In my family, it was a second appetizer. At a festive meal, it came after the gefilte fish. In an attempt to give chopped liver the refinement of, say, French pâté, kosher restaurants, catering halls, and the dining rooms of Catskill hotels would always present it scooped in a ball and set in an iceberg lettuce "cup." It is, in fact, more like a rustic French *pâté de campagne*, and may, as some Jewish food historians say, indeed derive from an Alsatian Jewish version of pâté.

Also, as parodied by Hollywood, chopped liver was always served at wedding and bar mitzvah receptions molded into outrageously fanciful, sculptural shapes. The Ten Commandments tablets in chopped liver is not a joke.

Everyone has an opinion about how to make chopped liver. I prefer a blend of beef and chicken livers because that's what I grew up eating. The chicken livers add softness and delicacy, while the beef liver gives body and deeper flavor. This is the way my mother made it, the way my grandmother made it, and the way it was made at the now sadly defunct 2nd Avenue Deli, which was famous for its chopped liver. At the deli, when the line for a table got too long and snaked out onto the street, a waitress would go outside and pass pieces of rye bread spread with chopped liver. You shouldn't go hungry while waiting to eat.

Until my grandmother's day, the liver, eggs, and fried onions were either chopped in a wooden bowl with a *hochtmesser*, a chopping tool with a curved blade that mirrored the curve of the bowl, or passed through the coarse blade of a hand-cranked meat grinder. Then the food processor came along and made the job easier, but also easier to do badly. With a processor, you must be very careful not to overprocess the liver into too fine a paste. Good chopped liver has a slightly rough texture and a certain fluffiness that it gets from coarser chopping and a good quantity of hard-cooked eggs. When hand-chopped the old-fashioned way, it was difficult to make too fine. Your chopping arm would fall off from exhaustion before the liver became pasty. I never liked the pasty chopped liver produced by a meat grinder. In a food processor, using the pulse function, be sure to chop the eggs separately from the liver so they maintain some of their volume.

This recipe follows Jewish dietary rules that require liver to be broiled to make it kosher. It contains too much blood to be koshered by the usual soaking and salting method, which is generally done by kosher butchers today. Not only does liver need to be broiled to be kosher, but it must also be broiled within 72 hours of the slaughter. If it is not, then it cannot be recooked, meaning that after the koshering broiling process it cannot be sautéed. Cooks who are not strictly kosher, or those kosher cooks who are guaranteed by their butcher that the liver is from a slaughter within the 72-hour time limit, then sauté the liver, usually in the same pan in which they have just fried the onions. Fully broiled livers definitely have a different flavor; they are neither better nor worse, just different.

Serves 8

³/₄ pound chicken livers

³/₄ pound beef or calf's liver, in 1 slice

2 tablespoons peanut, corn, or canola oil

2 pounds onions, sliced and fried until very brown (page 7)

6 hard-cooked eggs, peeled

³/₄ teaspoon salt

¹/₂ teaspoon freshly ground black pepper

2 tablespoons (or more) Schmaltz (page 9)

Griebenes (page 10), if you have them

To prepare the livers, cut away any membranes, blood vessels, or fat. Especially pay attention to any green globes or spots, the bile and bile ducts that will make the chopped liver bitter. (Today, most liver is sold quite clean, but it pays to look.) Cut off the tough skin from the beef liver.

To broil the livers, line a broiler pan or sheet pan with aluminum foil. Preheat the broiler.

Cut the chicken livers in half. Cut the beef or calf's liver into strips. In a small bowl, toss the chicken livers with 1 tablespoon of the oil. Place the livers on the pan. Brush the remaining 1 tablespoon of oil on all sides of the beef liver strips and place the liver on the pan. Broil the livers 6 to 7 inches from the heat for 4 minutes, then turn the livers and broil for another 3 to 5 minutes, until the livers are fully cooked but still pink inside. Let cool to room temperature.

Alternately, you can fry the livers. In a 10- to 12-inch skillet (preferably the same pan used to fry the onions), heat the 2 tablespoons of oil and fry the livers until fully cooked, but still pink inside, 8 to 10 minutes. Set aside to cool to room temperature.

In the bowl of a food processor fitted with the metal blade, combine about half the cooked liver and half the fried onions. Pulse until the liver is finely chopped, but not pasty. You may need to scrape the sides of the bowl and stir the mixture up from the bottom once or twice. Scrape the mixture into a large bowl. Repeat with the remaining liver and onions, and a few spoonfuls of *griebenes* and their caramelized onions, if using. Scrape into the bowl.

Without cleaning the processor bowl, pulse 3 eggs at a time, until finely chopped.

Add the chopped eggs to the liver mixture. Stir to combine, adding salt, pepper, and at least 2 tablespoons of schmaltz. Taste for seasoning and adjust the salt, pepper, and schmaltz.

Chill briefly before serving.

The chopped liver is best when eaten the day it is made, but it can be kept in the refrigerator, tightly covered, for several days with minimal loss of appeal. If well chilled, bring it to room temperature before serving.

Black Radish

Ritach

The black radish (*ritach,* in Yiddish), is a globe about the size of an orange, with a matte gray-black skin and snowy white interior. It's milder than red radish, but more aggressively flavored than daikon. In the spring, it's reasonably easy to find in New York City's vegetable markets and farmers' markets and one of the seasonal treats of Passover.

Although many old-timers incorporate shredded black radish into their chopped liver, the radish is also served separately, dressed with chicken fat (schmaltz) and seasoned with chopped or coarsely grated raw onion, salt, and pepper. This is called *ritach mit tzibeleh,* black radish with onion. It is delicious just like that, as an appetizer salad, eaten with black pumpernickel, or as a side dish with chopped liver, to mix in or not.

To prepare the radish, peel away the black skin (it's easiest with a swivel-bladed peeler), then shred it on the coarsest side of a box grater. Or use the julienne blade of a food processor. For a salad, use about 1 small onion, chopped, per 2 large radishes. Dress immediately with room-temperature schmaltz and season with salt and pepper. It will keep in the refrigerator, tightly covered, for several days. ✍

Vegetarian Chopped Liver

Mock chopped liver is another name for this dish that was a specialty of the dairy restaurants, which had largely vegetarian menus (although they also served fish). Vegetarian chopped liver was, and still is, also made at home. Nowadays in New York City, you can even buy prepared vegetarian chopped liver in a plastic container in the supermarket dairy case. It will be next to the prepared hummus and baba ghanoush, the Arab spreads that New York Orthodox Jews have adopted, being that Israel is in the Middle East.

Old-fashioned mock chopped liver was made with canned peas or canned string beans (now called green beans because they no longer have a string-like fiber on their sides), and with canned peas and canned green beans together. Other versions use roasted eggplant, fried mushrooms, or lentils, all with either almonds or walnuts and sometimes crackers as filler. The usual brand of cracker is Manischewitz's Tam Tam (pronounced "tom tom," *tam* being the Yiddish word for soulful flavor), but a popular old recipe uses Ritz crackers. Some might also call eggplant salad (page 16) a kind of vegetarian chopped liver. Whatever—the secret to making any recipe taste almost like real chopped liver is lots of fried onions.

"Does it really taste like liver?" you may well ask. Not really. It has a sense of chopped liver, but I have friends who won't touch liver in any form and love this stuff. You might want to call it something else: vegetarian pâté? Still, the words "vegetarian chopped liver" strike a resonant chord with many Jews.

I prefer to use fresh green beans, rather than canned, but they must be cooked through, not crisp-tender, not al dente. A recipe for mushroom-based vegetarian chopped liver follows this one.

This recipe tastes better if made a day ahead of serving.

Makes 7 cups

2 tablespoons plus 1 teaspoon salt

2 pounds fresh green beans, trimmed
  and washed (do not buy thin,
  new beans or slim French-style
  haricots verts)

4 medium onions, chopped
  (about 4 cups), fried until
  well browned (page 7)

1 cup shelled walnuts

5 hard-cooked eggs, peeled and
  cut into chunks

1/2 teaspoon freshly ground
  black pepper

To cook the green beans, in a large pot, bring about 5 quarts of water to a rolling boil over high heat. Add 2 tablespoons of the salt and the green beans. From the time the water returns to a boil, cook the beans for 8 to 10 minutes, depending on their maturity, until they are fully tender. Drain and set aside to cool.

In the bowl of a food processor fitted with the metal blade, combine half the fried onions, half the walnuts, and half the cooked green beans, then add half of the egg chunks. Pulse until the mixture is quite fine (but not pasty) and resembles chopped liver, scraping down the mixture once or twice during processing. Turn into a mixing bowl. Repeat with the remaining onions, walnuts, green beans, and eggs.

Combine the two batches, adding the remaining 1 teaspoon salt and the pepper.

Refrigerate, tightly covered, for at least a few hours before serving. It tastes even better the next day.

Mushroom Vegetarian Chopped Liver

 ————————————————————————

Although the mushrooms and onions can be fried separately, and at different times, it is best for flavor, and easier, to sauté the mushrooms in the same pan in which the onions were just fried.

Makes about 2³/₄ cups

3 tablespoons peanut, corn, or
   canola oil

1 pound white mushrooms, brushed
   clean and sliced ¹/₄ inch thick

2 or 3 medium onions, chopped
   (2 to 3 cups), fried until well browned
   (page 7)

¹/₂ cup shelled walnuts

3 hard-cooked eggs, peeled and
   cut into chunks

¹/₂ teaspoon salt

¹/₄ teaspoon freshly ground
   black pepper

In a 10- to 12-inch skillet, heat the oil over medium-high heat until very hot but not smoking. Add the mushroom slices, tossing constantly. Cook until the mushrooms release their moisture and those juices evaporate. Then cook about another 5 minutes, until the mushrooms have shrunk and become browned. Remove from the heat and let cool.

In the bowl of a food processor fitted with the metal blade, combine the cooked mushrooms, fried onions, walnuts, eggs, salt, and pepper.

Pulse to chop the mixture coarsely. Stop the machine and scrape the mixture from the rim of the bowl down and then from the bottom up to blend well. Taste and adjust the seasoning as necessary. Pulse again until the mixture is fine (but not pasty) and holds together enough to spread.

The mixture will keep in the refrigerator, tightly covered, for up to 1 week.

Romanian Eggplant Salad

Unlike other types of Ashkenazic restaurants, the Romanian steakhouse served vegetables besides cabbage and roots—namely sweet peppers and eggplant. The peppers and eggplant were roasted over charcoal and dressed with vinegar and garlic (see page 26). Without a charcoal fire—a fixture in the old Romanian steakhouses—you can also bake the eggplant, as suggested here.

I use a wooden spoon to beat in the olive oil and to give the eggplant a final mash. It feels good to do so, and, besides, the dish looks so appealing served in its wooden chopping bowl with its diced vegetable garnish arranged around it. But you can use a food processor for the whole job.

Makes about 1¹/₂ cups

1 medium eggplant
   (about 1¹/₂ pounds)
3 tablespoons extra virgin olive oil
Juice of ¹/₂ lemon
¹/₂ teaspoon salt
1 or 2 large cloves garlic, crushed with
   the side of a knife or pressed

Freshly ground black pepper
1 small onion, finely minced, for garnish
¹/₂ small green pepper, finely minced,
   for garnish
12 black or purple olives
Pita, rye bread, or pumpernickel, fresh
   or toasted, for accompaniment

Preheat the oven to 400°F.

To prepare the eggplant, place it directly on an oven rack or on a baking sheet set on a rack. Roast until it collapses when you press it down, about 40 minutes. Remove from the oven and let it rest until cool enough to handle.

Slit open the eggplant and, with a sharp knife and a wooden spoon, scrape the eggplant flesh from its skin into a wooden chopping bowl, or onto a wooden board.

With a *hochtmesser* for the wooden bowl, or the same knife on the board, coarsely chop the eggplant. If it is not already in a bowl, scrape it into one, preferably wooden.

Using a wooden spoon, beat and mash the eggplant against the sides of the bowl, until it looks mashed, not chopped.

While beating the eggplant with the spoon, add the olive oil in a thin stream, beating well between each tablespoon addition of oil.

When all the oil has been incorporated into the eggplant, the mixture should look like a rough puree. Beat in the lemon juice, salt, garlic, and a few grinds of black pepper.

Taste again and correct with more lemon juice, salt, and garlic, if desired. Do not add much pepper at this point.

With a rubber spatula, scrape the sides of the bowl to shape the eggplant into a mound. Surround the eggplant with a garnish of piles of diced onion, green pepper, and dark olives. Present the salad in its wooden bowl with a wooden spoon. Serve with bread or toasts to hold the eggplant spread and some diced vegetable garnish. Pass the peppermill.

For a presentation close to that of the Romanian restaurants, serve the eggplant already blended with the diced vegetables, mounded on a few lettuce leaves, topped with an olive.

Although hardly native to Eastern European cuisines, pita is now as everyday to Ashkenazic Jews as it is to every American, and I should add, to every Arab. I make this comment mainly to point out that pita has become wonderfully cross-cultural and that it is an ideal bread to dip into or scoop up eggplant salad, or to spread eggplant salad on. Rye bread, especially onion rye, as we used to call rye bread coated with oven-toasted chopped onion, would be more traditional. I love the salad on very grainy whole grain bread, too.

2nd Avenue Deli's Health Salad

The 2nd Avenue Deli, of blessed memory, put a stainless steel bucket of this sweet-and-sour slaw on every table, along with a bucket of the more usual brownish sour pickles, pale-green half-sours, and pickled green tomatoes.

At a deli, this type of coleslaw is called "health salad," presumably because it doesn't contain mayonnaise, like most coleslaws. It is lightly dressed (albeit with sugar), and it has more vegetables than mere cabbage. It was indeed a veritable tonic compared to the other salty, fatty foods that are the hallmarks of a Jewish delicatessen.

Mysteriously, you can get the same salad in an appetizing store, where they add black olives and bits of pickled herring and call it Greek salad for some reason that nobody knows. It could be the olives, which are fat Greek purple ones in a classy version.

Both slaws are getting harder to find. Most New York Jewish delicatessens and appetizing stores today serve or sell a more all-American, mayonnaise-based coleslaw.

This salad needs to chill for at least 8 hours before serving to develop the flavors.

Makes about 8 cups

1 small head green cabbage
  (1 1/2 to 2 pounds)
2 medium carrots, peeled
1 small green bell pepper
1 large rib celery, cut crosswise
  into thin slices

3/4 cup distilled white vinegar
2 tablespoons extra virgin olive oil,
  peanut, corn, or canola oil
1/2 cup sugar
1 tablespoon salt
1/2 teaspoon freshly ground pepper

To prepare the salad, halve the cabbage, cut into quarters, and remove the core in each section. With a large, sharp knife, shred the cabbage as finely as possible and transfer to a large bowl.

Using the coarsest side of a box grater, shred the carrots into the shredded cabbage. Halve the green pepper and remove the seeds, ribs, and stem. Wash and dry the pepper halves, then cut them into extremely fine strands; add them to the slaw along with the celery.

To make the dressing, whisk together the vinegar, oil, sugar, salt, and pepper in a small bowl. Pour the dressing over the slaw. Toss well.

Refrigerate the slaw, tightly covered, for at least 8 hours before serving. As the slaw will not wilt much, it should remain crisp and fresh tasting for 2 to 3 weeks.

"Kosher" Dill Pickles

A comely young woman is eating her dinner of dry bread and green pickles …
Pickles are a favorite food in Jewtown. They are filling and keep the children
from crying with hunger.

—Jacob Riis, *How the Other Half Live: Studies Among the Tenements*
of New York (1890)

My paternal grandfather, Bernard (Barney) Schwartz, was a professional pickle man at one point in his life. From a pushcart, he sold pickles, along with coleslaw, potato salad, and Manhattan clam chowder, to bars and grills in Manhattan. Later in life he continued to make all of these for his family and friends. I have great memories of making pickles with him. Always given the most menial job in the kitchen (isn't that what children are for?), I was put to scrubbing the cucumbers. The important work was stuffing them into gallon and half-gallon jars, which my grandmother did under the strict supervision of my grandfather, a stern man. The cucumbers needed to be firmly packed so they didn't float to the top. Barney did the seasoning, using mixed pickling spices that you can buy in the supermarket that he doctored, removing the hot pepper, but adding extra bay leaves, whole cloves of garlic, and sprigs of fresh dill that were going to seed. (I still like eating the pickled garlic.)

The jars would be left with their covers unscrewed but in place to allow for air circulation, lined up in the dark pantry at the back of his kitchen. After a few days, they would be ready as half-sours, which some people call green pickles. We liked them best at this light stage of pickling, but you could leave them at room temperature longer if you wanted a full-sour. Once they were as sour as you liked, they needed to be refrigerated. We would eat them all before they could spoil, but they will spoil eventually. In any case, they will get so sour and soft that they may not be to your taste. They weren't to ours.

By the way, there is nothing intrinsically kosher about pickles, but people call them "kosher" because they are a famous item of Jewish delicatessens. The combination of pickles with a pastrami, corned beef, or salami sandwich is unbeatable.

Because this style pickle is naturally fermented, things can go wrong. A bitter cucumber will also make a bitter pickle. Taste a raw cucumber from your batch: it should have a cool, refreshing flavor. Use small to medium Kirby cucumbers, the best for pickling. Larger cucumbers will, of course, take longer to pickle than smaller cucumbers, so try not to mix sizes in one jar, unless you want the variety of pickle strength that will result.

Makes 3 quarts

4 quarts water

3/4 cup kosher salt

20 (3- to 4-inch) Kirby cucumbers, scrubbed

12 to 16 whole cloves garlic, unpeeled, lightly crushed

2 tablespoons mixed pickling spices

6 bay leaves

1 large bunch dill, preferably going to seed, with tough stems, washed

To make the brine, bring the water to a boil in a large pot over high heat. Add the salt and stir until dissolved. Set aside to cool to room temperature.

To prepare the jars, either run them through a hot cycle of the dishwasher or fill them with boiling water, then pour out the water.

Pack the jars tightly with cucumbers, which prevents the cucumbers from floating to the top when the brine is added. As you pack the jars with cucumbers, distribute the garlic, pickling spices, and bay leaves equally among the jars and around the cucumbers.

For each jar, pour in enough brine to cover the cucumbers. Add sprigs of dill and dill seed, pushing them in wherever you can. If you have dill with woody stems, jam them into the shoulders of the jars to help keep the cucumbers in place.

Cover the jars loosely with their lids or with pieces of cheesecloth secured with rubber bands. Store in a cool, dark place. After 3 days, the cucumbers may be pickled enough to your taste. After 4 or 5 days, they should definitely taste like green pickles. For really sour pickles, let them ferment for about 6 days.

Once the pickles are at the stage you like, refrigerate them. They will get more sour as time goes by, but at a much slower pace.

Variation

For pickled green tomatoes, select very firm and small green tomatoes at the end of the tomato-growing season. Wash them well, then prick them all over with the point of a sharp knife. Proceed as for dill pickles.

Sours

At my mother's table, whenever we ate a big Jewish meal, as opposed to her daily, totally American meals, there was always a pretty plate of sours in the middle. She actually referred to them as "the sours." This is the word that is used for, collectively, "Kosher" Dill Pickles (meaning pickled Kirby cucumbers, page 20), Pickled Green Tomatoes (Variation, above), Romanian Steakhouse Roasted and Pickled Bell Peppers (page 26), perhaps Pickled Beets (page 24) in a separate bowl, and maybe sauerkraut.

We didn't always eat the sours. My mother always served fresh vegetables. But they were colorful decor, and to my mother a necessary reminder, a vestige, of where we came from. I can think of no other reason.

These days, this sour mix is available in jars in the refrigerator case, near the dairy, in New York City supermarkets. And still, in some New York delicatessens, a plate or tub of sours is always offered gratis. The tangy mix of vegetables known as health salad (page 19) would come under this category.

The Ashkenazic love of sours makes sense. In climates where fresh green vegetables were available only at the end of summer, and where most calories were derived from starch and fat, pickled (preserved) vegetables were all that were available during the cold months, and their acidity was a welcome counterpoint to the stodgy food.

In America, meat and poultry may have started to dominate the diet of Ashkenazic Jews, but still, when the starchy, fatty traditional foods were served, pickled vegetables remained appropriate. It is only in the last twenty years that Orthodox Jews in New York City have fully embraced fresh vegetables, and, after all, not much longer for Americans in general. ✣

Pickled Beets

My mother made pickled beets all the time. She opened a can of sliced beets, blended vinegar and sugar with some of the canning juices, added rings of sliced sweet onions, and refrigerated the mixture for a few hours or overnight. My father loved them. Delicatessens and family-style restaurants—even those that were not particularly Jewish—used to put them on the table with their pickles and coleslaw. Nowadays, only Junior's in its downtown Brooklyn location and Manhattan branches serves pickled beets this way. Pickled beets can be part of a sours array and are also an excellent side dish to grilled meat or roasted chicken, especially in the summer.

Serves 2 or 3

1 (15-ounce) can sliced beets, or 2 cups
  sliced boiled fresh beets
¹/₂ cup distilled white vinegar

¹/₂ cup cold water
2 teaspoons sugar
1 small onion, thinly sliced

Drain the beets, canned or fresh, reserving the liquid from the can or ¹/₂ cup of the cooking water. Combine the vinegar and the water in a bowl, then add the sugar and stir to dissolve. In a small bowl, combine the beets, vinegar mixture, sliced onion, and just enough of the reserved beet liquid to cover the beets.

Refrigerate, tightly covered, for several hours or overnight, until well chilled. Serve cold or at room temperature. The beets will keep in the refrigerator for at least a week, getting more vinegary as time goes by.

Romanian Steakhouse Roasted and Pickled Bell Peppers

In general, not many green vegetables found their way into the Ashkenazic-American kitchen, but green peppers, and the occasional red bell pepper, did appear on the Romanian and Hungarian Jewish table. The so-called Romanian steakhouses (see page 120) put these roasted peppers dressed with garlic and vinegar on the table as soon as you sat down, to nibble on with bread before any real food came. Romanians also put green bell pepper in their eggplant salad (page 16). Home cooks and delicatessens stuffed green peppers with ground meat and rice and braised them in sweet-and-sour tomato sauce, as they did for Stuffed Cabbage (page 118). Bell peppers were part of a good sours mix, too (page 22). Chunks of green pepper made their way into the appetizing store's Greek salad, and, in the 1950s, New York Jewish cooks became enamored of Chinese Pepper Steak (page 140).

These peppers get better as they sit. Give them a day or more to develop their flavor, if you can, before eating.

Makes 5 or 6 peppers

5 or 6 medium mixed green and red bell peppers (about 2$^{1}/_{2}$ to 3 pounds)

1$^{1}/_{4}$ cups distilled white vinegar

1$^{1}/_{4}$ cups water

$^{1}/_{2}$ teaspoon salt

2 tablespoons sugar

2 rounded tablespoons finely chopped garlic

To prepare the peppers, roast them over a direct gas flame or under a broiler until they are well charred. Turn them regularly and watch them carefully, especially if broiling. When the peppers are roasted, immediately place them in a covered pot or a paper or plastic bag to cool. As they cool, they will steam and become more tender—but they should not be soft.

Halve each pepper from pole to pole, but don't cut through the cap or stem; leave the cap and stem intact. Place the peppers in a large bowl, discarding any juices that collect in the bowl as they cool.

Hold each pepper half by its stem and scrape off the charred skin with the blade of a sharp knife. It's fine to leave a speck of black here and there; in fact, you should. I set a paper towel under the peppers to catch the skin and to periodically wipe off my blade. Remove the seeds and the ribs, but leave the peppers connected at the stem end if you can. Place the peppers in a large, clean, nonreactive bowl.

To make the dressing, in a small saucepan, combine the vinegar with the water. Bring to a boil over high heat. Stir in the salt, sugar, and garlic. Remove from the heat and pour over the peppers in the bowl.

Let the pepper mixture stand, covered, at room temperature for at least 12 hours before serving, although it is even better after 24 hours and perhaps best after several days. Pack the mixture into a jar and store in the refrigerator for up to several months.

P'tcha

Jellied Calf's Feet with Garlic

 ———————————————————————————

My family was divided on the hot or cold preference for p'tcha, *but only my Polish father liked it cold. The rest of us made a meal of the hot stuff with an entire large loaf of fresh challah. And when calf's feet went the way of unborn eggs (nearly impossible to find), my Mom used veal bones! Not quite the same. And cold* p'tcha *would be out. The ordinary veal bones didn't have enough gel power to make a yoich. If you were eating it hot, beaten eggs with a little vinegar and mashed garlic were stirred into the hot broth, added correctly so as not to curdle! The garlic strength of the mixture would be dependent on where you were going, how many days you planned to be locked away with* p'tcha *breath, and your personal garlic preference.*

    —A memory of Sylvia Marksman

Most people remember *p'tcha* as jellied calf's feet with chopped raw garlic and, in some versions, slices of hard-cooked egg or chopped hard-cooked egg embedded in the firm gelatin (*yoich*) just to make it look a little better. In French, *p'tcha* would be called an aspic, which sounds elegant. But even with a name like *p'tcha*, the dish has a cult following. Hardly anyone makes it anymore at home, and it is nearly impossible to find in a restaurant, so it has become legendary.

P'tcha possibly started out as a soup, not a jelly. Refrigeration is required to get the broth to jell. And, certainly in the old tenements of the Lower East Side, in the poor housing of Brownsville and East New York in Brooklyn, not to mention the shtetls of Eastern Europe, even ice boxes, which preceded the invention of the refrigerator, were a luxury appliance. Maybe in the shtetls they chilled their *p'tcha* outside in the frigid air, as people in Siberia would freeze their pelmeni (dumplings).

In the following recipe, chopped fresh parsley is a contemporary touch to improve the looks of the jelly as well as its flavor. If, however, in your memory, *p'tcha* is not *p'tcha* if it doesn't resemble a brownish, suspiciously quivering brick, leave out the herb.

Serves 6 to 8

2 calf's feet or knuckles or both (about 3 pounds), sawed into 2-inch pieces by the butcher

10 cups water, plus additional water for soaking

2 medium onions, quartered

2 cloves garlic, coarsely chopped, plus more for the broth

1 teaspoon salt

1/4 teaspoon white pepper

2 tablespoons distilled white vinegar

1 cup finely chopped fresh flat-leaf parsley, for garnish

3 egg yolks, for thickening the hot broth, or 2 hard-cooked eggs, peeled and sliced or chopped, for garnish (optional)

Finely minced garlic, for garnish (optional)

1 lemon, cut into wedges, for garnish (optional)

Wash the meat thoroughly. Put the pieces into a large bowl, cover them with water, let soak for a few minutes, then drain. Scrape the skin with a sharp knife until it is smooth. (Sometimes, these days, the calf's feet are already well cleaned.) In a 4-quart pot, bring the 10 cups water to a boil over high heat.

Place the pieces in the boiling water along with the onions, the 2 cloves of coarsely chopped garlic, salt, pepper, and vinegar. Continue to boil until the meat and gristle begin to separate from the bones, about 3 hours. You will probably have to add more water to keep the feet covered, but it is supposed to reduce. Strain the liquid, saving both liquid and solids.

Pull the meat from the bones and cut it into small pieces. Taste the broth and adjust the salt, pepper, and vinegar to taste.

To serve hot, combine the meat and broth and return to boiling. Remove from the heat and add as much chopped raw garlic as you like. Do not simmer the broth after adding the garlic.

Serve the hot broth in individual soup bowls with meat and garlic, garnished with chopped fresh parsley. Or, beat the 3 egg yolks together in a mixing bowl, then mix in some of the hot broth. Pour this mixture into the broth; do not allow the broth to boil after adding the raw eggs or the eggs will curdle. Another way to serve the broth is with chopped hard-cooked egg, instead of the raw egg enrichment.

To serve cold, which is more typical, arrange the pieces of meat and gristle in a deep heatproof dish. Add the parsley and chopped garlic. Pour in the broth and refrigerate, covered. Before the gelatin firms completely, place slices of hard-cooked egg over the top. Or, alternately, chop the hard-cooked egg and add it to the broth before you refrigerate it and it starts to jell.

In either case, hot or cold, *p'tcha* can be served with wedges of lemon.

Chicken Fricassee

 ————————————————————————————

My grandmother made chicken fricassee regularly, though as a child I never appreciated the boney chicken necks and wings, or the giblets. I didn't understand why it was called chicken fricassee if the meatballs and the brown gravy were the most interesting, delicious things about it. To this day, I consider chicken fricassee to be about great gravy, for which I now know the giblets and boney necks and wings are essential. And I can't eat it without soft bread, preferably challah, to sop up that gravy. The boney but succulent chicken pieces are secondary.

The following is an update of our family recipe. Like most stewed or braised dishes, it tastes best when made ahead and reheated.

Serves 6

2 pounds chicken wings or
   mixed wings and necks
2 tablespoons peanut, corn,
   or canola oil
2 medium onions, chopped
   (about 2 cups)
½ cup all-purpose flour
8 cups water
½ pound chicken gizzards,
   coarsely chopped

2 teaspoons salt
1 teaspoon freshly ground
   black pepper
1 large imported bay leaf (or 2 small)
½ teaspoon dried thyme
1 tablespoon sweet Hungarian paprika
1 pound lean ground beef
1 egg
½ cup dry unseasoned breadcrumbs
Challah or rye bread, for accompaniment

To prepare the chicken pieces, with a sharp knife or poultry shears, cut the chicken wings at their joints into three pieces. Don't discard the wing tips. They have no meat to speak of, but they will add flavor to the gravy. Hack the necks in half.

In a large pot, warm the oil over medium heat and, without crowding the pan, cook the chicken wings and necks until browned lightly on all sides, about 10 minutes. Remove with a slotted spoon or tongs to a bowl. Reserve.

Drain off all but 3 tablespoons of the fat left in the pot. Sauté the chopped onion until wilted, about 5 minutes.

Stir in the flour and cook, stirring frequently over medium heat, for 5 minutes, scraping up any browned bits left from the chicken.

Stir in the water, increase the heat to medium-high, and bring to a boil, stirring frequently.

Stir in the gizzards, and the reserved chicken wings and necks. Season with 1½ teaspoons of the salt, ½ teaspoon of the pepper, bay leaf, thyme, and paprika. Reduce the heat to low, partially cover, and let simmer gently and steadily for about 1 hour.

Meanwhile, make the meatballs. In a mixing bowl, combine the beef, beaten egg, breadcrumbs, the remaining ½ teaspoon salt, and the remaining ½ teaspoon pepper. With a fork or your hands, mix thoroughly. Using about 1 tablespoon of meat for each, shape into meatballs no more than 1 inch in diameter (you should have 26 to 30).

When the chicken has cooked for about an hour, add the meatballs, increase the heat to medium, and simmer briskly for another 15 minutes. Taste the gravy and adjust the salt and pepper.

The dish is best if made ahead and reheated. Serve very hot in shallow bowls, with plenty of bread to sop up the gravy.

Gefilte Fish

How can you tell the gefilte fish from the other fish in the sea?
The gefilte is the one with a slice of carrot on his back.

　　　—Old Jewish joke

Gefilte means "stuffed" in Yiddish. Nowadays, this iconic Jewish dish is fashioned into single-portion oval cakes and sometimes into "party-sized" loaves or tiny "cocktail balls." But originally, gefilte fish was packed back into the fish skin from whence the fish flesh came. For all the Borscht Belt jokes about its bad aroma, its gray color, and its too-often fishy flavor, when gefilte fish is well made, it is actually the most refined of Yiddish fare, a very highly manipulated way to serve freshwater fish elegantly, without their many bones. And it was meant to be fancy, because it was devised to be served on very festive occasions.

Once the fish's flesh is carefully separated from the bones, head, and tail, it is ground or chopped into a paste, seasoned well, possibly extended with a starchy ingredient (matzo meal and potatoes are the most usual), bound with eggs, then poached in a broth so rich in protein it jells when chilled. An aspic! It is every bit as clever and as elegant as a French quenelle in lobster sauce.

During the very last days of Soviet rule in 1988, I was in Vilnius, Lithuania (Vilna, to the Jews), a center of Jewish learning and Yiddish culture for hundreds of years. On the first day the Lithuanians were able to fly their flag in seventy-five years, I encountered, at a festive luncheon, a dish that must have been much like the original gefilte fish. This specimen was a large, whole carp, decorated with vegetable cutouts on a background of milky white aspic, a French-style chaud-froid. Even in this fancy guise, my band of mainly Jewish fellow travelers all looked up from our plates and, in unison, said, "gefilte fish?" When we asked the chef what she called her masterpiece, she said it didn't have a name, but that it was a recipe that came from the city's Jewish heritage.

Gefilte fish is the traditional Ashkenazic way to begin the Friday night Shabbos dinner. Sephardim have other fish preparations, but it is custom among all Jews to begin the Sabbath meal, the Passover seder, the Rosh Hashanah dinner, and, actually, any celebratory meal, with a fish course. As in Chinese tradition, fish symbolize prosperity and fertility. In some traditions, the head of the family is supposed

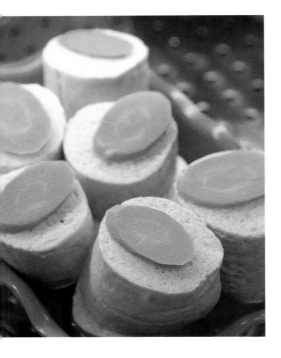

to be served the head of the fish, and it still is the custom of some Jews, especially for Rosh Hashanah.

As a food, gefilte fish can be much beloved. But that name! New York Jews looking to call it something less Yiddish, more elegant, came up with things like "stuffed sweet water fish," which I found on a menu from the Borscht Belt's famous Concord Hotel.

My Russian family tradition is for peppery gefilte fish, but many Jewish families with roots in Germany, Austria, and Poland prefer a sugar-sweetened fish. This difference in taste is typical of the two main divisions of Yiddish cooking: Litvak, referring to people who came from the easternmost areas of the Pale, and Galitzianer, referring specifically to Galicia, then part of the Austrian Empire, now divided between Poland and Ukraine, but also coming to mean all those who don't agree with Litvaks about the seasoning of food.

In the end, the Galitzianers have prevailed, probably because their taste for sweet food aligns with American taste. In New York City today, it is hard to find unsweetened gefilte fish. Every supermarket carries at least one, if not several, brands of gefilte fish, both peppered and "Vienna-style." But sweetened fish prevails in the few restaurants, delis, and appetizing stores that still make their own. These are of varying quality. Some, unfortunately, deserve the ridicule and embarrassment that Jews often make and have about this dish.

As preparing gefilte fish is something of a project—and an expensive one at that—many a *balabusta* gave in to the convenience of jarred gefilte fish when it was introduced in the 1950s. To assuage the guilt of not serving homemade fish—there is no other way to explain it—they would doctor the fish by recooking it in what amounted to a French-style court-bouillon. Of course, they didn't know they were making something called court-bouillon when they boiled water with a few vegetables and seasonings. Rather than "refresh" the fish, which is what everyone said they were doing, the fish became overcooked. Some brands of jarred gefilte fish are truly quite appealing, especially if you spike each bite with horseradish (see page 35), the condiment that is *the* necessary accompaniment to gefilte fish.

In the following recipe, my grandmother's, I have added some contemporary cooking touches. There are instructions for using a food processor and a stand mixer for preparing the ground fish, and instructions for using the microwave to test the seasoning of the fish. In my grandmother's day it was apparently somewhat safer to taste raw freshwater fish, but today we are told that they may harbor parasites. The fish can actually be cooked entirely in the microwave, which results in a fresher tasting gefilte fish if you cook it until just done—a very different dish, but delicious.

Family traditions differ on the combination of fish used. Carp is relatively inexpensive compared to whitefish, pike, or perch. All-carp gefilte fish can be very dense and dark in color, but it is definitely to some people's taste—as are, if I might say disparagingly, hard matzo balls. Gefilte fish with no carp, just whitefish and pike, which is the most popular combination, can be very delicate. Some carp in the mix adds body.

Serves 8

Broth
1 pound mixed fish head, skeleton, and skin
1 medium onion, sliced
1 carrot, peeled and sliced into rounds
1 large rib celery, cut crosswise into several pieces
1 teaspoon salt
$1/4$ teaspoon ground white pepper

Fish Cakes
2 pounds fish fillets (a combination of two or more of the following: whitefish, carp, perch, yellow pike; see headnote)
1 medium onion, coarsely chopped

1 carrot, peeled and coarsely chopped
1 rib celery, coarsely chopped
2 egg yolks
$1^1/2$ teaspoons salt
$1/2$ teaspoon ground white pepper
$1/2$ cup seltzer
Carrot rounds, for garnish
Sliced onion, for garnish
Horseradish (see page 35), for accompaniment

To prepare the broth, place the fish head, skeleton, and skin in a large pot, preferably enameled cast iron. Add the onion, carrot, celery, enough cold water to cover the solids, and the salt and pepper. Heat to boiling over high heat, decrease the heat to medium, and simmer for 30 minutes. Remove from the heat and reserve.

Meanwhile, prepare the fish. Examine the fillets carefully for bones, removing any with tweezers. Cut the fish into 1-inch chunks and place half of them in the bowl of a food processor fitted with the metal blade. Pulse until finely ground.

Transfer the ground fish to the bowl of a stand mixer fitted with the paddle. Grind the remaining fish in the processor and combine with the first batch in the mixer bowl.

Without washing the food processor bowl, fill it with the chopped onion, carrot, and celery. Process until very, very finely chopped. Add to the ground fish, along with the egg yolks, salt, and pepper.

With the mixer on low speed, mix well, scraping the bowl frequently, and gradually blend in the seltzer. Let the machine work the fish mixture for 5 minutes.

Check the seasoning as follows so you don't taste raw fish: Form a small ball of fish, place it on a small plate with 1 or 2 spoonfuls of broth, and cover loosely with plastic. Microwave on high until cooked. If the mixture is not to your taste, adjust the salt and pepper accordingly.

To cook the fish mixture in the microwave, measure about $^1/_2$ cup of clear broth into a 9-inch glass pie plate or other shallow microwave-safe dish.

With wet hands and a wet rubber spatula, shape the fish mixture into oval cakes, using $^1/_2$ cup of fish mixture for each one. Set about 4 in the 9-inch plate, cover loosely with plastic wrap, and place in the microwave oven. Cook at 50 percent power for 10 to 11 minutes, or longer. If there is no turntable, rotate the dish a third around twice during cooking. Test for doneness by cutting one fish cake in half; when cooked, the fish mixture is firm and no longer translucent. (Since every microwave oven is slightly different, your first batch may have to be somewhat experimental.) Repeat with the remaining fish cakes.

Remove from the microwave, let cool to near room temperature, then refrigerate, tightly covered, to chill thoroughly. Serve each with a carrot round, fresh sliced onion, or horseradish, or all three.

To cook conventionally, have the broth at a simmer. Shape the fish cakes as above, then ease them into the simmering broth on top of the bones and skins. Cover the pot and simmer gently for about 40 minutes.

When done, remove the fish cakes. Strain the broth. Arrange the fish in a shallow baking dish, top each cake with a slice of carrot salvaged from the broth, and pour over the broth (*yoich,* in Yiddish). This will encase the gefilte fish in jelled broth. Or pack the fish and *yoich* separately. The jelled broth can be cut into cubes to garnish the fish, but it is traditional to serve each cake of gefilte fish topped with a round of carrot, which also symbolizes prosperity.

Horseradish

Chrain

A favorite condiment on the Yiddish table, horseradish is absolutely essential with Gefilte Fish (page 31). Some people like it with P'tcha (page 27), although I think it conflicts with the large amount of garlic in the dish. It is, however, great with Boiled Flanken or Brisket (page 114).

The fresh root is available in New York City markets most of the year because it stores well. But it is an early spring specialty, and for many people freshly grated horseradish is strictly a Passover treat. It is, in fact, the "bitter herb" on the Passover seder plate alongside the other symbolic foods used during the ritual reading of the Haggadah.

There are two kinds of grated horseradish sold in bottles and jars: the fully pungent white type and the red type, colored and slightly sweetened with beet juice. Gold's Horseradish Company, founded in 1932, used to have the largest root cellar in the world, in Brooklyn, just for storing horseradish for New York's Jews. Nowadays, the company is in Hempstead, New York, on Long Island, and it has diversified into bottled horseradish sauce, mustard (to which horseradish is related), salsa, and other condiments, all nationally distributed.

Freshly grated horseradish has a very different flavor than jarred, which is preserved with salt and vinegar. This is not to diminish the appeal of jarred horseradish. It's great stuff. On the other hand, there is a discouraging fact about freshly grated horseradish: it loses its pungency very quickly, even within minutes, and its color turns an unappetizing gray unless it is preserved with vinegar, just like the bottled variety. Hand-grated horseradish with vinegar should keep for at least several weeks in the refrigerator before turning gray.

If you want to serve freshly grated plain horseradish, it must be put on the table immediately after it is grated. Otherwise, per 1 cup of grated horseradish (grated by hand on the medium side of a box grater or in a food processor), combine with $^1/_4$ cup distilled white vinegar, 1 teaspoon of salt, and 1 teaspoon of sugar. If you grate fresh horseradish in a food processor, be careful when you open the processor bowl. The fumes of horseradish—like its cousin, mustard—can burn your eyes or sinus passages.

Sweetbreads and Mushrooms with Egg Barley

Stuart Somerstein is the fourth generation of Somerstein Kosher Caterers. Although no longer affiliated with a synagogue, as most kosher caterers used to be, he is still producing Jewish weddings, very glamorous ones, at The Water's Edge, the restaurant and party venue he owns and operates with his wife, Marika, on the Queens side of the East River, facing the magnificent Manhattan skyline.

I remember, and Stuart confirms, that sweetbreads were a required item on every kosher wedding and bar mitzvah menu from at least 1930, when Somerstein was founded, until the mid-1970s. At first it was served after the fruit cup and before the soup, like a pasta course, except it was the sweetbreads course. It was, however, accompanied by egg barley, also called farfel (see page 37), which is a form of egg pasta that imitates the shape of the grain. Sweetbreads were a delicacy then, appearing on the menus of fancy mainstream New York restaurants as well. Serving them at your "affair" denoted your generosity to your guests at this time of great *naches*—pride derived from your children.

As the fashion for sweetbreads waned, however, the dish became relegated to the smorgasbord, an over-the-top buffet of hot and cold hors d'oeuvres and many, many chafing dishes of meat, poultry, and fish choices, any one of which could easily suffice as a complete meal. But then you sat down to five to seven more courses—with dancing in between. The Jewish smorgasbord survives today, but the stations are likely to include a sushi bar and a pizza bar. And dinner is probably only four courses.

Serves 4

2 tablespoons peanut, corn, or canola oil

1/4 cup minced shallots

1 tablespoon minced garlic

4 ounces white mushrooms, thinly sliced

1/3 cup dry white wine or dry white vermouth

2 cups Ratner's Vegetarian Brown Gravy (page 146), made with oil instead of butter

1 pound veal sweetbreads, blanched, peeled, and cubed

2 tablespoons finely chopped fresh flat-leaf parsley

Freshly ground black pepper and salt

8 ounces egg barley (farfel)

To make the sauce, warm the oil in a small saucepan over medium heat and sauté the shallots and garlic together for 2 minutes without letting them brown. Add the mushrooms, increase the heat slightly, and cook until the mushrooms release their moisture and those juices evaporate. Add the white wine and let it reduce by half. Add the vegetarian gravy. Stir well and bring to a simmer. Add the sweetbreads and parsley. Season with freshly ground black pepper, and add some salt, if necessary. Keep warm.

To prepare the egg barley, bring about 8 cups of water to a boil in a medium (no less than 3-quart) saucepan over high heat. Add 1 teaspoon of salt, then boil the egg barley until tender, about 10 minutes, depending on brand and type. Drain, then return it to the saucepan in which it was cooked.

Add the sweetbreads mixture to the egg barley and stir well to blend. Adjust the seasoning, if necessary. Serve very hot.

Farfel

The word *farfel* is fun to say, and it has symbolism. It is related to the Yiddish word *farfaln,* "fallen away" or "over and done with." On Shabbos, when all business and debts are supposed to be settled, and all hard feelings put aside, dishes with farfel take on extra meaning. In High German, on which Yiddish is based, *varveln* are noodles in the form of pellets or granules, which are what farfel are, too.

In one method, stiff egg dough is grated into tiny beads of pasta. In another, thin ropes of dough are pinched off into bits that are rolled into tiny balls between the thumb and forefinger. In a third, thin sheets of pasta are chopped with a knife or *hochtmesser* into little pieces, which are dried for future use. Today, and since the turn of the twentieth century, farfel has been made industrially into perfectly even little beads that, because of their vague resemblance to the grain, are also called "egg barley." Streit's is the only company in the U.S. that markets the more home-style farfel, which they label "heimishe farfel," chopped sheets of pasta that have been dried and toasted. New York City's kosher markets also import Israeli brands of "heimishe farfel" that are more like huge dried breadcrumbs. All these products can be used in the same recipes, but adjustments need to be made in the amount of liquid used, because their absorption qualities are quite different.

The word *farfel* is also used for matzo that has been crumbled into pieces a little smaller than a dime. During Passover, it is used to garnish chicken broth, but it is also used to make kugels (see page 70) and stuffings. There is also a traditional matzo farfel and honey candy, Ingberlach (page 189). ✎

CHAPTER 2

⁃❦ Soups ❦⁃

Many a Yiddish meal has been made of only a bowl of thick soup. Some bread wouldn't hurt—rye, pumpernickel, challah, a hard roll, or an Onion Bun (page 215). But that's all. Among the most popular thick soups are Mushroom-Barley (page 49), Split Pea (page 51), Potato (page 62), and Sweet-and-Sour Cabbage Borscht (page 53). And let's not forget Knubble Borscht (page 59), full of meat, beets, and *knubble* (garlic, in Yiddish).

My grandfather, Bernard (Barney) Schwartz, was a curmudgeonly waiter at the famous Famous dairy restaurant in Crown Heights, Brooklyn, then an affluent Jewish neighborhood, now the world headquarters of the Chabad Lubovitch Hasidic movement. He used to tell us about the "cheapskates" who would come to his restaurant, order a mere bowl of soup, eat an onion bun, then take the remainder of the bread basket home in their handbag or pockets. These soups didn't even have meat (the Famous was a *dairy* restaurant), yet they made a meal of them.

Of course, the most famous Yiddish soup is that divine golden broth called Chicken Soup (page 40). It doesn't have to support matzo balls (Knaidlach, page 43), but these days it more often does than doesn't. When it doesn't, even sometimes when it does, it may be graced with *lukshen*, fine egg noodles, making it quite substantial. Kreplach (page 47), meat-stuffed pasta dumplings, are another addition—let's call them a garnish—to chicken soup. However, because kreplach are such a fuss to make, and require advanced skills as well, they have always been reserved for important holiday meals.

Then there are the other clear soups, all of them with garnishes that can turn them into a meal unto themselves—okay, a near meal. In the summer, Clear (Cold) Borscht (page 57) can have additions of boiled potato and sour cream. Schav (page 64), cold sorrel soup, is not clear. It is green and murky, but it is light—that is, until you add chopped cucumber, scallions, and, but of course, lots of sour cream.

Chicken Soup (page 40) with Knaidlach (page 43)

Chicken Soup

When a poor man eats a chicken, one or the other is sick.
—Old Yiddish saying

Matzo ball soup, as chicken soup *with* matzo balls is so irritatingly called these days, is itself practically a New York City tourist attraction. But Jews hardly have a monopoly on great chicken soup. In fact, today you are more likely to get great broth in an Asian restaurant than at a Jewish delicatessen or kosher restaurant. Still, chicken soup continues to be called "Jewish penicillin," and the ability to make a great pot of *goldene yoichle*, golden broth in Yiddish, is still the measure of a *balabusta's* culinary ability.

By the way, it was doctors at Mount Sinai hospital in Miami, Florida (where else?), who first scientifically documented the connection between chicken soup and the common cold that the soup supposedly cures. To put it politely, hot soup, actually any kind of hot soup, promotes sinus and nasal drainage. If that's the case, then chili and vinegar-laced Chinese hot-and-sour soup does a better job.

These days, but not always in every family, the expectation for New York Jewish chicken soup, with or without matzo balls, is that it should be gorgeously golden, be crystal clear, and have the unmistakable flavor of chicken accented by root vegetables. This high standard is not easy to achieve, given the lamely flavored, factory-produced chickens of today. Even top caterers, restaurants, and, I have to say, a few sneaky home cooks, add powdered chicken soup base or bouillon cubes to what would otherwise be their thinly flavored broth. When chicken soup is very yellow, or if the soup doesn't jell when refrigerated, I guarantee that the cook has cheated.

I find it takes many pounds of chicken to make a good broth. To get the best chicken flavor and a golden color, I have to supplement a whole chicken with an almost equal weight of chicken wings, backs, or feet, or all three. These gelatin-rich parts, especially the feet, also give the soup body. You don't even need a whole chicken. You can make great soup with just parts, but I like the feeling of having a whole bird in the pot. I just do.

An old hen or fowl doesn't suffice any longer. Years ago, it was only an old bird that was used for broth. In the Old Country, as in many poor cultures, you didn't kill the hen that gave you eggs, an important protein source. Only when the old girl began laying few eggs, or not laying at all, did she become a candidate for the soup pot. If you couldn't afford a chicken for Shabbos, there had to be a special occasion or reason for chicken soup—a religious feast day or holy day, a celebration, or someone who was sick and needed the sustenance of easily digestible broth.

In America, many Jews could eventually afford to buy a boiling bird for Shabbos. A chicken in every pot! From the Bronx to Brighton Beach, it became the main event at Friday night's Sabbath feast. And certainly, at least through the 1960s, the bird would be flavorful enough that you could eat its meat even after it had flavored the broth. Not everyone liked what we called "soup chicken," but to some it was a reward at the end of the workweek. Today, even when using the best chicken available, all the flavor of the meat will be boiled out and transferred to the soup, and it is not worth salvaging. You have a choice: good soup or good chicken.

Good home cooks add vegetables to their chicken soup for additional flavor. In the Yiddish kitchen, they would be root vegetables—onion, carrot, parsnip, and occasionally turnip. I've even read recipes calling for zucchini.

The special ingredient to some Jewish cooks, however, is parsley root (*petrishke,* in Yiddish; *petrushka,* in Russian). It's a thin white root, 6 inches long at most, that looks like a miniature parsnip but has an intense flavor that is a cross between celery and parsley. It gives the soup herbal oomph without giving it a green cast, as fresh herbs can. (The root is difficult to find outside Orthodox Jewish neighborhoods.) For the same reason—that it doesn't add a green cast to the soup—I also prefer celery root (celeriac) to celery ribs, but celery leaves have a good strong flavor, too, and you don't need many. I prefer leek to onion, but often use onion or both. Too many vegetables in the pot can, however, overpower the delicate chicken flavor, and if you use fresh herbs, put them in only for the last 30 minutes of cooking. In New York City, we're likely to eat green matzo balls on St. Patrick's Day, but nobody wants to eat green chicken soup.

To get a clear soup, it is very important to wash the inside of the chicken very well under cold running water, loosening and removing every bit of liver or other brown material. The initial simmer is important to bring the *schmutz*, the scum, to the surface to be skimmed off. But once the bubbles that are surfacing have become white, lower the heat to a very gentle simmer.

Makes 3 quarts

7 pounds of chicken, a whole bird and
   parts (for instance, 1 (4-pound) whole
   chicken, plus 3 pounds of a combination of wings, thighs, backs, and feet)

14 cups cold water

1 tablespoon salt

2 medium-large carrots, peeled

$1/2$ large celery root, peeled and halved,
   or 2 large stalks celery

1 medium or $1/2$ large parsnip, peeled,
   and split if large

1 large leek, split lengthwise and well
   washed, with several inches of green

1 medium onion, peeled and halved

Several sprigs of parsley and dill

In a large pot, combine the chicken, water, and salt. Bring to a simmer over high heat. Reduce the heat and let simmer for at least 15 minutes, skimming off any scum that comes to the surface (I use a fine mesh skimmer for this. A slotted spoon works well, too.) Stir the chicken once or twice during this process, which helps loosen the *schmutz* for skimming.

When the liquid is releasing only white foam, add the carrots, celery root, parsnip, leek, and onion. Simmer, uncovered, very gently but steadily, for 3 to 4 hours. Add the parsley and dill for the last 30 minutes only.

Remove from the heat, let the soup cool to tepid, then refrigerate overnight so that the fat will harden on the surface and can be easily removed. Don't skim off every last bit of fat; a few beads of fat in each bowl of soup add aroma and flavor. (Reserve the skimmed chicken fat—schmaltz. It is an excellent cooking fat.)

Strain the broth through a colander. Pick out the carrots and parsnip you may want to use to serve in the soup. Press the remaining solids slightly to extract all the soup. If you press hard, then the soup will become cloudy, but that's an option to get even more flavor into the soup. What you gain in flavor, you lose in clarity. Discard the solids.

Reheat the broth and serve as a clear soup, with additions of either matzo balls, kreplach, *lukshen*, or soup nuts (*mandlen*). "Unborn eggs," the yolks that could be found in the tubes of a slaughtered pullet (young hen), used to garnish chicken soup. Now they are very hard to find, but you can easily fake it by adding hard-cooked egg yolks to the hot soup.

To have vegetables fresher than the soup vegetables to put in the soup, ladle off just enough broth to cook a carrot and a parsnip until tender. Or use water to do this. Serve each bowl of soup with a few rounds of carrot and a chunk or strip of parsnip. If you have used broth, you can add it back to the soup.

Knaidlach

2nd Avenue Deli's Matzo Balls

You know a food must be beloved when scornful jokes are told about it. In the case of matzo balls, the jokes are usually about how heavy they are ("sinkers" or "belly bombs"), and how they cause heartburn and indigestion. But a great matzo ball, often flavored lightly with chicken fat, airy or firm, always savory, in a bowl of steaming potent chicken broth, is a primal and iconic food for Jews of Eastern European heritage.

One might think that matzo balls were once a treat reserved for Passover, when Jews are required to give up bread and eat only unleavened bread—matzo. Actually, however, moistening matzo during the eight days of Passover is forbidden by custom in some very observant communities; über-observant Jews do not make matzo balls. They eat matzo balls only on the last day of, or *after* Passover, using up the matzo that is left over from the holiday.

I'd speculate that matzo balls became a Passover treat, and then an everyday treat, only after the Ashkenazim arrived in America. Still, nowadays, at home, *lukshen*, fine egg noodles, are a more typical soup addition, especially for Shabbos, because the word can be divided into syllables that sound like *lo kashen*, which means "no hardships" in Hebrew. For some holidays, Rosh Hashanah in particular, Kreplach (page 47), meat-filled pasta dumplings, like tortellini but bigger, are the special addition.

I always used to wonder how restaurants and delicatessens made perfectly round matzo balls that keep their shape for hours and hours while waiting to be immersed. My matzo balls, the ones I learned to make from my maternal grandmother, always come out misshapen at best, and they often deflate while they await their fate. These are no different than the matzo balls of a million other Jewish mothers and grandmothers. For that matter, they are all more or less the same matzo ball recipe that is printed on the back of matzo meal boxes. Great matzo balls, I believe, are not just about the formula. The same recipe in different hands comes out light or as a "sinker." There is mystery—call it karma—in matzo balls.

The late Abe Lebewohl, founder of the now defunct 2nd Avenue Deli, one day confided to me the deli man's secret ingredient for matzo balls: baking powder. Such leavening used to be forbidden during the eight days of Passover. Like many dumplings, traditional matzo balls were and still are leavened only by eggs. Abe was able to use baking powder all year because his deli was closed for Passover. Meanwhile, somehow, recently, through what must have been some pretty intense Talmudic arguing, there is baking powder approved for Passover use.

Baking powder makes matzo balls well-risen and light, while helping to produce a batter that is stiff enough to form gorgeously round dumplings. I have also found that they freeze perfectly. To reheat, just put the frozen matzo balls in a pot of hot soup and keep the soup at the merest simmer until the matzo balls are defrosted and heated through, at least 20 minutes.

The only trick to this recipe is that the batter must be beaten vigorously and very, very well, or left to stand until it thickens well. My tip, never offered by the 2nd Avenue Deli but learned from my grandmother, is to use a very wide pot, not narrow like a stock pot, so that when the matzo balls rise to the surface, they each have their own surface space. Because my grandmother, Elsie Sonkin, usually made so many, she used her aluminum oval roaster with the high cover, the same pot she used to make gefilte fish. I use my largest enameled cast-iron casserole.

Makes about 12

4 large eggs
$^1/_3$ cup Schmaltz (page 9)
$^1/_4$ teaspoon plus 1 tablespoon salt

$^1/_4$ teaspoon freshly ground black or, even better, white pepper
1 tablespoon baking powder
$1^1/_3$ cups matzo meal

Crack the eggs into a large bowl and beat with a fork to mix thoroughly. Beat in the schmaltz, the $^1/_4$ teaspoon salt, pepper, and baking powder. Stir in the matzo meal, then mix vigorously with a wooden spoon until completely blended and very stiff. Let stand for 30 minutes. It can be refrigerated, covered with plastic wrap, until ready to use, up to 8 hours.

Fill a large, wide pot three-quarters full with water. Add the remaining 1 tablespoon salt and bring to a boil over high heat.

Wet your hands with cold water so the batter doesn't stick to them, then holding and rolling the mixture between your palms, shape it into perfect balls about $1^1/_4$ inches in diameter. They will double in size when cooked.

Gently place the matzo balls in the boiling water. When all have been added, decrease the heat so the water simmers briskly, but isn't at a rolling boil, when the pot is covered. Cook for 25 minutes, preferably without removing the pot lid.

Remove the cooked matzo balls with a slotted spoon. Serve in hot chicken soup.

To hold matzo balls for serving at a later time, transfer them from the cooking pot to a platter or tray. Cover with plastic wrap. Just before serving, reheat them in the simmering chicken soup.

These matzo balls can be frozen. Arrange on parchment or wax paper on a baking sheet and freeze until hard. Then pack the matzo balls in a plastic bag or container. Reheat from the frozen state: Place in simmering soup over high heat. When the soup returns to a simmer, reduce the heat so the soup remains just under a boil, and simmer until the matzo balls are soft in the center and heated through. This can take as long as 20 minutes or so. Test the softness of the matzo balls with a skewer or point of a sharp knife. The only way to know whether they are hot enough is to cut one open and taste it.

Fluffy Knaidlach

Matzo Balls II

I first learned about this recipe only a few years ago from Estelle Forman of Brooklyn, who called them fat-free matzo balls, which they are if you don't count the fat in the egg yolks. The name is reflective of our times, but the recipe dates back to at least 1930, when an almost identical version was called "Fluffy Knoedel" in *Tempting Kosher Dishes*, an English-Yiddish cookbook published by Manischewitz. Interestingly, the book also has four other recipes for matzo balls—three called *knoedel*, the other called "Matzo Dumplings." But this is the only one made wholly with matzo meal. The others are based on soaked matzo boards, a method that is hardly ever used today. Besides being as fat-free as a dumpling can be, these balls are astoundingly light and flavorful, given that they are made from nothing but eggs, matzo meal, and salt.

Makes 6

$^1/_2$ to $^3/_4$ teaspoon salt,
  plus more for the pot
3 eggs, separated
$^3/_4$ cup matzo meal

Bring a large pot of water to a rolling boil over high heat. Salt it enough so that it tastes salty.

Meanwhile, in a large bowl using a hand-held electric mixer on medium speed, or in the bowl of a stand mixer with the whisk attachment on medium speed, beat the egg whites until stiff.

In a small bowl, beat the salt into the yolks just until the yolks are well mixed.

Gently, carefully, but also thoroughly, fold the beaten yolks and the matzo meal into the beaten whites. Let stand at room temperature for 20 minutes.

With moistened hands, form 1-inch balls and gently place them in the large pot of boiling, salted water. Cover and boil rapidly for 20 minutes.

Remove the cooked balls with a slotted spoon and drain in a colander. Transfer to paper towels to further drain and cool.

These can be frozen: see Knaidlach (page 43).

Kreplach

The word *kreplach* is plural and it is always used that way. Though it is a legitimate word, who ever heard of a *kreple*? Who could eat just one? The word is related to the French word *crêpe* and the Italian word *crespelle*. The casings of kreplach are not thin pancakes, however. They are made of egg-noodle dough. They are filled pasta dumplings. Kreplach are, in fact, Jewish tortelloni. The dough is the same, the shape is the same. The only thing different, and only slightly, is the filling. But who knew from such fancy Italian dumplings? Jews used to compare kreplach to Chinese wontons, and you can, in fact, make pretty good kreplach with store-bought wonton skins.

In the Jewish kitchen, kreplach are considered to be the most sublime addition you can have for a bowl of chicken soup, mainly because they are a great deal of trouble to make. In the old tradition, they take the place of honor in the chicken soup that is served at the Rosh Hashanah dinner that welcomes the New Year, at the auspicious evening meal before Yom Kippur, and at the Purim feast, as Purim is considered the single most joyful holiday of the year. But kreplach are becoming extinct. Hardly anyone bothers to make them anymore and there are few commercial sources. Until quite recently, there were women who made them at home and sold them for the holidays, but they are mostly all gone now, too.

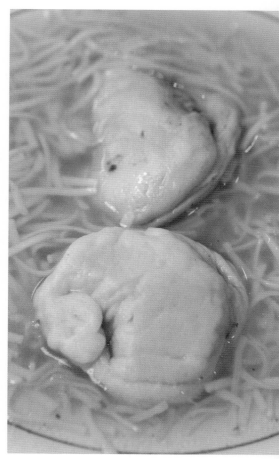

This recipe, which was passed on to me with personal, hands-on instruction, is from Cindy Klotz, whose kosher muffins are sold in the fanciest of fancy New York City (not necessarily kosher) grocers. She, in turn, learned to make kreplach from her Grandma Sarah. Both women prove the point that great home cooks are often fashionable women that you'd never expect to don an apron.

Makes about 2 dozen

Filling

3 tablespoons peanut, corn, or
  canola oil

3 to 4 pounds boneless beef chuck
  (shoulder), in one piece

4 cups coarsely chopped onion
  (about 4 medium onions)

2 cloves garlic, peeled, coarsely chopped

2 medium carrots, peeled

2 large ribs celery, halved crosswise

1 1/2 teaspoons salt

1/2 teaspoon freshly ground
  black pepper

1 beef bouillon cube (optional)

Dough

2 cups bleached all-purpose flour

2 extra-large eggs

1/4 cup lukewarm water

To make the filling, in a 4- to 5-quart Dutch oven, heat the oil over medium-high heat and sear the meat on all sides until well browned. Remove the meat from the pan to a large bowl and set aside.

Add the onions to the pan and stir well, using the liquid released by the onions to deglaze the pan. Sauté over medium heat, until the onions are tender and lightly colored, 10 to 12 minutes. Add the garlic for the last few minutes.

Return the meat to the pan with the onions and garlic and arrange the carrots and celery around it. Add enough water to come halfway up the side of the meat. Add the salt and pepper. Bring to a simmer over medium-high heat, cover, and adjust the heat so the liquid simmers gently for about 2 1/2 to 3 hours. During the last 40 minutes, check the water level. The pot should never cook dry, but the juices should be very reduced.

Taste the pot juices. If they lack flavor, add the bouillon cube and stir to dissolve.

Let the meat cool in the pot. It can be prepared ahead and refrigerated for several days. When ready to finish the kreplach filling, drain the meat, keeping the juices and onions and garlic, but discarding the carrots and celery. Cut about 1/4 of the meat into chunks and force through the medium blade of a meat grinder with the onions, garlic, and juices. Or pulse together in a food processor fitted with the metal blade. Or shred the meat in its juices with a fork, then mash in the onions and garlic. The filling should be fine, but not pasty. It will be slightly stringy. (Reheat, slice, and serve the remaining roast as such.)

To make the dough, make a mound with the flour on a wooden board (or in a large mixing bowl). Make a well in the center. Break the eggs into the well, then add 2 tablespoons of the water. With a fork, beat the eggs and water together, incorporating a bit of the flour. As the liquids become blended, continue to push flour into the well. Eventually, you will have to use your hand to mix.

When well blended, lightly flour the board and start kneading the dough on it. With a bench scraper, turn the dough and press it with your fingertips, then knead a few strokes again. The dough should remain slightly sticky but become smooth and elastic. Form into a ball and let rest on the board, covered with a bowl or a piece of plastic wrap, for 30 minutes.

Using half the dough at a time, and keeping the other half covered, roll the dough out very thinly on the floured board. This may take some stretching as you roll. Alternately, you can use a crank-handled pasta machine, eventually rolling the dough on the thinnest setting.

To fill and shape the kreplach, cut the rolled dough into 3-inch squares. Put no more than 1 teaspoon of filling in the center of each square. Brush the edges of the squares with some of the remaining water. Fold the dough from point to point, forming a triangle, and seal carefully. This is the final shape of the kreplach for some people, while others take the two points of the long side of the triangle and press them together, forming exactly the same shape as tortellini, but larger.

To cook the kreplach, bring a large pot of well-salted water to a boil over high heat. Add the kreplach and boil for 6 to 8 minutes, until the dough is cooked and tender. They can be drained and cooled now, to be reheated in the chicken soup.

Cooked kreplach freeze perfectly. Defrost either in the refrigerator or at room temperature, then reheat in simmering chicken soup.

Mushroom-Barley Soup

It took a trip to Lithuania in 1988, when it was still part of the Soviet Union, for me to understand why wild mushrooms were so much a part of my people's home cooking. Mushrooms are free for the gathering, and the many woods of Eastern Europe are filled with them. New York City is such a Jewish town, that after World War II and until recently, dried black mushrooms used to be available in the supermarket.

Mushroom-barley soup is made with fresh mushrooms, too, but wild dried boletus—Lithuanian, Polish, or Italian (porcini)—give it enough flavor to be a good vegetarian soup. Still, I think it is best when made with good chicken soup as the base, an extravagance that would never have been used in a traditional kitchen. Grandma would have put a piece of flanken in it to give a little extra flavor.

I devised this recipe more than thirty years ago. It was meant to imitate the dried soup mixes that come in a long cellophane bag. I still see these soup mixes in the supermarket—made by Mother's, Horowitz Margareten, and Manisch-ewitz (actually, now, three labels of the same company). Besides the named ingredients, the packets contain bouillon crystals, which are mostly salt and MSG. To avoid those bouillon crystals and to substitute real broth, I weighed out the barley, beans, split peas, and dried mushrooms that came in the mushroom-barley blend so I could come up with a fair approximation of the packaged soup. Of course, once you use good chicken soup as the base instead of the package's chicken "flavoring," the soup becomes significantly elevated.

For a vegetarian soup, substitute 4 quarts water or vegetable broth for the chicken soup plus water.

Serves 10 to 12

3 tablespoons peanut, corn, or canola oil

2 medium onions, chopped (about 2 cups)

1 large carrot, peeled

2 outer ribs celery, chopped (about 1 cup)

1¼ cups barley (½ pound)

½ cup dried baby lima beans

½ cup split peas (green, yellow, or mixed)

1 ounce dried mushrooms (see headnote), coarsely crumbled

12 cups (or more) Chicken Soup (page 40)

4 cups (or more) water

1 teaspoon salt

¼ teaspoon freshly ground black pepper

In a 5-quart or larger pot, heat the oil over medium-high heat; sauté the onions until tender and beginning to brown, 8 to 10 minutes.

Grate the carrot into the pot, using the coarse side of a box grater and holding the carrot perpendicular to the grater so the pieces are short. Add the celery. Sauté the vegetables 3 to 4 minutes more.

Add the barley, lima beans, split peas, dried mushrooms, broth, and water. Bring to a boil, then partially cover the pot and decrease the heat to low so the soup simmers gently. Cook at a slow, steady simmer for about 1½ hours, until the lima beans and barley are tender and the split peas have dissolved. After about 45 minutes, add the salt and pepper.

At the end of cooking, add a little more water or chicken soup, as necessary, to bring the soup to a thickness you like. Then taste and adjust the salt and pepper.

Serve very hot.

The soup can be kept refrigerated, tightly covered, for several days or frozen for several months. Reheat gently, stirring frequently, thinning it out with water and adding more salt and pepper as needed.

Split Pea Soup

 ——————————————————————————

Split pea soup can be prepared without meat, in which case it can be eaten at a meal that contains dairy products. Or it can be made with meat, usually a slice or two of flanken and sometimes with chicken broth. Naturally, everyone's grandmother and mother had a special recipe for split pea soup. And many an American Jewish mother or *bubbe* (grandma) floated rounds of sliced frankfurters on the surface just to prove she was a real "Yankee," as they used to say.

Vegetarian or not, split pea is supposed to be a very hearty soup. In fact, many a maker lives by the rule that if a wooden spoon doesn't stand up in the soup on its own then the soup isn't thick *enough*. Crisp croutons can add some needed textural contrast. Rye bread croutons are perfect. You might arrange to have some days-old rye bread around that you can cut into cubes and toast or fry. You can use yellow split peas instead of green, but I don't mix them because the resulting color is too muddy.

Serves 8 to 10

10 cups water

1 pound green or yellow split peas

1 large clove garlic, coarsely chopped

2½ cups grated carrots (about 4 medium)

1½ cups finely chopped onion (1 large)

1 cup coarsely grated parsnip (1 medium)

¾ cup finely chopped celery (1 large outer rib)

1 parsley root, minced (if available)

2 teaspoons salt

¾ to 1 teaspoon freshly ground black pepper

2 tablespoons chopped fresh dill, for garnish (optional)

2 hot dogs, thinly sliced, for garnish (optional)

Croutons, for garnish (optional)

In a 5-quart pot, combine the water, split peas, garlic, carrots, onion, parsnip, celery, parsley root, salt, and pepper. Bring to a simmer over medium heat, partially cover the pot, and adjust the heat so the soup simmers gently for 1¹/₂ hours. Stir occasionally.

At this point, the peas should have fallen apart and the soup will be a thick, rough porridge. It can be eaten immediately, as is, but pea soup is usually pureed. Puree the soup in a food processor or blender, or with a food mill or immersion blender.

Reheat the soup and dilute it with additional water as necessary to get a consistency you like. Add the dill and hot dogs at this point, and bring to a simmer before serving. Serve croutons on the side.

Meat Variation

Before adding the peas and other ingredients, bring 1 to 1¹/₂ pounds of beef flanken to a boil in the water. Simmer for 30 minutes. There is no need to skim the scum, but you can if you want.

Add the peas and remaining ingredients, except the garnishes. When the soup is fully cooked, remove the meat from the bones. Discard the bones and cut the meat into small pieces. Garnish each bowl of soup with pieces of meat, as well as other optional garnishes. For a chicken-based soup, use 10 cups of chicken soup instead of water, or at least 5 cups of chicken soup and the rest water.

Sweet-and-Sour Cabbage Borscht

My maternal grandmother, Elsie Binder Sonkin, made spectacular sweet-and-sour cabbage soup using canned tomatoes and canned tomato puree, adding granulated sugar and sour salt crystals (citric acid) to create the balance of sweet and sour that she called "winey." When I first tasted the following formula at the *glatt* kosher Crown Restaurant in the Boro Park section of Brooklyn, I thought it was pretty close to Elsie's. I was astounded when the Polish-born cook told me that ketchup was the main ingredient. If you think about it, ketchup has the sweet-sour balance that Eastern European Jews crave. And as Heinz ketchup was only the second commercial food product (after Heinz vegetarian beans) to sport a *hechsher*, the stamp of approval of a kosher supervising agent, it's no wonder it became a substitute for cans of tomatoes and tomato puree, sugar, and sour salt.

Serves about 8

2 pounds boneless chuck, cut into
  2- to 3-inch chunks
4 quarts water
1 tablespoon salt
1 large head green cabbage
  (about 3 pounds)

1¹/₂ cups ketchup
1 (6-ounce) can tomato paste
2 tablespoons sugar
¹/₂ teaspoon (or more) freshly ground
  black pepper

In a 5-quart pot, combine the meat, water, and salt. Bring to a simmer over high heat. Adjust the heat and simmer gently, uncovered, for 1 hour.

Meanwhile, halve the cabbage through the core, cut out the core in each half, and shred the cabbage as finely as you can. Rinse well in a colander.

Add the cabbage, ketchup, tomato paste, and sugar to the pot with the boiled beef. Return to a simmer and cook, partially covered, for 2 hours longer.

Let the soup rest for several hours at room temperature before reheating and serving. Skim off most if not all of the fat that rises to the surface. Even better, make the soup a day ahead, refrigerate, remove the congealed fat, and reheat.

The soup can be kept in the refrigerator, tightly covered, for at least a week.

The Borscht Belt (The Catskills)

Though the food hit your stomach quite heavily
At the Borscht Belt resorts like the Nevele,
It was kosher, at least!
Jewish guests used to feast
Through the day and all night until reveille.

　　—Anonymous

When a waiter put down the breakfast menu, guests would look it
over and say, "Fine! I'll have it."

　　—Alan King, *Is Salami and Eggs Better Than Sex?*

Food dominated life at the hotels. Huge meals of great variety were the
Catskills signature, and the source of much analysis, humor, and deprecation
by guests, dining room staff, and comedians.

　　—Phil Brown, *In the Catskills: A Century of the Jewish Experience*
　　in "The Mountains"

It was Abel Green, an editor at *Variety*, the entertainment industry newspaper, who first referred to the Catskill Mountain resorts as the "Borscht Belt." Jews in New York City just called it "The Mountains," as if there were no other.

Actually, technically, the Borscht Belt wasn't really in the Catskill *Mountains*. At best, these hotels that made a name for themselves through their world-class entertainment and opulently heaped dining tables were in the foothills of the Catskills, in neighboring Sullivan County. It was like Las Vegas without gambling, although the area is about to get gambling.

Without traffic, it would take about four hours to get from Manhattan to the Nevele during the 1930s, 1940s, and into the mid-1950s. With better roads, mainly a rebuilt Route 17 ("The Quickway," a joke of a name if there ever was one), which opened in 1958, the drive came down to two hours, maybe less with no traffic. It depended on how fast you drove, and how often you had to stop.

Of course, there never was *no* traffic, except in the middle of the night. The men who left work

Charles and Lillian Brown's hotel,
Loch Sheldrake, New York

in New York City at 5 P.M. on Friday often didn't get to greet their family ensconced in a Catskill bungalow or hotel until 10 P.M. The men would stay through Sunday, then drive back to "The City," leaving the Mrs. and the children to enjoy the "mountain" air.

Families that couldn't afford to go away for the whole summer often took a weekend or weeklong vacation in the Catskills, where the big hotels hired major name talent, and the small hotels hired no-name but often equally talented singers and comics.

The dining room at Grossinger's

In the winter, New Yorkers took getaway weekends, attracted not only by the entertainment in sprawling nightclub rooms, but also by the food. At first, it was just the normal food of Yiddish Jews. At the end of the Borscht Belt era, by which time home cooking had become much more American, people went to Grossinger's and The Concord, Kutcher's and the Nevele, for a taste of food they were no longer eating at home. It was the food of their past, sanctified by nostalgia.

Long before there were comedy clubs and the Comedy Channel, the Borscht Belt was the place where stand-up comics and young singers were nurtured. All the great names played the big hotels. On a single weekend in the 1950s through the 1960s, you could see Steve Lawrence and Eydie Gorme, Jerry Lewis (in the early years with, and in later years without, Dean Martin), Henny Youngman, Buddy Hackett, Jackie Mason. The list could go on and on. Sophie Tucker was still performing in the Catskills in the 1950s. We're talking here legendary entertainers at legendary hotels.

The Nevele and Kutscher's are the last of the big-name hotels in the Catskills. The Nevele was recently bought by Bobover Hasidim. Kutscher's attracts a kosher, *haimish*, modern Orthodox, but more secular Jewish crowd.

A seder menu from The Concord

One of the big attractions of the hotels was that you could eat all you wanted. You could order every dish on the menu and your waiter wouldn't blink, knowing the more food he brought, the better his tip.

The waiter and busboy culture of the Catskills is almost more important than the food they served. The food itself was the full repertoire of Yiddish dishes— the recipes in this cookbook, plus American breakfast items like pancakes and the gamut of egg dishes, plus hamburgers and grilled dinner entrees. The waiters were more or less ambitious Jewish high school and college students, all boys, all expecting to become businessmen or professionals. They intended to make enough money in the Catskills to pay for law school or medical school or to just put themselves through college. For two generations, this was a formative experience for so many Jewish men.

The Catskills today are still very Jewish, but it's a different crowd, "a different element," my grandmother would say. Many Hasidim have settled in this economically depressed, rural area, desiring a separation from secular society and culture.

Clear (Cold) Borscht

These days, before Passover in early spring, supermarket shelves become stocked with jars of borscht, because it is around Passover that less observant Jewish people become particularly nostalgic about their traditional foods. Actually, in metro New York, you can buy bottled borscht any time of the year.

There is, in fact, a special Passover borscht, made with *rosle*, which is the juice of fermented beets. Hardly anyone makes their own *rosle* these days. You need a large crock, a cool place like a basement, and a tolerance for the gray scum and stink it produces before it becomes this divine ruby red elixir, both sweet and sour, that can be used as a base for borscht. Today, however, you can buy *rosle* in a jar in kosher markets. The Pickle Guys on Essex Street on the Lower East Side of Manhattan stock it well into the summer.

This recipe is called clear borscht to distinguish it from meat borscht, which is also called Knubble Borscht (page 59) because *knubble* means garlic in Yiddish, and meat borscht, a Ukrainian specialty, is full of garlic.

Clear borscht is a great hot weather food. Served very cold, it is immensely refreshing. I remember well the summer days when my father and I would make a pit stop at Yonah Schimmel's Knishery, not for the knishes, which we didn't care for, but to have a glass of cold borscht blended with sour cream. Glasses of the thick pink drink were already poured and waiting in a refrigerated case behind the counter. At home, my father would drink borscht straight, without cream, downing it like a glass of iced tea or lemonade. Sometimes my mother would serve it in a soup bowl, with a big dollop of sour cream and a boiled potato. It was the first course before a summer dairy meal of egg salad or tuna salad, with cut-up tomato and cucumber and fresh Corn Bread (page 205), which is actually sour rye.

Serves about 8

3 pounds beets, washed, peeled, and halved

1 onion, coarsely chopped

10 cups water

1 tablespoon salt

1/3 cup lemon juice, or 1/2 teaspoon sour salt

3 tablespoons sugar

Sour cream, for garnish (optional)

Boiled potato, for garnish (optional)

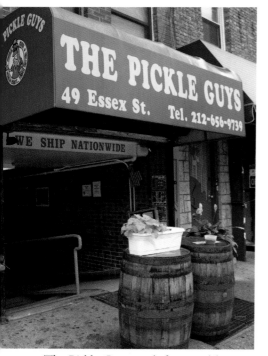

The Pickle Guys stock fermented beet juice to make rosle *borscht*

In a 5-quart pot, combine the beet halves, onion, water, and salt. Bring to a boil over high heat. Boil, partially covered, for 1 hour, or until the beets are very tender.

Remove the beets with a slotted spoon and cut them into julienne strips. Strain out the onion from the cooking liquid. Return the beets and any beet juice to the cooking liquid in the pot. Add the lemon juice and the sugar. Return to the pot and simmer, partially covered, 30 minutes longer.

Taste for sweet and sour seasoning, adjusting to please your palate.

Refrigerate in a tightly covered container and chill very well. Serve cold in a glass, as is or with about 2 tablespoons of sour cream blended into each cup of borscht, if desired. Or serve in a bowl with a spoon, garnished with a boiled potato and a big dollop of sour cream.

Knubble Borscht

Hot Meat Borscht with Garlic

Yiddish-speaking Jews call this *knubble* borscht because *knubble* means garlic, and the defining flavor of this soup, besides beets, is a large dose of raw garlic added just before serving. It is Ukrainian-style borscht with an underpinning of strong beef broth. Cubed root vegetables and shredded, roasted beets provide plenty of sweetness, although many cooks add additional sugar. In fact, to balance the soup's sweetness, I like to add an acidic edge with lemon juice.

Serves 6 to 8

2 pounds beef flanken or short ribs

12 cups water

2 teaspoons coarse sea salt

1 medium carrot, peeled

1 medium celery root, peeled, $^1/_4$ of the root left whole, the remaining cut into $^1/_2$-inch cubes

1 medium onion, with papery skin, studded with several whole cloves

8 whole allspice berries

3 medium-large beets (about $1^1/_2$ pounds without tops)

2 tablespoons peanut, corn, or canola oil

2 large onions, coarsely chopped (about 3 cups)

1 medium parsnip, peeled and cut into $^1/_2$-inch cubes (about $^3/_4$ cup)

2 medium white turnips, cut into $^1/_2$-inch cubes (about 2 cups)

1 large carrot, peeled, cut into $^1/_2$-inch cubes (about $^3/_4$ cup)

2 medium potatoes, cut into $^1/_2$-inch cubes (about 2 cups)

$^1/_2$ teaspoon freshly ground black pepper

1 well-rounded tablespoon tomato paste

8 to 10 large cloves garlic, crushed or pressed

Juice of $^1/_2$ lemon

3 tablespoons finely chopped fresh dill

3 tablespoons finely chopped fresh parsley

In a 5-quart or larger pot, combine the meat and water and bring to a boil over high heat. Decrease the heat to medium-low and skim off the foam.

When foam stops rising to the top, add the salt, the medium whole carrot, the quarter piece of celery root, the clove-studded whole onion, and the allspice. Simmer gently, partially covered, for $1^1/_2$ to 2 hours, or until the meat falls off the bone.

Preheat the oven to 400°F. Meanwhile, scrub the beets and wrap them in aluminum foil. Set the foil-wrapped beets on a rack in the middle of the oven and roast for about 1 hour, or until just tender. Poke through the foil with a skewer or the point of a sharp knife to check for doneness. Let the beets cool enough to handle. Peel them—the skins will peel or rub off easily—then shred them on the coarse side of a box grater. Set aside.

When the meat is very tender, remove it from the pot, strip it off the bones, and cut into small cubes. Place in a bowl and cover with foil. Strain the broth and set aside. Rinse out the pot in which the broth was made.

Place the pot over medium heat, warm the oil, and sauté the chopped onions for 5 minutes, until well wilted. Add the cubed celery root, parsnip, turnips, and cubed carrot. Sauté for another 5 minutes. Add the strained broth, potatoes, shredded beets, pepper, and tomato paste. Bring to a boil over high heat. Decrease the heat so that the soup simmers, uncovered, for at least 20 minutes, or until the vegetables are tender. Add the reserved meat.

Just before serving, and while the soup is simmering gently, stir in the garlic and lemon juice, and the dill and parsley. Immediately remove from the heat. Serve piping hot.

The borscht can be refrigerated, tightly covered, for up to a week. Do not freeze, as freezing changes the texture of the vegetables. When reheating, bring to a simmer and add more fresh crushed garlic just before serving.

Variation

In addition to the root vegetables or as a substitute for turnips, add 2 to 4 cups coarsely chopped cabbage.

Molly Goldberg

It says something about America during the Depression and through the post–World War II years that the biggest hits on radio, and then on the emerging medium of television, were two situation comedies based on ethnic stereotypes living in New York City. There was *The Goldbergs* of the Bronx and *Amos 'n' Andy* in Harlem.

What it might say is that Americans were ready to accept these ethnic groups as long as they remained the stereotype and made them laugh. Much of the humor of both shows was based on a misuse of the English language.

Amos 'n' Andy perpetuated the images of the shuffling, lazy, shifty, and ineffectual African-American male, but in this case he was outdone by hard-working, black family men and women, with emphasis on the strong women.

The Goldbergs perpetuated the stereotype of the all-wise, bossy, guilt-provoking Jewish mother. At the same time it showed how Old-World shtetl values meshed with New-World American values, and how the Goldberg children were able to assimilate fully into the American way of life.

Gertrude Berg, Harlem-born and with a degree from Columbia University, not only starred as Molly Goldberg but also was the creator and writer of the program, which began airing on radio in 1929 as *The Rise of the Goldbergs*, a 15-minute soap opera broadcast five days a week. It was the first family-based situation comedy and the prototype for every one that came after, from *The Adventures of Ozzie and Harriet*, through *Leave It to Beaver*, *The Cosby Show*, and *Everybody Loves Raymond*. The Goldberg family may have been Jewish, and from the Bronx, but their problems were universal.

From 1949 to 1955, *The Goldbergs* was a successful television series. Molly's greeting to her neighbor at the opening of each show—"Yoo-hoo, Mrs. Bloom!"—became a national punch line (although it has mistakenly come down to us as "Yoo-hoo, Mrs. Goldberg!").

In 1955, about the time the television show expired, Berg wrote a cookbook with Myra Waldo Schwartz (no relation). Because Myra Waldo was a professional food writer and thoroughly tested her recipes, the book remains one of the best on the subject of Ashkenazic cooking, with Molly's wry or merely whimsical commentary.

After TV, Gertrude Berg made a movie called *The Goldbergs*, later renamed *Molly*, and she starred on Broadway in *A Majority of One*, for which she won a Tony. She died in 1966. ✍

Potato Soup

Eastern Europeans became potato eaters after the middle of the nineteenth century. The potato competed with grain, although never surpassed its consumption. Bread was still the staff of life. But potatoes provided a good percentage of calories, as well as some essential nutrition, including vitamin C. The nutrients in milk complemented those of potatoes, and it was fortunate that Eastern Europeans kept cows and goats, giving them a constant flow of milk, cream, and the dairy products one could make with them.

Rich with butter and milk or cream, this is the kind of homey potato soup that many a cook from a Lower East Side tenement or poor Brownsville neighborhood could whip up when the budget was exhausted. Soups like this were also served in the kosher dairy restaurants, although they often had no milk or cream. Flour dissolved in water or a thickening roux (*einbrin,* in Yiddish) was added to "cream" the soup. It was a cheap method of faking richness. I have even seen recipes using farina for that purpose. I like this formula from *The Molly Goldberg Cookbook*, which uses barley for creaminess, but also some real cream. Gertrude Berg called it "Mrs. Barnett's Creamed Potato Soup," referring to the fictional Molly's fictional neighbor. To give you some of the flavor of the cookbook's prose, which so well mimics the speech patterns of mid-twentieth-century New York Jews, I quote the introduction to the recipe:

> *This recipe was passed down to me from Mrs. Barnett, who lives upstairs in 6E. By me it's potato soup and by her it's vichyssoise (that's French). How it got so fancy I don't know, but if Mrs. Barnett likes her potato soup French and I like mine plain, what's the difference? It tastes the same and a name is only a name. So I don't mind at all what Mrs. Barnett calls her soup because she's Dora's mother and My Sammy and Dora are going steady together. A good soup is only soup but Dora could be a daughter-in-law, and I ask you, what's more important?*

Serves 4

3 tablespoons butter

2 cups finely chopped onions
(about 2 medium onions)

1 cup diced celery

2 pounds potatoes, peeled and
cut into 1/2-inch cubes

6 cups water

2 tablespoons pearl barley

1 cup whole milk or light cream

2 teaspoons salt

1/4 teaspoon ground white pepper

In a 3-quart saucepan, melt the butter over medium heat and sauté the onions until golden, about 10 minutes.

Add the celery, potatoes, water, and barley. Bring to a boil over medium-high heat and boil vigorously, partially covered, for 30 minutes, by which time both the potatoes and the barley should be very tender. With a wooden spoon, smash some of the potatoes into the side of the pot to add a little extra thickening.

Add the milk and stir well. Check for and adjust the salt. Stir in the pepper. Return to a simmer before serving.

Potatoes

Starting in the middle of the nineteenth century, potatoes were a mainstay in Eastern Europe, a major and dependable source of calories and therefore an inspiration to invention. Potato Latkes (page 78), Potato Kugel (page 76), Potato Knishes (page 90), and potato Blintzes (page 149), as well as potato-based Vegetable Cutlets (page 145) are just a few Jewish creations. Potatoes go into Cholent (page 103), too, as if the dish weren't starchy enough with its base of beans and barley.

Mashed potatoes are very popular, and there is a Yiddish twist to them. Because butter and milk are forbidden when eating meat, mashed potatoes meant for a meat meal are enriched with schmaltz and fried onions, *griebenes*, too, if there happen to be some (page 10). As a guide for these seasoned mashed potatoes, use the recipe for knish filling on page 93. ✍

Schav

Schav translates from Yiddish as "sour grass," and "sour grass soup" or *schav* was indeed what my American-born grandmother called this sorrel soup. I hated the sour taste and mucky gray-green color then, and so I dreaded the day in early summer that she would bring home big, brown-paper grocery bags full of sorrel, the sour grass itself. These days, by me in Brooklyn, a little bunch of tender sorrel costs five dollars.

Fortunately, perfectly good *schav* comes in a jar, from Manischewitz, Mother's, and Gold's, and is available in New York City supermarkets. If you have a garden, sorrel is a very easy to grow perennial.

Makes 4 quarts

4 pounds fresh sorrel

4 quarts water

Salt and freshly ground black pepper

Lemon juice (optional)

4 eggs, raw or hard-cooked, for garnish (optional)

Sour cream or yogurt, for garnish (optional)

Chopped cucumber, for garnish (optional)

Chopped scallions, for garnish (optional)

Chopped red radishes, for garnish (optional)

A medium boiled potato per serving, for garnish (optional)

Pick over and wash the sorrel well. Remove the tough stems, then finely chop the leaves. In an 8-quart nonreactive pot, bring the water to a rolling boil over high heat. Drop in the sorrel and boil for 10 minutes. Remove from the heat. Season with salt and pepper. Taste, and add a little lemon juice if desired.

To enrich the soup with raw egg, beat the eggs well in a small bowl. Bring the soup to a boil, remove from the heat, then beat some of the hot soup into the eggs, then return the egg mixture back into the soup, which at this point should be very hot, but not boiling. Alternatively, you can add whole or chopped hard-cooked eggs to the *schav* when it's served.

To store, refrigerate, tightly covered. Without eggs, the *schav* should keep well for about 10 days. With eggs, do not keep longer than 3 days. Do not freeze.

Serve very well chilled in deep or shallow bowls with a hefty dollop of sour cream, either floating in the soup or beaten into it, chopped cucumber, chopped scallions, chopped red radish, and a boiled potato.

Cold Fruit Soup

Russians and Poles love cold fruit soups in hot weather. One of the delights of promenading on Brooklyn's Brighton Beach boardwalk in the summer (now the heart of Little Odessa, a Russian neighborhood since the 1970s) is that you can stop at a boardwalk café and get a big bowl of chilled fruit soup. Sour cherry is my favorite, with a dollop of sour cream. In the old days, the dairy restaurants would serve it. This is the fruit soup I have been making at home for decades. You can drink it by the glassful rather than sip it from a bowl with a spoon.

Makes about 5 quarts

5 medium MacIntosh apples, washed and cored but not peeled

5 medium ripe peaches, peeled and pitted

5 large ripe plums (any kind, but preferably soft, juicy, and dark), pitted

1 pint ripe strawberries, hulled

1/2 pint fresh blueberries

1 to 1 1/2 pounds assorted seedless grapes

1 pound pitted prunes

1/4 pound dark raisins

10 cups water

Apple juice, as needed (optional)

Heavy cream, sour cream, or yogurt, for garnish (optional)

Cut the apples, peaches, and plums into small pieces. In an 8-quart or larger nonreactive pot, combine all the fruit, fresh and dried, with the 10 cups of water.

Cover, bring to a boil over high heat, then decrease the heat to medium-low and simmer steadily, partially covered, stirring occasionally, for about 45 mintes, or until the fruit has disintegrated.

Press all the fruit through a coarse sieve, a chinois (cone-shaped sieve), or a food mill. Or puree in small batches in a food processor fitted with the metal blade. (If a food processor is to be used, peel the apples.) The puree will be very thick, just pourable (you can thin it with more water or with apple juice if you like).

Chill very well. Serve in bowls or mugs, with or without a dollop or swirl of heavy cream, sour cream, or yogurt. The soup can be kept refrigerated, tightly covered, for up to 1 week. Do not freeze.

A dried fruit "arrangement" and bulk dried fruits; Golan, a huge fruit market on Coney Island Avenue and Avenue J in Brooklyn, an Orthodox Jewish shopping area

CHAPTER 3

⊰ Side Dishes ⊱

If you want a green vegetable, eat a pickle.
 —Jewish advice

J ews from Eastern Europe didn't eat as many vegetables as other Europeans, other than root vegetables. For the most part, the climate was too harsh or the soil was too poor, or both, to support many vegetables. There were plenty of onions and garlic for seasoning, plus cabbage, carrots, parsnips, turnips, and beets. During the brief summer growing season, there would be what would become known as "garden vegetables"—cucumbers, scallions, radishes of various shapes and color, and tomatoes. In Hungary and Romania, they ate eggplant. And by the end of the nineteenth century just before the Yiddish-speaking Jews emigrated to America, peppers and tomatoes, both New World ingredients, had become established all over Europe. Let's not forget that paprika, one of only a very few spices used in Yiddish food, is dried, ground peppers.

Beginning in the mid-nineteenth century, potatoes became popular, although grains remained the starch mainstays—barley, rye, buckwheat (kasha), and wheat. Wheat was turned into flour for bread and used to make many noodle products.

Being in America didn't change much. At the end of the nineteenth century, vegetable markets were not as common as butcher shops. Indeed, Americans, with the exception of Italian-Americans, didn't eat a large variety of fresh vegetables until fairly recently. The following recipes are the traditional Eastern European repertoire. That's why there are no recipes for broccoli or dark leafy greens, but that doesn't mean they shouldn't be served with Yiddish food, as, of course, they are today. We even have broccoli and spinach knishes.

Kugel

Kugel, more or less "pudding" in Yiddish, is usually made with a starch ingredient base like noodles, potatoes, rice, or bread. It was originally cooked overnight alongside the long-cooked Sabbath casserole, Cholent (page 103). Actually, some cooks put a kugel mixture on top of their cholent and let the two cook together. On the other hand, some cooks would call this starchy mixture a *knaidle*, a dumpling. Now to make this even more confusing, before there was kugel, there was matzo *schalet*, noodle *schalet*, and *weck schalet*, *weck* being the northern and western German dialect word for a bread roll. (By the way, in Buffalo, New York, *weck* is still the word used for a Kaiser or Vienna roll. In fact, "beef on weck," sliced roast beef on a roll dipped in the drippings, is, after Buffalo chicken wings, that city's chief culinary claim to fame.)

In Poland, all these starchy dishes came to be known as kugel because they were baked in a round shape, and kugel is Yiddish for a ball or sphere. Nowadays, however, kugel can be any shape and is more likely baked in a rectangular pan than a round one.

Kugels baked overnight (like cholent) are still made in über-Orthodox communities. The most popular is Jerusalem kugel, a pudding made with fine egg noodles that are heavily sweetened with caramel, but usually also heavy with the balancing flavor of black pepper. After cooking in a very deep pan for 12 hours or longer, which further caramelizes the kugel, it becomes a rich brown. It is a creation of the Lubavitch Chabad Hasidim in Jerusalem, but it is now also standard fare for other Orthodox communities.

Haimish potato pudding is a similarly long-cooked and very thick kugel, unsweetened but caramel-colored from the long-cooked sugars in the potatoes. I find these puddings better bought than baked at home. They taste so much better when baked in huge, deep pans, which are way too big to even fit in a home oven, and make way too much for a normal-size American family to eat. Still, some people, with big families, make them at home.

Kugels are still among the most popular traditional dishes in kosher homes, even when the recipes are not traditional. For the most part, kugels can be baked ahead of time, and they reheat well or are delicious at room temperature, qualities that make them perfect for large family gatherings. As Orthodox families often have six or more children, these qualities are important. And there are so many varieties of kugel that you can serve several different ones together, as people often do.

By far the most popular kugel is noodle kugel (*lukshen* kugel, in Yiddish). The simplest and most traditional *lukshen* kugel is the one made to be eaten on the Sabbath with a meat meal. It is nothing more than boiled egg noodles mixed with salt, pepper, schmaltz or oil, and eggs, and sometimes fried onions. The proportion is usually 3 eggs to each $1/2$ pound of fine or medium egg noodles, with about 2 tablespoons of schmaltz or oil. Sometimes raisins or apples or both are added, too. They definitely add interest to this otherwise austere dish.

Dairy noodle kugels, on the other hand, are usually elaborate and rich. And here's where new American ingredients have been most adopted. Canned fruit cocktail, canned pineapple, corn flakes, and cream cheese are often added to dairy kugels.

Rice kugel, a baked rice pudding one rarely sees these days, was a specialty of the dairy restaurants, and my paternal grandmother, Rose Cohen Schwartz. At the restaurants, these tended to be overly sweet, served hot, and often sauced with cornstarch-thickened canned fruit cocktail. My grandmother's was very rich with egg yolks and topped with meringue that she made from the egg whites that didn't go into the custard. It was always served as dessert or on its own as a light meal or an afternoon snack. ❧

Anne Whiteman's Birthday Kugel

Anne Whiteman was the mother of Michael Whiteman, a Brooklyn native and the business and creative partner of the legendary Joe Baum in designing and operating many restaurant projects, among them the food services of the World Trade Center, including Windows on the World, and the restoration and operation of the Rainbow Room.

If this is the kind of food Michael grew up eating, then it's no wonder his palate is so finely tuned. This recipe is typical of highly evolved dairy noodle kugels, in that it is dessert-sweet and topped with corn flakes, although it doesn't call for the canned crushed pineapple that so many less refined recipes do. Here, the cottage cheese is pureed with the sour cream, milk, and eggs to form a silken custard to hold the noodles. Michael and I are not certain how his mother arrived at the odd amount of sour cream, but I have decided not to change it. It is called "birthday kugel" because his mother made it mainly for those celebratory occasions.

Serves 12

6 eggs
1¹/₂ cups 4-percent-fat cottage cheese
   (small or large curd, or California-
   style)
1 cup plus 2 tablespoons sour cream
³/₄ cup sugar
2¹/₄ cups whole milk
³/₄ cup raisins
6 tablespoons butter, melted

2¹/₄ teaspoons vanilla extract
1 teaspoon grated orange zest
1 teaspoon grated lemon zest
1 tablespoon salt
18 ounces wide, preferably flat
   egg noodles

Topping
1 cup coarsely crushed corn flakes
2 tablespoons butter, melted
2 teaspoons ground cinnamon

To make the kugel, in the bowl of a food processor fitted with the metal blade, whirl together the eggs. Add the cottage cheese, sour cream, and sugar. Process until smooth. Pour into a large bowl and stir in the milk, raisins, melted butter, vanilla, and orange and lemon zests.

In a large pot, bring at least 5 quarts of water to a boil over high heat, salt, and cook the noodles until just before they are fully cooked, about 5 minutes, but check package directions for exact timing. Drain and stir the noodles into the egg-cheese mixture, then refrigerate, tightly covered, overnight. (I think this step of preparing ahead was mainly for convenience. I have baked the pudding immediately, and it turns out lighter; the noodles don't absorb as much of the custard.)

Lightly butter a 9- by 13-inch baking dish. Preheat the oven to 350°F.

To make the topping, toss together the corn flakes, melted butter, and cinnamon in a small bowl. To bake the kugel, pour the noodle mixture into the baking dish and sprinkle evenly with the topping. Bake for 35 to 40 minutes, until lightly browned. Let stand at least 10 minutes before serving.

My Family's Yom Kippur Break Fast Kugel

This is the noodle pudding my maternal grandmother, Elsie Binder Sonkin, made to break the fast on Yom Kippur. We ate it only that one time during the whole year. It is so rich that it is certainly not the best thing to eat after an entire day of fasting, but we did and still do. It is not a sweet pudding, but we did eat it as a last course, if not dessert. After the table was cleared, and the first round of dishes was washed, we went on to coffee, cakes, and pastries. Before the kugel, we ate pickled herring with "wine" sauce and cream sauce, platters of smoked whitefish, sable, and kippered salmon (also called baked salmon), cream cheese, Munster and Swiss cheeses, egg and tuna salads, sliced tomatoes and cucumbers, and bagels and other breads—basically what used to be considered the quintessential New York Jewish Sunday breakfast or brunch, the festive family breakfast that my family did indeed indulge in when we all lived together in one house in Brooklyn.

This is the original kugel recipe with its full quotient of butter, but you can reduce that ingredient from three sticks to two. Relatively dry, large-curd pot cheese may be difficult to find, but you can substitute cottage cheese if need be, large curd, if possible. To further reduce the fat content, you can substitute low-fat sour cream for full-fat. Naturally, if you go for every possible fat reduction, it won't be the same recipe and I can't guarantee it will give the same pleasure.

1 pound wide egg noodles,
   preferably flat, not curly

8 large eggs

3 cups sour cream

1$^1/_2$ pounds pot cheese
   (preferably fresh bulk)

1$^1/_2$ cups (3 sticks) butter, melted

1 tablespoon salt, plus 1 teaspoon,
   or more to taste

$^1/_2$ teaspoon freshly ground
   black pepper, or more to taste

Preheat the oven to 350°F.

In a large pot, bring at least 4 quarts of water to a boil over high heat, add salt, and cook the noodles until done, but still firm to the bite. The time will depend on the noodles; see package directions.

While the noodles boil, in a very large bowl, beat the eggs together. Stir in the sour cream, pot cheese, and most of the butter, reserving about $^1/_4$ cup for the baking pan. Season with the 1 teaspoon salt and the pepper. Drain the cooked noodles and add to this mixture. Mix well. Taste and correct salt and pepper, as desired.

Pour the remaining butter into a 4-quart baking pan with 2-inch sides (a rectangular pan will measure about 10 by 15 inches). Tip the pan to coat the bottom and sides with the melted butter.

Pour in the noodle mixture and bake for 1 hour and 15 minutes, or until the top is lightly browned. Let cool at least 15 minutes before cutting. Serve hot or warm.

Store the baked kugel, tightly covered, in the refrigerator for up to 3 days. The kugel reheats well in a 350°F oven, the exact time depending on the size of the piece. It freezes well, too.

Potato Kugel

All the old recipes for potato kugel come out sort of heavy and gluey, which is not at all how good kugels taste today. These days, the kugel sold in the take-out shops and delicatessens, not to mention those made at home by modern *balabustas*, are still full of good onion flavor but they are high and light. What may seem like an inordinate number of eggs is the secret. Some recipes call for baking powder, too, but I've found the baking powder does absolutely nothing. Lots of eggs are definitely the ticket to lightness. It also helps to use russet potatoes, which were not nearly as available in grandma's day as they are today. Drier russets produce a fluffier kugel. Incidentally, this is a very low-fat recipe.

Besides serving potato kugel as a side dish for meat or poultry or fish, a larger portion of this egg-rich version makes a good lunch. If cut into small squares, it's also a good finger food to go with wine or cocktails.

Serves at least 12

3 pounds russet (baking) potatoes
12 eggs
2 medium onions (about 12 ounces), peeled and cut into chunks
2/3 cup matzo meal

1 tablespoon salt
3/4 to 1 teaspoon freshly ground black pepper
3 tablespoons peanut, corn, or canola oil (for a pareve pudding) or melted Schmaltz (page 9)

Preheat the oven to 350°F.

Peel the potatoes and cut into chunks to prepare them for the food processor. Reserve in a bowl of cold water until ready to process, but don't leave them there longer than 2 hours.

In a very large bowl, beat together the eggs until well mixed. In the bowl of a food processor fitted with the metal blade, pulse the onions until very finely chopped, but not liquefied. Scrape the onions into the bowl with the eggs and stir them in. Stir in the matzo meal.

Drain the potatoes, then set a strainer over a bowl. In the same processor bowl (no need to clean), process the potatoes in three batches, until very finely chopped. The pieces should be no bigger than a grain of rice and mostly smaller.

As each batch of potatoes is processed, immediately scrape it into the strainer. With a rubber spatula or the back of a spoon, press out the moisture so it drains into the catch bowl. Immediately stir the potatoes into the egg mixture. Discard the liquid and potato starch collected in the bowl. Season the batter with salt and pepper.

Pour 2 tablespoons of the oil into a 13- by 9-inch baking dish, preferably heatproof glass. Tip the pan so the oil coats the pan bottom and halfway up the sides. Warm the empty pan in the preheated oven for 5 minutes.

Protecting your hands, remove the hot pan from the oven and fill with the kugel mixture. The oil will rise up the sides of the pan, especially in the corners. It's a good thing when the oil spills onto the surface of the batter, as it adds crispness to the finished dish. Press the batter down near the corners lightly to fill them with potato batter. Drizzle the surface with the remaining 1 tablespoon of oil.

Bake for 1 hour and 15 minutes, until lightly browned. Let rest for at least 15 minutes before cutting and serving, preferably somewhat longer. Serve hot or warm, freshly baked or reheated.

The kugel reheats extremely well in a 350°F oven, uncovered so the top can re-crisp. Reheating time depends on the size of the piece being reheated and the temperature of the kugel before it goes into the oven. It can be kept in the refrigerator, tightly covered, for at least 4 days, and for several months in the freezer. It is best to defrost in the refrigerator before reheating.

Potato Latkes

Latkes are the Eastern European Jewish expression of Chanukah, which is an eight-day festival in December that commemorates the miracle when, after the Second Temple was desecrated by the Syrian Greeks, there was only one day's worth of sacred oil left to put in the eternal lamp over the altar. When the Temple was rededicated by the Jews, this one day's worth of oil lasted eight days, just the time needed to get more.

The celebration of Chanukah is therefore supposed to include fried foods. The ancient oil was olive oil, the main fat of the Mediterranean basin. In December, when the rededication of the Temple occurred, it was during the olive oil harvest, which is why more time was needed to replenish the supply.

In Central and Eastern Europe, potato pancakes were fried in poultry fat, Schmaltz (page 9), because potatoes were plentiful, as was poultry fat, December being the season for slaughtering geese and ducks. These days, however, we fry latkes in flavorless vegetable oil.

In the old days, when a little knuckle blood was considered a seasoning, the potatoes and onions were grated on the finest side of a box grater. I was often enlisted to help with this tedious job. But my maternal grandmother, Elsie Binder Sonkin, was young enough, and lived long enough, to adopt first the blender, then the food processor. The following recipe is my own, based on hers. I always use matzo meal instead of flour because I think it makes the surface of the latkes crisper. It also makes a pancake that reheats better, although reheating is always a compromise.

I used to be against reheating latkes, but I know many people would gladly compromise slightly on the quality of their latkes for the sake of being able to sit down with the family. As I get older, I understand these things better. To reheat, put the pancakes on a rack set in a baking pan and heat in a 425°F oven for about 3 minutes.

Keeping the potatoes from turning gray is a problem for some people. My grandmother's solution was to stir her batter with a very large, tarnished, silver-plated spoon that she'd inherited from her mother. I have it now. When not stirring, it was left in the bowl. I used to think the heirloom spoon had some

magic, but it is only the tartrates on the surface of *tarnished* silver that prevent the potatoes from turning dark. Short of a silver spoon, use a pinch of cream of tartar.

Makes about 24, serving 4 to 6

1 pound russet (baking) potatoes
2 eggs
1 medium onion, peeled and
   cut into 8 pieces
$^1/_4$ to $^1/_3$ cup matzo meal

1$^1/_2$ teaspoons salt
$^1/_4$ teaspoon freshly ground
   black pepper
Pinch of cream of tartar (optional)
Peanut, corn, or canola oil, for frying

To make the batter, peel the potatoes and cut into chunks to prepare them for the food processor. Reserve in a bowl of cold water until ready to process, but don't leave them there longer than 2 hours.

In a medium bowl, beat the eggs together to mix well. In the bowl of a food processor fitted with the metal blade, pulse the onions, scraping them down a few times, until very finely chopped, almost a puree. Scrape the onions into the bowl with the eggs and stir them in.

Drain the potatoes, then set a strainer over a bowl. In the same processor bowl (no need to clean), process the potatoes until very finely chopped, but still with some texture. Immediately scrape it into the strainer. With a rubber spatula or the back of a spoon, press out the moisture so it drains into the catch bowl. Immediately stir the potatoes into the egg mixture. Discard the liquid and potato starch collected in the bowl. Add the matzo meal, salt, and pepper. If not using a tarnished silver spoon, add a pinch of cream of tartar. Stir well and let stand while the oil is heating.

To cook the pancakes, heat about $^1/_8$ inch oil in a large skillet over medium-high heat until very hot. Spoon out the batter, using a scant $^1/_4$ cup for each pancake. The batter should sizzle as soon as it hits the fat, but not wildly. If the edges of the batter separate, the oil is too hot. If there are just slight bubbles when the batter touches the oil, the oil is not yet hot enough. The first round of latkes is inevitably less good than later batches. Consider the first try a cook's share.

Fry the latkes for about 4 minutes on the first side, slightly less time on the second. They should be well browned before turning them. Drain on absorbent paper or on a rack. Serve immediately. See the headnote for reheating directions, although reheating always compromises quality.

Shlishkas

Potato Dumplings with Onions and Breadcrumbs

Shlishkas are Hungarian potato dumplings, but they are nearly identical to Italian gnocchi; the only difference is their shape and the way they are served, but sometimes even the shape is the same. *Shlishkas* can be oval dumplings, sometimes with a dimple in the center, or they can be 2- to 3-inch lengths of ¹/₂-inch-thick rope, while gnocchi are usually stubbier, and as long as they are wide. And *shlishkas* are sautéed briefly with browned onions and breadcrumbs (or breadcrumbs alone), while gnocchi most frequently take tomato sauce (if Sorrento-style, with mozzarella, too), or Ligurian basil pesto, or a creamy mixture of cheeses.

When well made, *shlishkas* should be light, not dense or hard, and taste of potato, not flour. My maternal grandmother, Rose Cohen Schwartz, often sautéed *shlishkas* in chicken schmaltz or goose fat (which is also called schmaltz, incidentally) and served them as a side dish to pot roast, or roasted meat or chicken. I prefer them with butter, however, and I like to eat them for their own sake, as a main course, with a green vegetable, preferably steamed broccoli or briefly sautéed spinach.

Makes about 5 dozen, serving 6 to 8 as a side dish, about 4 as a main course

2 pounds russet potatoes
¹/₂ cup bleached all-purpose flour, plus
   3 tablespoons or more for the board
¹/₂ teaspoon salt
1 egg, lightly beaten

To dress:
6 to 8 tablespoons butter or
   Schmaltz (page 9), or a mixture
   of 4 or 5 tablespoons corn, peanut,
   or canola oil with 1 tablespoon
   schmaltz for flavor
3 medium onions, cut into ¹/₄-inch dice
1 cup plain dry breadcrumbs

Preheat the oven to 400°F. Scrub the potato skins and puncture them in a few places with the point of a knife. Place the potatoes directly on the oven rack. Bake for 45 minutes to 1 hour, depending on the size of the potatoes, until they are soft enough to push a skewer through them easily. Let cool to room temperature.

Peel the potatoes and puree them using a potato ricer or a food mill held over a large bowl. Do not use a food processor.

Sprinkle the ¹/₂ cup flour and the salt over the potatoes and add the beaten egg. With a fork, mix until well blended. Turn the mixture out onto a board sprinkled with 3 tablespoons of flour. Knead the dough, incorporating the flour on the board, just until it holds together, a few seconds. The dough should no longer be sticky. If it is still a bit sticky, sprinkle another couple of teaspoons or as much as a generous tablespoon of flour on the dough, and knead it in.

Using about one-sixth of the dough at a time, roll the dough into ¹/₂-inch-thick ropes. With a knife or bench scraper, cut the ropes into 2- to 3-inch lengths. Spread them out on baking sheets lined with wax paper.

The *shlishkas* can be cooked immediately, or up to one day later if kept tightly covered with plastic in the refrigerator. Or freeze for up to 3 months. Freeze on the baking sheet, well separated, and when the *shlishkas* are hard, pack them into tightly sealed containers or plastic bags. Boil them frozen, directly from the freezer, adding a couple of minutes of cooking time.

Bring a 4- to 5-quart pot of well-salted water to a rolling boil. Cook half the dumplings at a time. Carefully drop half of the dumplings into the water. When they come to the surface and the water has returned to a boil, let them cook for 2 minutes. (Frozen dumplings will take about 4 minutes, at least.) With a slotted spoon or skimmer, remove the *shlishkas* from the water and place in a bowl. Set aside.

In a large skillet over medium heat, melt the butter or heat the schmaltz or oil. Sauté the onions until golden, about 12 minutes. Add the breadcrumbs and mix well with the onions. Add the boiled *shlishkas* and toss in the breadcrumb-onion mixture for about 2 minutes until they are heated through. Serve immediately.

Simche Torenheim of Hungarian Kosher Catering in Brooklyn displays a tray of shlishkas.

Kasha Varnishkes

In Jewish cooking, kasha refers to buckwheat groats, although it is a generic word for cereal in Russian. The word *varnishkes* is connected to the word *vareniki*, which is today the Ukrainian word for a filled dumpling, on the general order of Kreplach (page 47) and Polish pierogi (*pierogen* in Yiddish). However, the word *vareniki* originally meant a rectangular noodle. Today, and for as long as anyone alive can remember, kasha varnishkes is kasha tossed with bow-tie egg noodles, and seasoned with fried onions. Bow ties are made by pinching a pleat into a rectangular noodle.

In Yiddish cooking, kasha is also one of the traditional fillings for knishes (see page 90), which, arguably, were not created in Europe but in New York.

At my family's table, as at many others, kasha prepared with water and no onions or bow ties was the usual accompaniment to a pot roast, and, more often than not, a brisket. The real treat was pouring the meat juices full of onions and vegetables over the nutty flavored grain.

Chicken fat makes all the difference in the flavor of kasha varnishkes. Vegetable oil, such as corn, peanut, or canola, will do, but then I would want the broth to be particularly flavorful and I might use a full quart of broth and not half water, as follows. When I make kasha as a side dish to roast chicken, I deglaze the roasting pan and use those juices to flavor the kasha.

This recipe can easily be cut in half, if desired. It reheats very well. I think it even improves with reheating.

Serves 8

3 medium onions, chopped (about 3 cups), fried in Schmaltz (page 9) or peanut, corn, or canola oil until well browned (page 7)

2 cups water, for deglazing (optional)

1/2 to 1 teaspoon salt

1/4 to 1/2 teaspoon freshly ground black pepper

2 cups chicken or beef broth or bouillon (vegetarians can use vegetable broth), plus 2 cups water (see headnote)

2 cups medium or coarse kasha

1 egg, lightly beaten

4 to 8 ounces dried egg pasta or macaroni bow ties, depending on the balance of noodles and kasha you'd like

To prepare the kasha, if possible, deglaze the pan from frying the onions with 2 cups of water. Pour the deglazing water into a 1-quart measuring cup. Add $^1/_2$ teaspoon salt and $^1/_4$ teaspoon pepper, then add the 2 cups of broth (to make a full quart of liquid) and set aside. If the onions have been fried ahead of time and there is no pan to deglaze, use 4 cups of broth or all water. If using water, not broth, add an additional $^1/_2$ teaspoon salt and $^1/_4$ teaspoon pepper—that is, double the salt and pepper.

In a small bowl, mix the kasha and beaten egg together well. Put the egg-coated kasha in a dry, 10-inch skillet or medium saucepan that has a cover. Place the pan over medium-high heat and stir constantly until the kasha separates into individual grains again, 2 to 3 minutes. The grain's earthy aroma will come up from the pan. Immediately add the reserved liquid. As soon as the mixture begins to simmer, cover the pan, and decrease the heat to medium-low. Cook for 7 to 9 minutes, until the kasha is tender. Fluff the kasha with a fork and set aside, partly covered to let the steam escape.

In a large pot, bring about 3 quarts of well-salted water to a rolling boil over medium-high heat. Add the bow ties and cook until tender. Drain well. Add the fried onions and boiled bow ties to the kasha and toss together until well mixed. Serve hot. The dish can be made ahead and reheated, covered with a lid or foil, in a 300° to 350°F oven.

Mushrooms and Egg Barley

This remains a much beloved, standard Jewish delicatessen item in New York City, and, of course, it is made at home, too. There are several ways to approach it. For one thing, it is pareve if made with vegetable oil, dairy if made with butter. For a meat meal, it can be made with schmaltz. It can also be nothing but farfel boiled in water, like any macaroni, served with Ratner's Vegetarian Brown Gravy (page 146). The following recipe, with fried onions and mushrooms and good broth, is baked in a casserole, but the exact same ingredients can also be cooked on top of the stove.

Serves 4 to 6

2 cups coarsely chopped onions
  (2 medium onions)
3 tablespoons peanut, corn, or canola
  oil, Schmaltz (page 9), or butter
8 to 10 ounces white mushrooms
  (or fresh exotic mushrooms, like
  shiitake, oyster, morels), thickly sliced

8 or 10 ounces plain or toasted egg
  barley or farfel
2½ to 3 cups Chicken Soup (page 40)
Salt and freshly ground black pepper

Preheat the oven to 300°F.

In a 2½- to 3-quart stovetop casserole or ovenproof saucepan, sauté the onions in oil over medium-high heat until they begin to brown, about 10 minutes. Add the mushrooms and continue to sauté, stirring frequently, until the mushrooms have shrunk and browned. If they start to exude liquid, increase the heat so no liquid collects in the pan.

Add the egg barley and the soup. Season with salt and pepper to taste, which will depend on the seasoning of the soup. Taste the broth; it should be highly seasoned, as the egg barley will absorb its flavor when fully cooked. Bring to a simmer over high heat. Cover the pot and place it in the oven. Bake for about 30 minutes, stirring and fluffing the barley with a fork after about 20 minutes. Serve immediately. Or reheat, covered, in a 350°F oven.

Kishka

Stuffed Derma

Kishka means "guts," "intestines," "entrails," or "stomach," as in, "He kicked me in the kishkas." Or, "The movie was so sad it grabbed me in the kishkas." I could go on. It is a very useful Yiddish word. As food, kishka refers to a starch and fat sausage packed into the large intestine of a cow. The starch can be flour, matzo meal, barley, or potatoes. In Lithuania, even today, where there are few if any Jews living, potato-stuffed sausage casings are a popular food. Gentile Polish kishka, which one can readily buy in the Polish stores of Brooklyn's Greenpoint, is stuffed with kasha (buckwheat groats) that is enriched with pig's blood, basically a type of blood sausage. Nothing could be less kosher.

Kishka was actually mentioned in *halachic* literature (Jewish law) more than 700 years ago, originally called P'shtida or Pashtida, and it has been a staple of Shabbos and *yom tov* (holiday) meals for centuries.

Among secular Jews today, kishka is totally out of fashion, but it used to be served at every special Jewish occasion, even elegant weddings and bar mitzvahs where, otherwise, no Yiddish food was served, not even a ball of gefilte fish. It was called "stuffed derma," or even more pretentiously, "derma farci." The only explanation for its presence alongside the prime rib roast and green beans almondine was to remind the guests that they were Jewish, even though they ate shrimp, lobster, and pork lo mein in their everyday lives. Indeed, a friend of mine who got married in the mid-1970s, at the end of kishka's era as an iconic Jewish dish, says his mother claimed she would not attend his "affair" unless kishka was served.

Traditional kishka is made with either beef suet (fat) or chicken fat, often ground, not rendered, and flavored with onion, sometimes also with a tiny bit of carrot, and even celery. I've created a lighter, less pasty, and leaner mixture with matzo meal, and a larger than traditional proportion of vegetables, which allows for a smaller quantity of fat—largely vegetable oil, but blended with a little chicken fat for flavor.

You can still get kishka in Jewish delicatessens in New York, but they are, besides being pasty and served with horrible brown gravy, usually formed in plastic tubes that are not edible. Not that a cow's intestine is such a nice thing to eat. You can still order casings (*bungits*) from a kosher market, but they require intensive cleaning. I remember well my grandmother spending hours at the sink turning the casings inside out and cutting off any suspicious looking fibers. These natural-casing kishkas made with ground fat needed to be boiled first, rubbed with fat to crisp the tough casing, then browned in a roasting pan. Here, the stuffing, which would also serve well inside a chicken, is baked in aluminum foil that holds it in a cylindrical shape. It's so easy you can make it any day of the week. There's no need to wait for a celebration.

Serves 8 to 10

2¹/₂ cups matzo meal

1 tablespoon paprika, preferably sweet imported Hungarian

2 teaspoons salt

¹/₂ teaspoon freshly ground black pepper

³/₄ cup shortening (preferably ¹/₄ cup cold Schmaltz, page 9, plus ¹/₂ cup peanut, corn, or canola oil, all oil, or all schmaltz)

1 cup, firmly packed, very finely chopped carrot (2 medium carrots, chopped in the food processor)

1 cup, firmly packed, almost pureed onion (2 medium onions, chopped in the food processor)

In a large bowl, stir together the matzo meal, paprika, salt, and pepper. Add the shortening and, with a spatula or wooden spoon, blend the ingredients together well. Add the carrots and onions and mix again, until the mixture is a homogenous paste.

Divide the mixture between 2 sheets of aluminum foil, each about 15 inches long. On the bottom third of the narrower side of the foil, compress the mixture with your hands to form a roll about 10 inches long and 3 inches in diameter. Using the foil as a form, start compressing and rolling the kishka up, tucking in the sides as you go. The formed kishka may be refrigerated for up to 1 day before baking, but the kishka is, in fact, better reheated.

For initial baking, preheat the oven to 350°F.

Place the rolls on a baking sheet and bake for 1 hour and 30 minutes, turning the rolls a quarter turn every 20 minutes. Remove from the oven and let the unwrapped kishka rest for at least 15 minutes before opening and slicing.

To reheat as a whole kishka, preheat the oven to 350°F and reheat, in foil, for about 30 minutes if the kishka comes directly from the refrigerator. Or slice the cold kishka and reheat in a dry nonstick skillet over medium heat until crusted on both sides.

If desired, serve with brown gravy, with the sweet-and-sour sauce from potted flanken (page 109), with the onions from a potted brisket (page 105), or with Ratner's Vegetarian Brown Gravy (page 146).

Potato Knishes

Knishes as we know them today were probably created in New York, modeled after an unknown European prototype. According to Eve Jochnowitz, a culinary ethnographer, in a piece by Erica Marcus in Long Island's *Newsday,* "The knish probably had its origins in Western Europe and…it accompanied the Jews eastward when, in the fourteenth century, they were expelled from France." This dating, says Jochnowitz, explains why early European references to knishes have them stuffed with meat or cabbage: the potato didn't make its way from the New World to Europe until after Columbus' journey in the late fifteenth century.

Maybe Jochnowitz is right. I don't think so. She certainly is correct that "those Eureka moments—like that shish kebab was invented by William the Conqueror's wife—are almost never true." Still, the Yonah Schimmel Knish Bakery on Houston Street, one of the few Lower East Side businesses still left from immigrant days, claims to have created them. And there are other stories as well.

Whatever their origin, they apparently did not exist as they are today in anyone's Old Country. The word itself is related to the Italian word *gnocchi,* the Austrian word *knoedel,* and the Yiddish word *knaidlach,* all of which are kinds of dumplings. My sketchy etymological research on this produced the word *lump* as the meaning of the *gn* and *kn* root.

The New York knish is a kind of dumpling, too, a baked dumpling, like people call apples baked in pastry "apple dumplings." It is stuffed pastry. The traditional New York fillings are potato and kasha (buckwheat groats), although the old-timers of my youth also liked dusty, dry liver-filled knishes. These are nearly impossible to find today. That palate and that taste are gone. Today we have fillings like spinach and broccoli, which are blended with the potato. I'm told by Les Green, the owner of Mrs. Stahl's Knishes, that the popularity of broccoli is about to exceed pure potato. Sweetened cheese knishes have been around for decades—Yonah

Schimmel started baking them. But, as Erica Marcus notes, at least there are no sun-dried tomato knishes—yet.

In the classic delicatessen knish, the pastry encloses only the bottom and sides of the filling, leaving the top of the filling exposed. But there are various styles, including a strudel style in which the filling is made into a pastry-wrapped roll that is sliced. The first knishes were baked, as most delicatessen knishes are today.

Yonah Schimmel, a Romanian immigrant, began selling this type of knish from a pushcart in 1890, just as Eastern European foods were being introduced into the previously German-style Jewish delicatessen. In 1910, he opened the bakery (he called it a "knishery") on Houston Street, where it stands today, near the corner of Chrystie Street.

Yonah Schimmel's knishes have had their ups and downs over the years. When I was a boy, it was a regular pit stop for my father and me on our Sunday morning food adventures, but we stopped more for the glasses of cold borscht and "sour milk," a kefir-like drink, as for the knishes, which, even then, in the 1950s, were not as good as those we could buy at our local Brooklyn delicatessen. Today, the knishes are back to delicious form thanks to the current proprietor, Alex Volfman, a Russian immigrant.

In 1921, Elia and Bella Gabay created a different kind of knish. It was a square knish, totally enclosed by a different sort of dough, a heavier, thicker pastry jacket,

Old and new fillings for knishes at Aidell's Delicatessen, Kings Highway, Brooklyn

Gabila's square knishes

and it was deep-fried. The company, Gabila & Sons Knishes, which is still going strong, although moved from their original plant in Williamsburg, Brooklyn, produces more than 1.5 million knishes a year. It is the most popular knish in New York.

It is "The Original Coney Island Square Knish" the company claims, "square" being the operative word here. Many other knishes were sold on the beaches of New York, and Gabila was not the first. Knishes for some strange and unknown reason became popular on the Atlantic Ocean beaches and boardwalks of Brooklyn sometime during the Depression. And not just on Coney Island, but also on Brighton Beach, which is the residential and beach area next to Coney Island, and all the way out to the boardwalk of Long Beach, in Nassau County (Long Island).

How a hot item like a knish was deemed appropriate food for stifling New York summer days is one of the mysteries of the universe. Could it be its compactness, its manageable size, and that it is self-contained? And knishes were enormously popular, one of the enticing features of going to the beach. Knish stands, often selling hot dogs as well, lined the boardwalks. And hawkers even walked the sand to sell them to the beach-blanket crowd.

The last of the Brighton Beach knisheries, Mrs. Stahl's, opened in 1935 and closed in 2003, although the knishes are still made and sold wholesale. Les Green, the current owner, explained that the Russian community of today's Brighton Beach, often called "Little Odessa," doesn't eat knishes. Most of his customers were coming from far away to stock up. He sells them now to delicatessens, restaurants, and take-out shops that cater to the Jewish Diaspora in the suburbs of Long Island and New Jersey.

That Gabila's knishes were made to withstand reheating—and that knishes go so well with a hot dog—does, however, explain how potato knishes came to be one of New York City's most popular street foods, split and spread (or not) with mustard. Knish carts were common on the streets of Manhattan since the early twentieth century, and after World War II, Gabila's knishes were sold from the same carts as Sabrett's hot dogs. For supposed health reasons, Mayor Rudolph Giuliani's administration banned them from the hot dog carts in the mid 1990s, leaving hot dogs bereft of their perfect starch accompaniment, and New Yorkers just plain bereft. We never lost a New Yorker, or, even more important, a tourist, to a knish. But go fight City Hall.

It doesn't pay to make just a few knishes. This is a party amount. If you want to freeze these, add $^1/_2$ cup instant mashed potatoes to the real mashed potatoes. It will stabilize the filling, preventing it from becoming too wet when defrosted. The directions here are for making knish rolls that can be cut into individual finger-food servings after they are baked. These will have open sides, like a piece of strudel. To make a small knish with closed sides, use a bench scraper to pinch the dough together at $1^1/_2$-inch intervals. Press straight down as if you were trying to cut the dough, but do not use a sawing motion. Just press. Even if the dough does not pinch to a seal, it will be more enclosed when you cut the roll after it is baked.

To form classic, open-topped knishes, make the rolls as instructed below and cut into 2-inch pieces. Take the piece of dough that is overlapping on the side and twist it so it now covers one of the open ends of the slice. Dab the end with a bit of egg wash and bring it back up to meet the side of dough. Push the knish into shape and bake as directed below.

Makes about 4 dozen

Potato Filling
5 pounds russet (baking) potatoes
1 tablespoon salt, or more to taste
$^1/_2$ teaspoon freshly ground
    black pepper
6 cups coarsely chopped onions
    (about 6 medium onions), fried
    in peanut, corn, or canola oil or
    Schmaltz (page 9) or a combination
    until medium brown (page 7)

Dough
$^1/_2$ cup hot water
$^1/_2$ cup canola, peanut, or corn oil
2 large eggs
1 teaspoon salt
$^1/_4$ teaspoon freshly ground pepper
$3^1/_2$ cups all-purpose flour
1 teaspoon baking powder

Egg Wash
1 egg, beaten well

To make the filling, peel the potatoes, cut them into chunks, and place them in a large pot. Cover with cold water by about an inch and bring the water to a boil over high heat. Boil the potatoes until very tender, about 15 to 20 minutes, depending on the size of the chunks. Drain immediately in a colander.

Using a food mill with the medium blade or a potato ricer (do not use a food processor), work the potatoes into a smooth puree. Stir in 1 tablespoon of the salt and the pepper. Stir the onions into the mashed potatoes. Taste and adjust the seasoning (I like mine peppery), then cover tightly and refrigerate until chilled.

To make the dough, in the bowl of a food processor fitted with the metal blade, combine the water, oil, eggs, salt, and pepper. Process briefly to mix well. Add 3 cups of the flour and the baking powder. Process again until the dough is smooth.

Flour a work surface with some of the remaining $^1/_2$ cup flour and scrape the dough out onto this surface. Knead the dough briefly, just a minute or so, to incorporate just enough additional flour to make a dough that is just slightly sticky. Wrap the dough in wax paper or plastic wrap and let it rest for 1 hour in the refrigerator before rolling it out.

To make knish logs, cut the dough into 4 pieces. Roll out one piece at a time to an 18- by 8-inch rectangle. The long side of the dough should be facing you. With your hand, take enough cold potato filling to make a long, approximately 2-inch-wide roll of potato along the long side of the dough, about 2 inches up from the bottom edge. Bring the bottom edge of the dough over the potato roll and brush the upper edge with egg. Bring the upper edge of the dough over the egg-washed edge. Repeat with the remaining dough and filling.

Lightly grease 2 baking sheets. Transfer 2 rolls to each baking sheet, seams down. Brush the logs with beaten egg.

Preheat the oven to 375°F. Bake the rolls until golden, about 50 minutes.

To serve, cut the rolls into crosswise pieces about 1 to 1$^1/_2$ inches wide. Or follow the instruction at the end of the headnote.

A hot, fluffy potato knish at Katz's

Carrot Tzimmes

In Yiddish, the word *tzimmes* means "a fuss," an unduly long procedure, a complicated mess. Few recipes for carrot tzimmes live up to the name. They may contain many ingredients, but they are throw-everything-in-the-pot-and-let-it-cook dishes.

For several reasons, carrot tzimmes has special meaning as a dish for Rosh Hashanah, aside from the rest of the year when we eat it because we like it. First, the word for carrots (plural) in Yiddish is *mehren*, which is also the word for "be fruitful and multiply." In essence, eating carrots is asking for that blessing. To add meaning on top of superstitious meaning, we cut the carrots in rounds to resemble golden coins. In addition, tzimmes is a sweet dish—indeed, a *sweetened* dish—and eating sweet foods on the New Year is supposed to bring sweetness the rest of the year.

Serves 6 to 8

1¹/₂ to 2 pounds flanken or chuck stew meat, cut into large chunks

1 medium onion, coarsely chopped

2 pounds carrots, peeled

1 teaspoon salt

¹/₂ teaspoon freshly ground black pepper

¹/₂ pound large prunes, preferably sour prunes, preferably not pitted

Preheat the oven to 250°F.

In a large stovetop casserole, over medium-high heat, sear the meat a few pieces at a time. When browned, remove and set aside on a platter. When all the meat has been browned, add the onion to the pan and sauté for about 3 minutes, scraping up the brown residue on the bottom with a wooden spoon. In the casserole on top of the onion, layer half the carrots, then half the meat, then the remaining carrots, and the remaining meat, seasoning each layer with salt and pepper. Add just enough water to barely cover everything. Bring to a simmer.

Cover and transfer to the oven. Cook for 1 hour. Add the prunes, pushing some to near the bottom of the pot. Return to the oven for another hour. Uncover the pot, and continue baking in the oven for 1 more hour.

It is best to let the tzimmes cool, then reheat it, even a day or two later. If made ahead and refrigerated, you can easily skim the fat from the top of the casserole.

Variations

- Many families like their tzimmes sweeter than this one. After cooking the prunes for 1 hour, taste, and stir in as much as $1/2$ cup of honey or firmly packed brown sugar into the liquid.

- For sweet potato and prune tzimmes, follow the recipe for Carrot Tzimmes, but substitute 2 pounds of sweet potatoes, peeled and cut into very large pieces (each 8-ounce potato can be cut into quarters), for the carrots. In addition to the prunes, you may want to add as much as $1/2$ pound of dried apricots.

- Some cooks make a combination tzimmes using both carrots and sweet potatoes. You can divide the poundage of vegetables evenly or unevenly between the two vegetables.

Cabbage and Noodles

In the brutal climate of Eastern Europe, easily storable cabbage was one of the few vegetables Jews could eat most of the year. According to Claudia Roden in *The Book of Jewish Food*, "Every shtetl smelled immensely of cabbage." As late as the 1960s, it wasn't much different in the apartment houses of Flatbush (Brooklyn), Forest Hills (Queens), Washington Heights (Manhattan), or the Grand Concourse ("duh" Bronx).

Long cooking is supposedly what causes cabbage to smell bad, but I find that only long boiling does it. Smothering it in a covered pot with only its own moisture and some fat—butter, schmaltz, or vegetable oil, depending on how you intend to serve it—doesn't produce the bad odor. And it is delicious at every stage of cooking, from just wilted, still pale green, through golden tender shreds, then brown, sweetly caramelized tendrils of amazingly intense flavor.

Marion Gold, a Hungarian cook and the late mother of cookbook writer Rozanne Gold, taught me to first salt the cabbage, then leave it for 24 hours to leach out excess moisture before cooking it slowly in a whole stick of butter until it becomes deeply caramelized. Only then did Marion toss the cabbage with egg

noodles, either wide ones or bow ties. Gilding the lily, I like mine with a big spoon of sour cream, too, which makes it a main course. Sometimes, I'll use cottage cheese instead, which also makes it substantial enough to eat for its own sake. And some Hungarians add poppy seed toward the end of the cooking.

The caramelized cabbage is also used as a filling for a savory strudel. Just wrap the cooked cabbage in several layers of phyllo pastry, each sheet brushed with melted butter and lightly sprinkled with dry breadcrumbs, and bake.

Unless you are buying just-picked cabbage, however (what old recipes call "new cabbage"), salting is unnecessary. I find that most supermarket cabbage does not have much moisture. Without salting, the cabbage just takes about 20 minutes longer to get deep brown, and it is just as delicious. You might add a sliced onion to the cabbage, as Marion said she used to do until she realized it didn't make much of a difference.

Serves 4 to 8, depending on how it is served

1 (2½ to 3 pound) cabbage	1 pound (or less) egg noodles (wide, medium, bow ties, any shape but fine)
2 to 8 tablespoons butter, or ¼ cup Schmaltz (page 9) or peanut, corn, or canola oil	
	Freshly ground black pepper
1 medium onion, thinly sliced or chopped (optional)	About ¼ cup poppy seed, for garnish (optional)
1 teaspoon salt, or more to taste	Sour cream or cottage cheese, for garnish (optional)

Core the cabbage, shred it finely and wash well, then dry in a clean kitchen towel or salad spinner. In a large pot, melt the butter over medium heat. (A whole stick of butter is what Marion Gold used, and it does make the cabbage divine.) Add the cabbage, onion, and salt. Toss the cabbage in the melted fat. Cover the pot and let steam until well wilted, about 10 minutes.

Toss again. Cover the pot, decrease the heat to medium-low, and cook for 1½ hours longer, tossing the cabbage every 20 minutes or so. If the juices have not evaporated after the first hour, increase the heat.

After about 2 hours, the cabbage will have begun to brown. Raise the heat and continue to cook, uncovered, tossing more often, until the cabbage is a deep brown.

As the cabbage is delicious at any point, you can toss it with egg noodles or serve it alone as a vegetable, in either case seasoned with freshly ground black pepper and, if necessary, more salt. Garnish with poppy seed and sour cream.

CHAPTER 4

❧ Meat Main Courses ❧

[My mother] liked food from special parts of the animal, the container, or the store. It was her form of geography. "Take it from the back. Cut it from the middle. Reach down to the bottom of the barrel."

—Alan King, *Is Salami and Eggs Better Than Sex?*

Like every other nineteenth-century immigrant group, Eastern European Jews became heavy meat eaters in America, which they were not necessarily in their old countries. America was practically founded on beef production, on cattle on the range. Think cowboys and Manifest Destiny. In Europe, meat was precious, especially to the poor, as the majority of Eastern European Jews were.

Obtaining kosher meat was a particular problem for Jews who forged into the American heartland. The peddlers and other merchants who went West to make their fortunes (and many of them did make fortunes as founders of great department stores) often had to subsist on only bread, fruit, and vegetables. Easy access to kosher meat and poultry was one reason Ashkenazic Jews remained in East Coast urban centers, especially in New York City. By the end of the nineteenth century, on both the Lower East Side and in Brownsville in Brooklyn, an observant Jew could find everything a kosher home could need. And by the 1920s, there were many other Jewish enclaves in Brooklyn and the Bronx, all with their own kosher butchers. At one time, in the 1950s, when one in four New Yorkers was Jewish, and not by a long shot all kosher, there were more than 2,000 kosher butchers in New York. Today, as in mainstream America, there are hardly any full-service butchers of any kind, much less kosher. Even in Brooklyn, the Orthodox Jewish heartland, most kosher meat is precut and sold wrapped in plastic in the refrigerated case in the supermarket, albeit a kosher supermarket. Even the small butcher shops of Orthodox Brooklyn are self-service now.

A glatt kosher meat store, owned by Satmar Hasidim, in Brooklyn

Cholent

Some scholars say that cholent, a Sabbath dish, is one of only three truly Jewish dishes, the others being the matzo and charosis of the Passover seder. However, except for matzo, there are cultural differences in the exact recipes. Still, these are the only foods that every Jew recognizes as Jewish, no matter where he lives.

A valid argument or not, cholent is a long-cooked dish always based on beans, and it is served as the midday Sabbath meal, having been prepared the day before and allowed to cook long and slow. In the shtetl and even in the midsized cities of Eastern Europe, the cholent was taken to a communal oven on Friday before the Sabbath began, then retrieved—often by a non-Jewish neighbor or servant, or a child young enough not to be responsible for keeping the Sabbath. In some communities, an *eruv* was arranged, a physical enclosure of the whole community that was created by a string or wire, which allowed certain tasks to be accomplished within it that might otherwise be forbidden on the Sabbath, such as carrying home the cholent (or, in these days, wheeling a baby stroller).

In New York City's kosher food markets, they now sell "cholent beans." There is even a major national brand that packages these. The usual mixture is equal parts kidney beans, pinto beans, and Navy beans. I prefer an old-fashioned lima-bean cholent with a little barley added for additional substance (like it needs it!), a big enough piece of meat for everyone to get some, and plenty of onions and some garlic for flavor. There are a zillion other cholent recipes. Today, in observant homes, cholent is usually made in a slow cooker that has a timer. Cholent can be made with meat or poultry. In the old days, a length of kishka was often cooked into it. Or a giant and rather indigestible *knaidlach* was steamed at the top of the heap. In this case, the *knaidlach* was not a matzo ball. It was a flour dumpling. It is no wonder that there are so many stories and jokes about the heaviness of cholent, and why Saturday afternoon is nap time for so many observant Jews.

Serves 8

1 pound large or baby lima beans

1¹/₂ to 2 pounds sliced flanken or
  beef cheeks

1 tablespoon salt, plus more for the meat

1 cup chopped onion (1 medium)

1 large clove garlic, finely minced

¹/₂ cup pearl barley

2 (8-ounce) all-purpose or boiling
  potatoes (not russet), peeled
  (unless they are a thin-skinned
  variety), and cut into quarters;
  or 4 (4-ounce) potatoes, peeled
  and halved

5 cups cold water

If cooking in the oven (as opposed to a slow cooker), preheat the oven to 250°F.

Rinse the beans in a strainer under cold water. Put them in a medium sauce-pan with enough cold water to cover by several inches. Bring to a boil over high heat and boil 1 minute. Set aside while searing the meat.

Season the meat on both sides with salt. In a very hot skillet (I like cast iron), sear the meat over high heat a few slices at a time, or a cheek at a time. Be sure not to let the drippings burn. If a spot on the pan bottom is getting too brown, cover it with the next piece of raw meat. Remove the meat to a platter as it becomes nicely browned.

In the same skillet, sauté the onion over medium heat. The moisture released by the onion will help deglaze the pan. Scrape up any browned bits and fry the onion until just wilted, about 3 minutes.

Drain the cooked beans and put half of them in a slow cooker or an oven-proof casserole, along with half the onion, half the garlic, and ¹/₄ cup of the barley. Make a layer of half the meat, then all the potatoes, then the remaining half of the meat. Pour on the remaining beans, onion, garlic, and barley.

Pour on the 5 cups of water, season with the 1 tablespoon salt, and jiggle the contents with a spoon to season the liquid throughout. Bring to a simmer over high heat; as soon as the liquid simmers, cover the pot and transfer the casserole to the oven. The cholent can also be cooked on top of the stove on the lowest possible heat. Either way, cook for 3 to 5 hours. Cholent is excellent reheated, and usually it is.

Pot-Roasted Brisket

Braised—in other words, pot-roasted—or any way you call it, moist-cooked brisket is the odds-on favorite celebration food in Jewish homes, the *ne plus ultra* of main courses. It is the centerpiece of the Passover seder, when, in deference to the sacrificial lamb that was roasted before the Exodus from Egypt, custom dictates that no dry-roasted meat be eaten. It is also the way to bring in the New Year at the Rosh Hashanah feast. It is prepared for birthday parties, for anniversaries, for "company," and for homecomings, pointing to the fact that it is a dish of memory, a dish that connects us to our past. Surprisingly, the only time it is not ritualistically served is for the festive Sabbath meal on Friday nights. That's usually a chicken dinner.

As in any American home, a huge hunk of meat represents attainment of the American Dream. That's probably why brisket, the most impressive and, at one time, the most succulent kosher cut of beef, became idolized, you should pardon the expression.

Unfortunately, brisket, a cut that comes from the underside of the steer, below the shoulder, has suffered greatly by the change in modern American beef production and eating habits, both of which emphasize leanness. To be good, brisket needs to be fatty, not only on the outside, but also within. Today's meat in general is vastly leaner than Grandma's. As a result, our briskets can never, well, hardly ever, be as good.

You are most likely to have a succulent roast if you cook a whole brisket. The cut is composed of two distinct muscles that run in different directions, which is why you must cut them apart after cooking to carve them properly. But they cook better together than apart.

The fattier top layer is called "second cut," "thick cut," or "deckle," and its fat lubricates the leaner bottom, which is called "first cut," "thin cut," "flat cut," or "point cut." The "second cut" deckle defines the word succulent. (By the way, these terms apply to corned beef, too, which is brine-cured brisket.)

Unfortunately, only the leaner bottom piece, trimmed of nearly all visible fat (*not* a virtue), is what one generally finds in the supermarket. The goodly layer of fat between the two pieces on a whole brisket keeps the meat very moist. Exterior fat is easy to trim off after the meat is cooked. Cooking a whole brisket is the optimum for succulence.

Because whole briskets are hard to find in a supermarket meat case, however, they often have to be ordered. In addition, a full brisket will weigh between 8 and 10 pounds, which may be too much meat for many families or occasions.

So, if you can only buy a "first cut" brisket, look for a more marbled piece, and take the one that has the most surface fat. Extremely lean pieces often cook up stringy or hard no matter how much care you take.

I learned to make pot roast from my mother, who tried many contemporized versions over her lifetime. Like most 1950s homemakers, she wanted to incorporate modern ingredients into her cooking, either to make the traditional dishes more American, or for novelty, or for added convenience and speed in the kitchen. She started with her mother's recipe for brisket, who possibly made it *her* mother's Russian immigrant way. But my modern 1950s mom also tried pot roast made with ketchup, and for a period, when we lived in the same house with a Neapolitan–American family, pot roast made with canned Italian tomatoes, really ragu made in the oven. Like the rest of America, she tried Lipton's dehydrated onion soup mix and, finally, the worst, in the 1970s, pot roast made with Harvey's Bristol Cream Sherry. That last had to have been a recipe devised to promote Harvey's, and an indication of how important the American Jewish market was for upscale products. In the end, with a little encouragement from her children, she returned to tradition and the essentials. That is, a whole brisket, fat and all, no browning or liquid necessary, and a lot, a lot, a lot of onions, which eventually become the substance of the "gravy," which is really just meat and vegetable juices.

Everyone always expects pot roast to be measurably better the second day. It isn't necessarily so, at least not with today's leaner meat. Its optimum moment of glory is 45 minutes to a couple of hours after it has come from the oven. Still, there are plenty of reasons to cook a pot roast a day ahead and reheat it. You gain convenience, the ability to skim off the fat with ease, and perhaps even a little more depth of flavor. What you lose is some juiciness.

This recipe can easily be halved for half the amount of meat.

Serves at least 12

2 very large cloves garlic, crushed with a bit of salt

8- to 10-pound brisket

1 1/2 teaspoons salt

1/2 teaspoon freshly ground black pepper

4 pounds onions, halved and sliced

3 medium carrots, peeled and sliced into 1/4-inch-thick rounds

2 large outer ribs celery, sliced crosswise 1/4 inch thick

4 small bay leaves

Preheat the oven to 350°F.

Rub the crushed garlic into both sides of the meat. Season the meat on both sides with salt and pepper.

Spread the onions, carrots, and celery on the bottom of a roasting pan just large enough to hold the meat. Set the meat over the vegetables. Put 2 of the bay leaves under the meat, 2 on top of the meat. There is no need to add any liquid to the pan. The vegetables and meat will produce enough moisture as they cook.

Cover the pan tightly with aluminum foil and bake for 3 to 4 hours, until the meat is fork tender.

Let the meat rest for 30 to 45 minutes. Then, cut the second cut off of the first cut and trim off and discard the layer of fat between them.

Slice both cuts across the grain, either straight down or at a slight diagonal angle.

Tip the roasting pan so you can skim off some of the fat on the surface of the juices. Serve the onions and vegetables with the juices as a sauce for both the meat and any starch accompaniment. If desired, you can puree some of the vegetables to make a thicker sauce.

Serve with kasha (buckwheat groats): follow the directions on the back of the box, and top each helping with onions and juices from the pot roast. Or prepare Kasha Varnishkes (page 85). Or serve with mashed potatoes. A green vegetable is up to you.

To cook ahead, remove the brisket from the oven before it is actually fully tender. Let it cool until just warm, then refrigerate overnight. The next day, the congealed fat will easily peel off the surface of the juices.

Slice the meat while it is cold. Use a long-bladed, preferably serrated knife (such as a bread knife) and slice the meat across the grain, about 1/4 inch thick. It will require a sawing motion. Do not disturb the conformation of the meat. Return the meat to the roasting pan, with all the juices, as if it were still a whole piece.

Let the meat warm up to room temperature. Return the meat to a 350°F oven, keeping it covered for the first 30 minutes. Then, uncover the meat, baste it with the pan juices, and return it to the oven for 45 minutes to 1 hour more to heat through, fully tenderize, and color a little. Baste it a few more times with pan juices during this cooking time. Serve hot.

Rib Roast, Rib Steak, and Mushk Steak

Perhaps because they were always so expensive, the forward ribs of beef, which is the most prized kosher cut, were not, until fairly recently, cooked as a roast in a kosher home kitchen. The ribs were more likely to be cut into steaks, and eaten as a great treat. Nowadays, however, rib roast, also called standing rib roast, and also called, but somewhat incorrectly, prime rib, is the most luxurious meat entrée on the kosher table. The fact that the true prime ribs are too far into the hind quarter to be kosher hasn't stopped generations of kosher caterers and kosher restaurants, not to mention kosher butchers, from giving their meat the "prime" imprimatur, even when it is USDA choice cut, not USDA prime, and not derived from the truly prime ribs.

Whatever. "Prime rib" was a cut reserved for high-end wedding and bar mitzvah receptions. (The low-end main course was chicken.) And the roast was served "au jus," using the same French that made kishka, "derma farci."

Rib steak is today the most expensive and fashionable item in a kosher meat restaurant or steakhouse, of which New York City has several. Until the 1950s, it was known as *mushk* steak in the old Romanian steakhouses and restaurants, but a *mushk* steak was only the center, round muscle section of the rib, what is properly called rib eye or club steak. These terms have unfortunately lost their significance today. Nonkosher and kosher butchers and restaurants alike now call a full rib steak a rib eye, even when it is bone in and still surrounded by the coarser, more marbled muscle, the deckle or top of the rib. (To my plebeian taste, the deckle is actually more the delicacy than the rib eye.)

Also until fairly recently, steaks, but roasts, too, were invariably cooked well done, not a trace of juice left. Many a middle-aged Jew still talks about his or her mother's propensity to incinerate steak in the name of kashruth. This stemmed from a misunderstanding of the dietary laws. As long as meat has been humanely slaughtered in accordance with the dietary laws, and it has been salted to leach out blood in accordance with dietary laws, it is kosher, whether it is raw, rare, or well done. In theory, there's nothing not kosher about beef carpaccio or beef tartare, much less a rare steak.

In Manhattan's *glatt* kosher steakhouses, the young, affluent, modern Orthodox clientele lunches and dines on a menu very different from their grandfathers'. Sushi has replaced gefilte fish as an appetizer. A thick, juicy rare rib steak follows. Neither kishka nor kugel are to be seen. ✑

Sweet-and-Sour Potted Flanken or Beef Cheeks

Gedempte Fleish

Gedempte fleish simply means "well-cooked meat," usually braised meat, as is pot roast. However, it has also come to mean "overcooked." For instance, when someone is served a leathery steak he could complain, "What kind of *gedempte fleish* is this?"

In this recipe, the *fleish* improves by being *gedempte*. It is braised in a subtly sweet-and-sour tomato sauce, a flavor profile that is very popular among Ashkenazic Jews. This is the same sauce as for Sweet-and-Sour Potted Meatballs (page 116), but it ends up tasting quite different because the meat is different. And it cooks much longer, giving more meat flavor to the sauce.

You can use the same recipe for any cut of meat that benefits from long cooking. In the kosher butcher shops of Brooklyn, beef cheeks are one of the offerings for Cholent (page 103), and they are spectacular when cooked this way. They produce a sauce that is full of gelatin and makes for some of the best, literally lip-sticking gravy you will ever have. It's great to top kasha, mashed potatoes,

or noodles, or for dunking bread. (Make mine challah.) Brisket or a chuck roast can be cooked this way, too.

This recipe can easily be doubled or tripled. And, like all *gedempte* recipes, it is best served the day after it is made, when the flavors will have melded and when it is easy to remove the solidified fat.

Serves 4 to 6

Salt
2 pounds relatively lean sliced flanken
  or whole beef cheeks
2 tablespoons peanut, corn, or
  canola oil
1 cup water

1 (15-ounce) can Hunt's tomato sauce
2 tablespoons brown sugar
$1/4$ teaspoon sour salt (citric acid), or
  juice of $1/2$ lemon

Preheat the oven to 250°F. Generously salt the meat on both sides.

In a heavy stovetop casserole just large enough to hold the meat (for instance, an enameled cast-iron casserole), heat the oil over medium-high heat until very hot but not smoking. Brown the meat well, a few slices at a time, or a cheek at a time, on both sides. As it is browned, remove the meat to a platter. Be careful not to burn the oil or any of the film on the bottom of the pan. If you see a spot getting too dark, put the next piece of raw meat on it.

When all the meat has been browned, pour off the fat from the pan. Add $1/2$ cup of the water to the pan, and scrape up the browned film and bits on the bottom of the pan. Let the water reduce by about half.

Add the tomato sauce, then fill the can with the remaining $1/2$ cup of water to rinse out any sauce that remains, and add that liquid to the pot. Stir in the brown sugar and sour salt or lemon juice. Place the meat in the pan with the sauce and any meat juices that may have accumulated on the platter. There should be enough liquid to almost, but not completely, cover the meat.

Bring the liquid to a gentle simmer over high heat, cover the pot, and cook in the oven for $1^1/2$ to 2 hours, possibly up to 3 or 4 hours, depending on the meat and the amount. When done, the meat should be fork tender.

If serving immediately, let the meat rest for at least 30 minutes, then tilt the pan and skim off any fat that has risen to the top. Better, however, is to serve the meat the next day. Let it cool to room temperature, then refrigerate overnight (the congealed fat will easily peel off the surface of the juices). To reheat, cover and let simmer gently over low heat until very hot, then serve.

Potted Flanken with Vegetables

To my taste, braised flanken seasoned as it is here with tomato paste and paprika, vegetables, garlic, and herbs, is every bit as delicious as the best French daube, and because flanken is such a well-marbled cut it is much more succulent. You could add some hunks of potato for the last hour, to absorb the gorgeous flavor. Or serve the potted meat with potatoes roasted separately with olive oil, salt, and pepper, until they become browned and crunchy on the surface, fondue-soft inside. I have to admit, with a dish like this, my mother would roast canned potatoes, perfect little globes called "Irish" potatoes. They came in a can with green shamrocks on a black background. I still crave that flavor. In a more Yiddish mode, the gravy is also wonderful poured over kasha or egg barley. Although carrots and celery cook with the meat, I would definitely add something green on the side. Broccoli is perfect, but sautéed spinach is excellent, too.

Serves 6

1 teaspoon salt

3 pounds breast flanken, sliced into 6 ($^3/_4$-inch-thick) pieces

1 tablespoon peanut, corn, or canola oil

1 cup water

2 tablespoons tomato paste

2 teaspoons sweet Hungarian paprika

$^1/_4$ teaspoon freshly ground black pepper

2 large onions, trimmed (leave root ends) and each cut into 6 wedges

3 large carrots, peeled and cut crosswise into 1-inch-thick rounds

3 large ribs celery, cut crosswise into 1-inch-long pieces, or 1 large celery root, peeled and cut into 6 wedges

6 large cloves garlic

1 large bay leaf

$^1/_2$ teaspoon dried thyme

Preheat the oven to 250°F. Salt the meat on both sides.

In a large stovetop casserole (for instance, enameled cast iron), heat the oil over medium-high heat until very hot, but not smoking. A few pieces at a time, brown the slices of flanken well. Remove to a platter as they are browned.

Discard any fat that has accumulated in the casserole. Add the water and scrape up the brown film on the bottom of the pot. Add the tomato paste and dissolve it in the liquid. Add the paprika and pepper. Return the meat to the pot with the onions, carrots, celery, garlic, and herbs. Cover and bake in the oven for about 3 hours, or until the meat is fork tender.

Serve very hot, each portion getting its share of meat, vegetables, and pot juices.

The meat reheats very well. In fact, it is even better the next day. Let it cool to room temperature, then refrigerate overnight (the congealed fat will easily peel off the surface of the juices). To reheat, cover and let simmer gently over low heat until very hot, then serve.

Flanken
Jewish Short Ribs

Flanken means "flanks" in Yiddish and it is, in essence, beef short ribs cut across the bone instead of parallel to the bone, as is customary in American butchery. Flanken may be an even more beloved cut of beef than brisket, but it was never considered as refined. Now that short ribs have become a cliché of fashionable American cuisine, can flanken be far behind?

There are actually two kinds of flanken, breast flanken (*brust* flanken, in Yiddish) and plate flanken. The former is a much longer, meatier piece than the latter, but the latter is the one you are most likely to find in a nonkosher market. When cooked, they both are immensely flavorful and bursting with fatty juiciness, even when merely boiled, which used to be the most popular way of cooking flanken for its own sake (see page 114). With vegetables from the pot and horseradish to spike it, it is as appealing now as then.

Flanken is also used as a flavoring meat for soups, such as Mushroom–Barley (page 49), Split Pea (page 51), and Sweet-and-Sour Cabbage Borscht (page 53). And its bones add gelatin, which gives body to the soup. It is also a popular cut for Cholent (page 103). It's great for pot-roasting (page 114) and cooked in a sweet-and-sour sauce (page 109). And, if you don't mind that it is somewhat tough, it has unbeatable beefy flavor when broiled or pan-broiled very rare. I confess: when searing flanken to braise it, I often cut off a piece of the browned meat as a prize for myself, the cook's share. ✍

Boiled Flanken or Brisket

Boiled beef is gray and not pretty, but oy is it good to eat, especially flanken and brisket, and especially when served with somewhat beautifying red horseradish.

This is a classic Ashkenazic dinner. For a first course, serve the broth with *lukshen* (fine egg noodles) or boiled egg barley, or, for a festive meal, with Kreplach (page 47). Or, as I do here, serve the broth and vegetables pureed together to make a thick soup with a garnish of chopped fresh dill and parsley. As a second course, you have the meat with the boiled vegetables alongside it. If you have used the vegetables for a thickened soup, serve the meat with potatoes that were also boiled in the broth.

Usually, boiled beef is cooked on top of the stove, where it should be kept at the barest simmer because high heat can toughen the meat. This requires more attention than I am often willing to give. Nowadays, I put the meat in a casserole with enough water to cover it, bring it to a simmer on top of the stove, skim it for about 15 minutes, then cover the pot and put it in 250°F oven, just as you would for potted meat. The liquid will gently perk away. The meat will be fork tender after 2 to 4 hours, depending on whether it is slices of flanken (the lesser time) or a big piece of brisket (the longer time).

Serves 4 to 6

2 to 3 pounds flanken or brisket, preferably deckle (top of the rib, the deckle of a rib roast, is also excellent for boiling, but available only in kosher markets)

8 to 10 cups cold water

2 teaspoons salt

4 medium carrots, peeled

1 large leek, halved and well washed

1 large or 2 or 3 small parsnips

About 15 sprigs fresh dill, plus some for garnish

About 15 springs fresh flat-leaf parsley

Croutons or soup nuts, for garnish (optional)

½ large celery root, peeled and halved

Coarse sea salt, for sprinkling

Red or white horseradish, for accompaniment

Mustard, for accompaniment (optional)

In a 5-quart pot, combine the meat with enough cold water to cover the meat by ½ inch and the salt. Bring to a simmer over high heat. Decrease the heat to medium-low and simmer gently for about 20 minutes, skimming off the foam that comes to the surface.

When the simmering liquid is no longer very cloudy, add the carrots, leek, parsnip, celery root, dill, and parsley. The water should barely cover everything. Add more water as necessary. Simmer very gently for at least 2 more hours, or until the meat is fork tender. Or, alternately, once the water comes to a simmer, place the pot in a preheated 250°F oven for 2 to 3 hours.

The soup (without the meat) can be served as broth with pieces of the vegetables in it, but I prefer to puree it all together, discarding only the herbs. Serve the pureed soup with a garnish of fresh dill and croutons or soup nuts. Serve the meat as a separate course from the soup, sprinkled with coarse sea salt and horseradish or mustard or both as condiments.

Ground Neck and Tenderloin

My mother's standard ground meat order was "2 pounds chopped neck and tenderloin." When I was old enough to walk the two blocks to the kosher butcher, these were the words she sent to the store with me. It wasn't until I was a teenager and became more aware of meat cuts that I thought, "Why is she using filet mignon, the most expensive cut, for chopped meat?"

However, in Jewish parlance, tenderloin is not filet. For one thing, filet is not kosher. Filet mignon is *trayf*, meat that is from the forbidden hindquarters of the animal. Tenderloin at the kosher butcher refers instead to a muscle that is now known as hanger steak in restaurants trying to seem trendy. *L'onglet,* in French, it is a cut often served as *steak-frites* in French bistros. In New York City it was called "butcher's tenderloin" by both kosher and nonkosher butchers because it was a cut that butchers often saved for their own families. It is related to, but not quite as flavorful as, its neighboring cut, skirt steak. They are both muscles of the diaphragm. Neck meat provides good flavor, too, but also some fat to balance the lean tenderloin. Ground neck and tenderloin is still a favored mix at kosher butcher shops in New York City, and the blend does, indeed, make particularly flavorful hamburgers and meatballs. ✥

I&D Glatt Meats and Poultry in Brooklyn

Sweet-and-Sour Potted Meatballs

Sweet-and-sour is a much beloved Eastern European taste. The flavor is usually accomplished in a tomato-based sauce, although there are exceptions, like the raisin-sweetened, vinegar-balanced sauce used for dressing smoked tongue.

Ashkenazic Jews hadwholeheartedly adopted tomatoes, a New World food that didn't become common in Europe until the early nineteenth century, by the time they emigrated to America at the end of the nineteenth century. Numerous dishes depend on them and on the sweet-and-sour flavor profile you get by adding sugar (or honey) and an acidifying agent, most usually sour salt, which is citric acid crystals.

Stuffed Cabbage (page 118), stuffed peppers, and Sweet-and-Sour Cabbage Borscht (page 53) are probably the best known dishes to offer that winey, tomato, sweet-acid taste. In New York City, we used to be able to buy sour salt in almost any supermarket. As the product began disappearing, cooks substituted lemon juice, which works nicely but doesn't have the same edge. Sour salt comes in crystals that look like the coarsest sea salt, or it is granulated like fine table salt. The latter is available by mail order from King Arthur Flour (www.kingarthurflour.com).

The tomato ingredient could be canned plum tomatoes, tomato paste, canned tomato sauce (such as Hunt's or Del Monte, both of which are kosher), or even ketchup. Sugar, brown sugar, or honey, as well as dried raisins or mixed dried fruits are typical sweeteners. Some more recent sweet-and-sour recipes use gingersnaps, which provide spice as well as sugar, and act as a thickener, too.

Makes 24 meatballs, serving 6 to 8

Sweet-and-Sour Sauce
2 tablespoons vegetable oil
1 medium onion, finely minced
2 (15-ounce) cans tomato sauce
$1/2$ cup water
$1/2$ teaspoon sour salt, or the juice of
  1 lemon (about 2 tablespoons)
$1/4$ cup firmly packed dark brown sugar
Salt and freshly ground black pepper

Meatballs
2 pounds ground chuck or a combination of ground neck and tenderloin
2 eggs, beaten
$1/3$ cup long-grain rice, parboiled for
  3 minutes
1 cup fresh breadcrumbs from challah
  or good-quality supermarket white
  bread (with crusts)
1 medium onion, grated on the coarse
  side of a box grater
$2^1/4$ teaspoons salt
$1/2$ teaspoon freshly ground black pepper

To prepare the sauce, in a 5-quart stovetop casserole or Dutch oven, heat the oil, then sauté the minced onion over medium heat until tender and golden, 8 to 10 minutes. Reserve $1/2$ cup of the canned tomato sauce to season the meatballs, then add the remaining sauce to the onions. Rinse out both cans with the same $1/2$ cup water to loosen any sauce that remains, and add that liquid to the pan. Stir in the sour salt and brown sugar. Bring to a simmer, uncovered, over medium heat. Remove from the heat and set aside.

To make the meatballs, put the ground meat in a large bowl and push it to one side. Put the reserved tomato sauce, eggs, rice, breadcrumbs, onion, salt, and pepper on the other side of the bowl and combine with a large fork. Incorporate the meat into the breadcrumb mixture a little at a time, until thoroughly mixed.

To cook the meatballs, bring the sauce back to a gentle simmer over medium heat. Using a $1/4$-cup measure, make compact meatballs and drop them gently into the sauce. By the time the pot seems full, the first meatballs will be cooked enough and firm enough to push them around gently to fit in more meatballs. You may have to go to a second layer. It's okay if a few meatballs are, at first, not covered with sauce.

Cover and simmer slowly for 30 minutes, gently rotating and pushing the meatballs around after about 15 minutes. Eventually, the sauce will increase enough, and the meatballs will shrink enough, for them to be all covered with sauce. Correct the seasoning with salt and pepper.

Serve very hot, preferably reheated. The meatballs benefit from at least several hours or overnight in the refrigerator. Store in the covered pot (if not aluminum) and reheat over low heat.

Stuffed Cabbage

Holishkes

Stuffed cabbage was a great favorite at our house. My mother did not use raisins but she did squeeze fresh lemon juice to taste. Anyway, at one point she began crumbling gingersnap cookies into the sauce. This was a very hush-hush ingredient that she learned about through someone connected to the kitchen at The Twin Cantors, the famous kosher catering establishment in Brooklyn. Our family did not like the new taste and so after a few meals it was discontinued. My mother did what any good cook would do. She took it off the menu.

—A memory of Barbara Rachman

You can call them *holishkes*, or *holipchess*, or *halubchas*, *golubtzes*, or *prakkes*. It's stuffed cabbage all the same, one of the most beloved dishes in the whole Yiddish repertoire. The idea for stuffing a cabbage leaf most likely comes from the Ottomans, who, after all, controlled Hungary and other parts of Eastern Europe for a couple of centuries; they stuffed grape leaves, as well as many vegetables. Many Sephardim lived under the Ottoman Turks. Perhaps they passed the idea along to the Ashkenazim. At any rate, most stuffed cabbage today uses a sweet-and-sour tomato sauce, with or without raisins or other dried fruit, which is the taste from Russia, White Russia, Ukraine, Poland, Lithuania, and Latvia. On the other hand, Hungarian, Czech, Slovakian, and Romanian cooks often make a brown sauce or a strictly savory tomato sauce, sometimes with a touch of sour from sauerkraut. Gingersnaps are an American addition. They add a bite to the sauce as well as serving as a thickener, too.

Makes about 15 pieces, serving about 6

Meatballs (page 116)
1 extra-large head green cabbage
  (4 to 5 pounds)

Sauce
2 tablespoons peanut, corn,
  or canola oil
1 medium onion, finely minced
1 (28-ounce) can imported Italian
  tomato puree

1/3 to 1/2 cup firmly packed
  dark brown sugar
3/4 to 1 teaspoon sour salt, or
  the juice of 2 medium lemons
1/3 cup dark raisins
6 gingersnaps, crumbled and soaked
  in 1/2 cup water (optional)
1 teaspoon salt

Prepare the meatball mixture as directed in the recipe, but don't form into meatballs; set aside.

To prepare the cabbage, have ready a pot large enough to hold the whole head of cabbage almost submerged in water. Fill the pot halfway with water and bring it to a rolling boil over high heat. Meanwhile, core the cabbage with a small sharp knife. Submerge the head in the boiling water for a few seconds. Spear the cabbage with a two-tined chef's fork, lift it out of the water, and peel off the outside leaf. Return the head to the water for another few seconds, and remove the next loose leaf. Continue to blanch the cabbage and remove outer leaves until the leaves become too small to easily stuff. You should have 12 to 15 leaves that are big enough to use. (There are other ways to soften the cabbage leaves—for instance, by freezing the whole head of cabbage—but I find this method is the easiest.)

Remove the pot from the heat. Shred the remaining cabbage, and layer the pieces on the bottom of a wide, deep casserole (I use one of enameled cast iron).

Cut out and discard the white central rib of each cabbage leaf.

Use ¼ to ⅓ cup (depending on the size of the cabbage leaf) of meat mixture for each leaf. Place the meat along the edge of the leaf opposite the core end, shaping it into a thick, oblong patty. Roll up the meat in the leaf, tucking in the leaf sides as you roll to completely enclose the filling. If you have a little extra leaf, trim it off. Place the stuffed leaves, seam side down, on top of the shredded cabbage.

To make the sauce, in a saucepan over medium heat, heat the oil and sauté the onion until tender and golden, about 12 minutes. Add the tomato puree, sugar, sour salt, raisins, gingersnaps, and salt. Stir well and, still on medium heat, uncovered, bring to a simmer. If using gingersnaps, simmer until they are dissolved. Otherwise, simmer for just 5 minutes.

Preheat the oven to 325°F.

Pour the sauce over the cabbage rolls. Shake the casserole to encourage the sauce to seep to the bottom. Cover with the pot lid or tightly with aluminum foil and bake for 2 hours.

Serve hot. Stuffed cabbage reheats beautifully. Some would say it improves after having rested a day in the refrigerator and then reheated. Reheat in a 350°F oven until heated through.

Romanian Steakhouses

Morris is sitting in a restaurant. He calls over the waiter.
"Are you the waiter who took my order?" he says.
"Yes sir, why do you ask?" answers the waiter.
"Because by this time, I thought you'd look a lot older."

No one really knows how it was that the Romanian steakhouse emerged, sometime around World War I, as the dominant form of Jewish meat restaurant after the corner deli. We're talking about restaurants that have tables with linen and waiters in bow ties, places like Gluckstern's and Pollok's, which both first opened on Delancey Street, the grand boulevard of the Lower East Side.

"It's very fancy on old Delancey Street, you know," wrote lyricist Lorenz Hart in 1925. Of course, it wasn't "very fancy" to a family on Park Avenue, or to the upwardly mobile assimilated Jews already living in the burgeoning boroughs. It was only fancy to those in the squalid tenements.

Uptown, which to Lower East Side Jews meant the garment center in Midtown, was and still is to a degree an essentially Jewish business quarter. The pattern makers, the coat and dress makers, the tailors, designers, wholesalers, and jobbers would meet at Pollok's and Lou G. Siegal, which closed only a few years ago. No surprise, its space is taken by Ben's, a kosher delicatessen and restaurant. Jews still dominate the garment industry. Gluckstern's eventually moved "uptown," too.

Seymour Kaye worked at several of these places and then owned three legendary Romanian (sometimes spelled "Roumanian") steakhouses. He started as a waiter at Pollok's in the early 1950s, then he moved briefly to Gluckstern's before he bought his own place, The Parkway, on Chrystie Street, in 1957. The Parkway was upstairs from where Sammy's, the last of the breed, is now.

The Parkway became The Parkway East when Seymour was forced to move around the corner to Allen Street. His final restaurant was Seymour Kaye's in Forest Hills, Queens. By that time, in 1971, he had a big name, a following. "I moved to Forest Hills because I thought it was a good Jewish neighborhood. But by then, the current generation, the younger generation, didn't want to eat their grandparents' food except on holidays. Even the grandparents didn't want to eat that food. So my customers in Forest Hills were coming from Manhattan and L.A. People were nostalgic for that food already in the '70s. Walter Matthau loved my place."

All the Romanian steakhouses had pretty much the same menu. Chopped liver was the almost obligatory appetizer, although the menus also listed such first-course delicacies as sliced brains; P'tcha, calf's feet jelly with a lot of garlic (page 27); Chopped Eggs and Onions (page 4); Gefilte Fish (page 31); and Romanian Eggplant Salad (page 16). Some groups—no, most groups—would order many or all of these, maybe with a side of unborn eggs, the yolks of an egg caught in the chicken's canal before the white and shells are formed. To this day, the mention of unborn eggs elicits great nostalgia, but really they taste just like egg yolks.

You could also get smallish starter portions (as opposed to gargantuan main-course portions) of Stuffed Cabbage (page 118), Chicken Fricassee, mainly giblets with tiny meatballs in gravy (page 29), and Sweetbreads and Mushrooms with Egg Barley (page 36).

Among the so-called broilings was the famous Romanian tenderloin (see page 126), which in most restaurants was skirt steak but in others was the shorter of the two diaphragm muscles, what we now call a hanger steak. Until the mid-1980s, this was an inexpensive cut of meat. When fajitas, the Tex-Mex specialty that is made from the same cut as Romanian tenderloin, became nationally popular, the price of skirt steak soared. Lately in New York, skirt steak is on mainstream menus. As expensive as it has gotten, it has become the inexpensive choice next to New York strip steaks on the city's steakhouse menus.

Mushk steak was the steak of the big spenders. It was a boneless rib eye and cost 50 percent more than Romanian tenderloin. Chopped steaks were popular, too. And then there was Karnatzlach (page 125), listed on Seymour Kaye's menu with the warning that these little sausages are "for garlic lovers only." The most popular item, says Seymour, was Boiled Flanken (page 114) served with noodles floating in the bowl, Kreplach (page 47), *and* Knaidlach (page 43)—"all three in the same bowl."

Seymour Kaye's Parkway East
New Year's Eve Menu

APPETIZERS

TOMATO JUICE
CHOPPED LIVER
SLICED BRAINS
CHOPPED EGGS & ONIONS
(Served with Radish, Onion & Chicken Fat)

SOUPS

A Cup of PARKWAY SPECIAL SOUP
Unborn Eggs, Kreplach, Noodle and Mandel

ENTREES

ROUMANIAN TENDERLOIN
SHELL STEAK
MUSHK STEAK
(Served with Kishka - Kasha Varnishkas and Parkway East
Silver Dollar French Fries)

DESSERTS

COFFEE AND COOKIES UNLIMITED

The above dinner also includes 4/5 of a bottle of Liquor for six persons.

Thereafter $22.50 - includes set-ups.

The cooking at these Jewish restaurants was done by women. "You would have a first cook," recalls Seymour. "She would be in charge of everyone. But then you would have a kreplach lady, and a gefilte fish lady, a lady who made chicken, one who made the flanken, one the brisket. Like that. Each woman had her specialty. Maybe the kreplach lady and the gefilte fish lady were the same person. Maybe she did two things very well.

"Then you had a *bruta*, a *bruta* is a broiler. He was proficient and able to broil anything by eye. He could broil rare, medium-rare, whatever you want. And we used to broil on charcoal. One of my favorite things was broiled sweetbreads. We used to weight them down and after they were cooked they'd be thin like a piece of matzo. Delicious.

"In the 1930s, '40s, even '50s, everyone ate at the Jewish restaurants," says Seymour. "The politicians would come, and the late-night crowd. The wise guys loved the Jewish restaurants. They called them 'Jew joints.' But a place like Moskowitz and Lupowitz would have been called a 'carpet joint' by the wise guys, a place with a carpet, a fancy restaurant. The wise guys liked to meet at the Jewish restaurants to be more discreet than they could be in their own Italian restaurants. But also to enjoy a good steak.

"At Moskowitz and Lupowitz," Seymour continues, "they had strolling violinists playing gypsy and Yiddish music. They had roast goose with kasha. You went to Moskowitz and Lupowitz for your birthday or anniversary."

As a child, I remember well that whenever we drove by the corner of Second Avenue and Second Street in the car, my father would point out "the fanciest Jewish restaurant ever." It was where he took my mother on their first anniversary, in 1946. Moskowitz and Lupowitz was so well regarded, in fact, that Ted Patrick and Silas Spitzer included it in their book *Great Restaurants of America*. It is interesting to read a non-Jewish perspective on the place.

"The flavors of the food are as exotic as the names of the dishes," wrote Patrick and Spitzer. "In one generous meal of five courses, your palate will taste in turn appetizers that are sour and winy, an unctuous soup, meat that blazes with the flames of pepper and garlic, intensely spicy vegetables or cereals [probably referring to kasha], and desserts sweeter than honey."

The owners of Moskowitz and Lupowitz were Max and Hy Anzelowitz, who by most accounts opened the restaurant in about 1910. It was to their credit, as well as testimony to the customers, that Patrick and Spitzer could write that the restaurant "fairly bounce[d] with humanity at its most expressively emotional level."

In Yiddish, "bounce" might translate to *tummul* (tumult, chaos), which was often a feature of these restaurants. Seymour Kaye was no slouch in the "bounce" department. On Queens Boulevard in Forest Hills, he provided music—Yiddish and Rat-Pack pop, some cha-cha and mambo, warning that no dancing was allowed in the aisles—and he didn't just serve food. He also sold—at discount, of course—fashions off the rack. He carried clothes to your table for inspection while you were cutting into your fried veal chop. It was anybody's guess where the Christian Dior, Pierre Cardin, and Ted Lapidus dresses and coats came from. No questions were asked.

By 1971, when Seymour Kaye's opened in Forest Hills, there were few women in the kitchens of Jewish restaurants. As Seymour explained, "The women sent their kids to college. The kids graduated, and what lawyer or doctor do you know who wants his mother making kishka in a kosher restaurant?" ✦

Seymour Kaye's old restaurant on Allen Street on the Lower East Side

Karnatzlach

Romanian Grilled Garlic Sausage

Hardly anyone knows what *karnatzlach* are anymore, but they used to be one of the most popular items served at the Romanian steakhouses. In modern–day Romania these are called *mititei*, and in the burgeoning post-Ceauçescu Romanian immigrant community in Sunnyside, Queens, they are sold in the butcher shops already mixed and shaped, to take home and cook. They're not kosher, though, as they are often made with a meat mix including pork.

In English, they are sometimes called sausage, and *karnatz* does indeed mean "sausage" in Romanian Yiddish, *lach* being a suffix that makes the word mean "little sausages." But they have no casing and are less a type of sausage than a variant of Middle Eastern kefta, which is seasoned ground meat grilled on a skewer. They must have been introduced by the Ottomans.

Make sure your meat is not overly lean. You need some fat to give the *karnatzlach* succulence. Besides a strong garlic presence, *karnatzlach* have a slightly funky, "high" taste created by the action of seltzer and baking soda and a ripening period in the refrigerator. Skip the ripening period for a fresher, although less authentic, taste.

These are best cooked over a charcoal grill, but well worth making indoors, too. If cooking them in an oven broiler, be sure to preheat the broiler tray on the rack position second down from the broiler element.

Makes about 20, serving 6 to 8 as an appetizer, 4 to 6 as a main course

1 pound not-too-lean stew beef, cut into ³/₄-inch cubes

1 pound stew veal, cut into ³/₄-inch cubes

¹/₂ cup seltzer

¹/₂ teaspoon baking soda

8 to 10 large cloves garlic, minced

2 teaspoons kosher or sea salt

1 teaspoon sweet Hungarian paprika

1 teaspoon freshly ground black pepper

¹/₂ cup finely chopped fresh parsley

To prepare the meat mixture, first grind the meat. Working with about ½ pound at a time, put the meat cubes in the bowl of a food processor fitted with the metal blade; pulse until the meat looks finely minced, but not a paste. Scrape each batch into the large bowl. Repeat until all the cubes have been ground.

In a small bowl, combine the seltzer and baking soda. Pour it into the meat.

Add the garlic, salt, paprika, pepper, and parsley. Combine all the ingredients with a wooden spoon or with your hands. The meat should be very well blended.

Cover the bowl with plastic wrap and refrigerate for at least 2 hours, but preferably for about 8 hours.

To make the sausage, wet your hands with cold water and form the meat mixture into tapering rolls about 3 inches long and 1 inch wide. Re-wet your hands every couple of rolls. Place the rolls on a platter or baking sheet.

Heat a charcoal grill until very hot or preheat the broiler and broiler tray.

Place the *karnatzlach* on the hot grill over direct heat or on the preheated broiler tray and cook 8 minutes for rare, or 10 minutes for medium-well. Turn the rolls a couple of times as they grill to brown on all sides. Serve hot, immediately.

Romanian Tenderloin

This is skirt steak, a muscle of the diaphragm, and was very inexpensive until fajitas, made from the same piece of beef, became a national rage in the early 1980s. It is an extremely flavorful cut, but it has a unique coarse grain not to everyone's taste, and it can be tough, which is why it is often mechanically or chemically tenderized in restaurants. It continues to be much more affordable than short loin steaks (New York strip steaks, T-bone, porterhouse) and filet mignon, which is why in New York City it has become a fashionable steakhouse-cut all over again in kosher restaurants, American bistros, and mainstream steakhouses where less expensive cuts are now in style.

Salt, pepper, and a hot broiler are all you need to make a great skirt steak, which should be cooked to no more than medium. But a garlic option was offered at the Romanian steakhouses. To give the steak the Romanian garlic treatment, make a paste of crushed garlic and vegetable oil and smear it on the steak before serving. Skirt steak is also often eaten with Smothered Onions (page 7). ✑

Breaded Veal Chops

At old Jewish restaurants the signs and menus may have featured "Roumanian Broilings." But my favorite main course was always the breaded fried veal chop, the gargantuan slab of meat, bone, matzo-meal breading, and nearly melted and therefore sublimely succulent clumps of veal fat. The cut was and remains veal arm shoulder chop, still sold in New York City supermarkets, both kosher and nonkosher. These chops can cover a dinner plate. (Let's not forget that Jewish restaurants originated the concept of super-sized. In delicatessens, the sandwiches were always said to be *ongeshtopt*, "overfilled." And that was a good thing.)

A veal arm shoulder chop, at about ¹/₂ inch thick—it can be no thinner to remain juicy—usually weighs more than a pound. It has a few small bones, often including a marrow bone, but even with the bones it is a lot of meat. In theory it should be enough to feed two people, but at Romanian steakhouses each chop was meant for one, and was generally consumed by one.

With shared side orders of mashed potatoes seasoned with onions fried in chicken fat, Kasha Varnishkes (page 85) seasoned with onions fried in chicken fat, and perhaps some stuffed derma, Kishka (page 88), which is essentially a starch and fat sausage, there was good reason that seltzer and antacids were considered the most appropriate finish to a meal. Now that was food and beverage pairing!

The chops can be single-breaded or double-breaded. In either case, a rest in the refrigerator will ensure that the breading solidifies and sticks to the meat as it is frying.

Serves 4

2 veal arm shoulder chops (about 1 pound each)	3 cups matzo meal (not all of it will stick to the chops)
Salt and freshly ground black pepper	Peanut, corn, or canola oil, for frying
2 eggs	

Season the chops with salt and pepper.

In a large shallow dish, beat the eggs with a fork until well mixed.

On a large platter or piece of wax paper, spread about half the matzo meal to the size of the veal chops.

Prepare 1 chop at a time. For each, dip the chop in the egg, coating well on both sides. Then, still dripping with egg, place the chop on the matzo meal. Pour the remaining matzo meal on top of the chop and, with a fork, press it down to make a good coating. Turn the chop, spoon some of the matzo meal on top of the chop, and press again. Be sure to press matzo meal onto the edges of the chop. As each chop is coated, place it on a platter or baking sheet. Set aside to let the breading set. When all are ready, refrigerate the chops, uncovered, for at least 30 minutes. If a thick breading is desired, repeat the whole process: dip the chops in egg then press on more matzo meal. Let dry again, as previously.

Preheat the oven to 200°F.

To cook the chops, in a large skillet heat about $1/4$ inch of oil over medium-high heat. When hot, slide a chop into the pan. It is unlikely you will be able to fry more than one at a time, although you could work two or three pans at a time. Fry until golden brown on one side, 3 to 4 minutes. Turn the chop and brown the second side, another 3 to 4 minutes.

Keep the cooked chops warm in the oven until all have been fried. Serve hot or warm. These are also not bad at room temperature, but in that case avoid eating the clumps of fat.

Jewish Delicatessen

It is deeply offensive to real New Yorkers—old-time New Yorkers, anyway, like me—that today any neighborhood grocery, indeed any convenience store, calls itself a "deli," a "gourmet deli" no less. The New York Jewish delicatessen is a venerable institution that dates back to the mid-nineteenth century. And, by definition, it is a store that sells delicacies, not Cheese Doodles.

The word is German, not strictly Yiddish. *Delikat* means, according to my German-English dictionary, "delicate, delicious, exquisite." *Essen*, in German, means "to eat." In English, or I should say in Old New York-ese, the word applies both to the store and to the products it sells. Those products are mostly of German origin and are mostly meats. The first delicatessens in New York were, in fact, German, not Jewish, and their cured, smoked, and otherwise processed meats were mainly, if not entirely, fabricated with pork. But as Jews generally adopt the foods of their homeland, German Jews had developed kosher versions of these. (The non-Jewish German delicatessen persisted, by the way, until only a few years ago, living on as New York's main form of neighborhood grocery.)

Jewish delicatessens gained their particularly Yiddish character in the 1880s, with the increase in Jewish migration from Eastern Europe. Most of the German-Jewish delicatessen meats, including frankfurters and corned beef, were foreign to the Eastern European Jews. But delis were the only kosher public eating places, so they went. In a short time, the delicatessens became an eating and meeting place for men who had emigrated to America for work without their wives and families. After that, it became not only a place you could take the family, but a store where they sold prepared foods to take home. Even as full-fledged kosher restaurants opened, the deli remained the most popular type of restaurant.

Romanian pastrami, spice-cured and lightly smoked beef, was added to the delicatessen menu sometime in the late 1880s. Patricia Volk, a New York writer and the daughter of a famous New York restaurateur, claims her paternal great-grandfather, Sussman Volk, was the first person to carry pastrami in a delicatessen. It may well be true that Volk, in 1888, as his descendent says, introduced pastrami into the already established German-style delicatessen he owned.

Eventually, other foods that had a more Eastern European flavor were incorporated into the delicatessen's repertoire. It was at the delicatessen that you could get hearty Polish-Lithuanian-Russian soups as well as the supreme soup of the Jewish kitchen—Chicken Soup (page 40).

Cucumber pickles, some half-sour and still bright green, others full sours and a drab green, got plunked down in front of you, along with a cabbage slaw and Pickled Green Tomatoes (page 22). These were put on the table even before the waiter—notoriously a sarcastic or grumpy older man—could say, "What'll you have?"

Added to the frankfurters, well-spiced salami, boiled tongue, corned beef, and pastrami, were roasted chickens to eat in or take out; sliced, freshly roasted turkey; Knishes (page 90) filled with kasha or mashed potatoes; a garlicky beef sausage called *knubblewurst* (the "k" *is* pronounced), *knubble* being the

Katz's Delicatessen • New York • 1932

garlic that laced it; and "specials," sausages as fat as knockwurst and spicier than a frank. Steaks and chops were added, too.

Frankfurters were a big item at the delicatessen. You could get them grilled and served on a plate with Heinz vegetarian beans. (In 1923, the beans became the first commercial kosher product in America. Jewish delicatessens invariably had cans of them stacked on a display shelf behind the counter.) Or you could get them on a hot dog bun topped with spicy brown mustard and sauerkraut. Jewish delicatessens never used to have onions in tomato sauce, as do New York's hot dog street carts, but nowadays they offer it. Every delicatessen grilled their hot dogs neatly lined up on a griddle in the window. It was an enticement as you walked by, one I could never resist. So perhaps it is just as well that the custom is dying out.

Next to the hot dogs on the griddle in the window were a few potato and kasha knishes that would develop a crisp bottom crust from standing on the heat. Today, I warn you, most delicatessens want to reheat refrigerated knishes in the microwave, which ruins them.

The Jewish delicatessen is not totally extinct, but it is certainly an endangered species. There are several in Manhattan. Most notably there is Katz's on Houston Street, on the Lower East Side, which isn't kosher but does have sublime pastrami and looks as old as its 1888 founding date. And in the Midtown theater district, there is Carnegie Deli and Stage Deli, both of which have become tourist traps, although on some days the Carnegie's pastrami and corned beef aren't half bad. Sarge's, on Third Avenue and 36th Street, is a notable holdout, with good pastrami and corned beef, and some outstanding specialties, such as lox, eggs, and onions on the all-day breakfast menu.

In Brooklyn there are more: the Crown Restaurant in Boro Park is *glatt* kosher and has very good cooked food, but lesser cold cuts. It is frequented mainly by ultra-Orthodox black hatters. In Williamsburg there is Gottlieb's, which is frequented by the insular Satmar Hasidim. Outsiders are not really welcome. In Mill Basin there is the Mill Basin Deli, which has better art on the walls than food on its plates. There are a few more delis in Queens and, it seems, only one left in the Bronx. The suburbs of New Jersey and Long Island, where many New York Jews moved late in the twentieth century, have restaurants that serve the classic old deli foods, too. Only a few are kosher. The rest, as do many in the City, serve shrimp salad and other *trayf*, forbidden foods, along with the chopped liver. Only in New York! ✍

Salami and Eggs

Salami has certainly suffered from American fat-phobia. It used to be that when you fried salami you rendered some fat, at least enough to fry a few eggs. Nowadays, if you don't make salami and eggs in a nonstick skillet, you're in trouble.

When my mother spent a day shopping or playing mah-jongg and didn't take the time to put a really good dinner on the table, which she usually did, one of the things she made was salami and eggs. My father loved it and so he didn't complain. Somehow, salami and eggs is more a man's dish. The comedian and actor Alan King wrote a book with food writer Mimi Sheraton called *Is Salami and Eggs Better Than Sex?* Most women would instead ask, "Isn't shopping better than salami and eggs?"

Serves 1

3 eggs
¼ teaspoon salt
A few grindings of black pepper

1½ to 2 inches of kosher salami, cut into ⅛-inch slices, small cubes, or sticks

In a small bowl, beat the eggs, salt, and pepper together with a table fork until well mixed.

Method 1

(Salami slices): Arrange the salami slices on the bottom of a nonstick skillet. Place over medium heat. As soon as the salami starts cupping, turn the slices over. When the second side cups, pour on the eggs. Let the eggs set, then slide the pancake onto a dinner plate or pot cover, flip it back into the pan, and cook the second side for a few seconds. Serve immediately.

Method 2

(Salami cubes or sticks): Heat a nonstick skillet over medium heat. Add the salami cubes or sticks and toss until they begin to color. Pour on the egg mixture and gently push the eggs and salami around the pan to form large-curd scrambled eggs. Serve immediately.

Garlic and Paprika
Rubbed Roast Chicken

Long before contemporary chefs used rubs to season food, Jewish mothers were massaging chickens with garlic, paprika, salt, and pepper. The later-day American version of this seasoning may have included garlic powder, or onion salt, or may have been based on Lawry's steak seasoning or another supermarket-bought mix that contains mainly salt and MSG, but it was an early-day rub, nevertheless.

Since I abhor garlic powder, I use crushed garlic. I add good imported Hungarian paprika, salt, and freshly ground pepper. This blend, made into a paste with the addition of some vegetable oil, I not only rub onto the skin, but also tuck under the skin. It makes such a Yiddish aroma as it cooks. Using a modern high-temperature, butterfly roasting method, my roasted chickens come out with juicy white meat and crisp skin. As I much prefer dark meat to white, I also use the same rub and high temperature for roasting thighs and drumsticks alone. Obviously, it works for breasts alone, too.

Serves 2 to 4

6 large cloves garlic, crushed
  or pressed
1 tablespoon sweet Hungarian paprika
1 teaspoon salt

1/2 teaspoon freshly ground black pepper
1 1/2 tablespoons corn, canola, or
  peanut oil
1 (3- to 4-pound) whole chicken

Preheat the oven to 450°F.

In a small bowl, blend together the garlic, paprika, salt, pepper, and oil.

On a cutting board, cut the chicken in half alongside the backbone. Cut out the backbone. (I like to roast the backbone alongside the chicken, allowing myself the pleasure of eating it—the cook's share.) Place the chicken, skin-side up, and press the butterflied chicken down to flatten it. Massage the chicken on both sides with the garlic-paprika paste, pushing some of it under the skin. Place the chicken, skin-side up, on a jellyroll-type baking sheet. Roast for 45 minutes.

Remove from the oven and let rest for 5 minutes before cutting it into serving pieces.

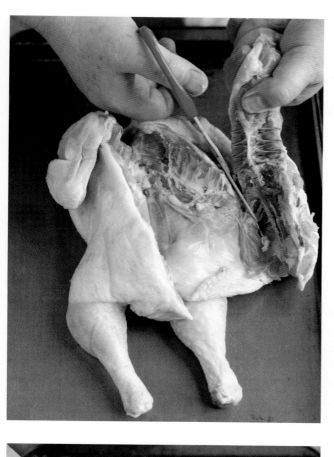 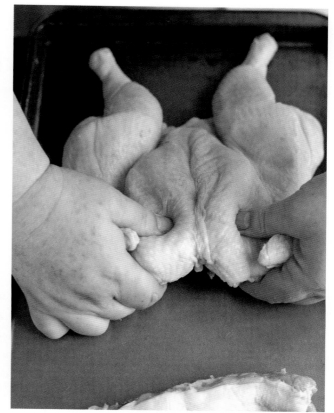

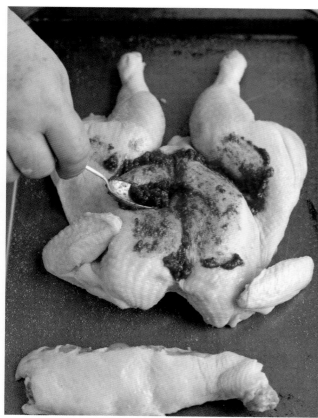 

Why Jews Like Chinese Food

Here's an old joke about Jews, Chinese people, and food:

> *Two Chinese men are walking out of Katz's Delicatessen. One says to the other,*
> *"The problem with Jewish food is that two weeks later you're hungry again."*

Here's another one:

> *If, according to the Jewish calendar, the year is 5764, and, according to the*
> *Chinese calendar, the year is 5724, what did the Jews eat for forty years?*

That Jews have an affinity for Chinese food is no secret. The Jews know it. The Chinese know it. Everyone knows it. Until the dispersal of middle-class Jews to the New York suburbs was complete in the 1970s and 1980s, Chinese take-out shops opened on every corner of the city. It was said that you could tell how Jewish a neighborhood was by the number of Chinese restaurants.

Going out "to eat Chinese" continues to be a Sunday ritual for many Jewish families; even kosher families know that there are many kosher Chinese restaurants. In Brooklyn, there's one called Shang Chai, a play on the Hebrew word for "life," *chai.* Any Sunday at 6 P.M., step into Shun Lee West on West 64th Street, the Upper

West Side's upscale Chinese restaurant, and you'd think they were holding a bar mitzvah reception.

Here's another joke, although it's no joke:

> *What do Jews do on Christmas? They eat Chinese and go to the movies.*

Eat Chinese because those were the only restaurants open on Christmas. Go to the movies because all the Christians were home, and you could get into the theater without waiting on line.

That the Chinese are not Christian is important to understanding the appeal of the Chinese restaurant to Jews. If you went to an Italian restaurant, which, aside from the coffee shop, the luncheonette, or the deli, was likely the only kind of restaurant in your neighborhood before the American food revolution, you might encounter a crucifix hanging over the cash register, or at least a picture of the Madonna or a saint. That was pretty intimidating to even a nonobservant Jew. The Chinese restaurant might have had a Buddha somewhere in sight, but Buddha was merely a rotund, smiling statue—he looked like your fat Uncle Jack. He wasn't intimidating at all.

Important, too, was that the Chinese were even lower on the social scale than the Jews. Jews didn't have to feel competitive with the Chinese, as they might with Italians. Indeed, they could feel superior. As Philip Roth points out in *Portnoy's Complaint*, to a Chinese waiter, a Jew was just another white guy.

Italians didn't go out to eat as much as Jews. Italian-Americans spent Sunday afternoons gathering in large family groups, eating Italian food at home. The Italians and Jews continued to live together when they left their immigrant ghettos on the Lower East Side and started moving to the boroughs, along with the Chinese who wanted to leave the impoverished conditions of the Lower East Side as much as any other group. The Chinese that lived among the Jews and Italians in the boroughs were the owners of the restaurants and the hand laundries.

So the Jews' proximity to Chinese restaurants was important, and let's not discount the fact that Chinese food tastes good and costs little. When I asked my parents why, when they were courting in the 1940s, their dates always ended with a Chinese meal, and why we continued to eat in Chinese restaurants as a family more often than at other kinds of restaurants, the answer was simple and obvious. They could afford it. In their youth, during and right after World War II, a classic combination plate of egg roll, fried rice, and usually chow mein cost 25 cents.

The attraction of the forbidden aspects of Chinese food should not be underestimated, either. Eating forbidden foods validates your Americanness: it is an indication that you have "arrived." Although both Italian and Chinese cuisines feature many foods that are proscribed by the Jewish dietary laws, such as pork, shrimp, clams, and lobster, there are two big differences. The Chinese don't combine dairy and meat in the same dish, as Italians do—in fact, the Chinese don't eat dairy products at all. And the Chinese cut their food into small pieces before it is cooked, disguising the nonkosher foods. This last aspect seems silly, but it is a serious point. My late cousin Daniel, who kept kosher, along with many other otherwise observant people I have known, happily ate roast pork fried rice and egg foo yung. "What I can't see won't hurt me," was Danny's attitude.

Even Jews who maintained kosher homes often cheated by serving Chinese takeout on paper plates. I had one neighbor who would only let her family eat Chinese on paper plates *in the basement*, lest the neighbors across the alley that divided the houses only by about ten feet should look into her kitchen window and see those telltale white containers on the table. ✍

Chinese Roast Meat on Garlic Bread with Duck Sauce

This is an exquisite example of Jewish crossover food, "fusion food" these days. It was a dish that made first- and second-generation Jews of the 1950s, Jews who no longer abided by the kosher laws, feel like they were truly Americans as well as urbane and sophisticated. Imagine what a scandal it was to observant parents and grandparents, what a delicious act of defiant assimilation it was, to eat Chinese roast pork on Italian garlic bread.

This was invented in the Catskills and brought back to Brooklyn where, today, substituting roasted veal for the *trayf* meat, the sandwich survives in kosher delicatessens in Brooklyn and Queens. (It is particularly well done at Adelman's, a delicatessen on King's Highway and Ocean Avenue in Brooklyn.) With pork, it is also a hot item in diners on the South Shore of Long Island, where Jews from Brooklyn and Queens moved decades ago.

By all accounts, the sandwich was created sometime in the mid-1950s at Herbie's in Loch Sheldrake, New York. It was the most popular Jewish-style deli-restaurant in the area. According to Freddie Roman, the Borscht Belt comic who

years later starred in the nostalgia show *Catskills on Broadway*, Herbie's was where all the entertainers would gather after their last shows at the hotel nightclubs. "Specifically for that sandwich," says Freddie. "And everyone else had to eat what the celebrities ate."

Herbie's sandwich of Chinese Roast Pork on Italian Garlic Bread was so popular among the summer crowd in "The Mountains," that it was imitated back in "The City." I remember when it was introduced at Martin's and Senior's, two fabulously successful, middle-class family restaurants on Nostrand Avenue in Sheepshead Bay, Brooklyn.

In just a few years, it seemed Chinese roast pork on garlic bread became so popular in the southern tier of Brooklyn communities—from Canarsie through Mill Basin to Bay Ridge—that every diner and coffee shop made it. The sandwich even made it to Manhattan in the 1960s, at a place called The Flick, an ice cream parlor and casual restaurant near the then-new movie houses on Third Avenue.

Eventually, Herbie's, which closed in Loch Sheldrake only several years ago, opened Herbie's International on Avenue N in the Flatlands section of Brooklyn, where many of its Borscht Belt customers lived. It, too, was a well-priced family restaurant, serving, as its name was meant to imply, a little of this and a little of that from all over. But, as would be expected in this neck of the woods, "international" was really limited to red-sauced southern Italian, Cantonese-American Chinese, and a few specialties of the Yiddish kitchen. Maybe they served French crêpes, too.

Herbie's original sandwich was undoubtedly made with something other than real butter. Who knows what grease Herbie used. And the garlic flavor may have come from garlic powder, not fresh garlic. There are garlic spreads available in some supermarkets that probably come pretty close to the original flavor. If making the sandwich with pork, you might as well use butter and chopped fresh garlic. Of course, to make it a kosher meat sandwich (using veal), the fat would have to be vegetable-oil based, like olive oil. If you are making a kosher sandwich with veal, using olive oil and chopped garlic not only makes it kosher but also more contemporary. In that case, leave off the Chinese duck sauce, too, and douse the meat with balsamic vinegar. There should be a certain "white bread" quality to the roll with either version. The duck sauce used to flavor the meat is an apricot-based, sweet condiment; Saucy Susan is a popular brand.

Serves 4

4 tablespoons softened butter or extra virgin olive oil

8 cloves garlic, finely minced

4 (6- to 7-inch) French-style loaves, not too crusty nor too firm

1 pound Chinese-style red-roasted pork, or plain roast veal

Duck sauce or balsamic vinegar, for drizzling

Chinese mustard (optional)

To prepare the bread, in a small bowl, make garlic butter by working the butter and minced garlic together with a fork until well combined. For an oil dressing, combine the olive oil and garlic. Let the spread stand at room temperature for 30 minutes or up to a few hours.

Preheat the oven to 350°F. Heat the bread directly on the middle rack of the oven for about 3 minutes, until hot. Leave the oven on. Remove the loaves from the oven; for each loaf, hold it with a potholder and halve it the long way with a serrated knife.

Spread the cut sides of each loaf with garlic butter or drizzle with the garlic oil. Place the loaf halves, spread-side up, on the middle oven rack and toast until the edges are browned.

To assemble the sandwiches, arrange a layer of sliced roast meat on the bottom half of each loaf. Drizzle the meat with about 2 tablespoons of duck sauce, and then very lightly with Chinese mustard.

Serve open with the top half of the bread, spread-side up, alongside the meat-filled bottom.

Chinese-American Chow Mein

There was absolutely nothing *trayf* about basic chow mein. The base was all vegetables. It could even be served in a dairy restaurant, and it was. Sure it could be topped with roast pork or shrimp, but it was just as Chinese topped with chicken or beef, or nothing. Chow mein became mainstream New York food in the 1930s. It was on the menus of kosher and nonkosher restaurants, and hardly a specialty of just Chinese restaurants. Even the chichi Stork Club had a whole list of different chow mein choices. At the other end of the spectrum entirely, Nathan's, the hot dog emporium on Coney Island, featured chow mein on a hamburger bun garnished with crisp fried noodles. It still does.

Serves 3 or 4

2 tablespoons peanut, canola,
   or corn oil
2 medium-large onions, peeled,
   cut in half through the root end,
   and thinly sliced (about 3 cups)
4 ribs celery, thinly cut on a
   sharp diagonal (about 2 cups)
1 large clove garlic, finely chopped
1½ cups sliced white mushrooms
   (about 5 ounces)
1¼ cups chicken broth

2 tablespoons dry sherry
2 tablespoons soy sauce
4 teaspoons cornstarch
1 cup fresh bean sprouts
½ cup sliced fresh water chestnuts
   (optional)
About 2 cups white meat chicken,
   cooked any way and cut into strips
   (or red-roasted Chinese pork or veal,
   or sliced steak or roast beef)
Fried Chinese noodles, available at
   any supermarket

In a large skillet over medium-high heat, heat the oil until very hot but not smoking. Add the onions and celery and stir-fry for 4 to 5 minutes, until the onions are slightly wilted.

Add the garlic and mushrooms and stir-fry just 1 minute. Add 1 cup of the chicken broth, cover the pot, and simmer for 3 to 5 minutes, until the vegetables are tender.

Meanwhile, in a small cup, with a fork, blend together the remaining ¼ cup chicken broth and the sherry, soy sauce, and cornstarch.

Uncover the pot and stir in the bean sprouts and water chestnuts. Give the cornstarch mixture a final stir to make sure the starch is dissolved. Add it to the pot and stir it until the liquid in the pot is thickened. Taste for seasoning. You may want to add more salt or soy sauce.

Serve immediately, topped with the chicken, on a bed of fried Chinese noodles. It is best when eaten immediately, but you can reheat it, gently, if need be, adding a bit more liquid as necessary.

Chinese Pepper Steak

Chinese pepper steak was a standard home-cooked dish of my youth in Brooklyn in the 1950s. Even kosher mothers made it. It was the Chinese dish we didn't have to go to a restaurant to eat—the one stir-fry in every mom's repertoire before anyone knew what stir-fry was.

The choice of meat is up to the cook. If you are kosher, skirt steak is terrific. Think of the dish as Chinese fajitas. Supermarkets in New York still sell "beef for pepper steak," but it is usually bottom round, which is not kosher.

In the old days, only green peppers were used, but the dish looks and tastes better if you mix red (or orange or yellow) peppers with the green.

Serves 4

1 tablespoon dry or semidry sherry

3 tablespoons soy sauce

1 teaspoon sugar

2 teaspoons cornstarch

1 pound steak, trimmed of fat and sliced into ¼-inch-thick strips about 3 to 4 inches long

3 tablespoons corn, peanut, or canola oil

1 heaping teaspoon minced garlic

1 medium green bell pepper, washed, cored, and cut into $^1/_2$-inch strips

1 medium red, yellow, or orange bell pepper, washed, cored, and cut into $^1/_2$-inch strips

1 medium onion, halved through the root end, then sliced thickly into half-moons

3 to 4 ($^1/_8$-inch-thick) slices of peeled fresh ginger

1 medium firm but ripe tomato, cut into 6 or 8 wedges (optional)

Place the sherry, soy sauce, sugar, and cornstarch in a medium bowl. With a table fork, stir to combine. Add the steak strips to the marinade and toss to coat. Refrigerate for 30 minutes or up to several hours, until ready to cook.

Place a 12-inch skillet or wok over high heat. When hot, add 1 tablespoon of the oil and swirl it to coat the bottom of the pan. Add the garlic, peppers, and onions. Stir-fry for 3 minutes. With a slotted spoon or skimmer, remove the vegetables from the pan and set aside in a bowl.

Return the pan or wok to high heat. Add the remaining 2 tablespoons of oil and swirl to coat the bottom of the pan. Add the ginger and stir-fry just a few seconds. Turn the meat in the marinade to coat it one final time and add it to the pan with all the liquid in the bowl, which should be very little. Stir-fry until the meat is no longer pink, about 2 minutes. Discard the ginger, if desired (I don't). Return the pepper mixture to the pan, add the tomato wedges, and stir-fry an additional minute or so, tossing constantly.

Serve immediately with plain white rice.

Dr. Brown's Celery Tonic (Jewish Champagne)

There never was a Dr. Brown, but Dr. Brown's Celery Tonic was, in fact, developed in 1869 by a physician who treated immigrant children on the Lower East Side. It is carbonated water—seltzer—flavored with celery seeds and sweetened with sugar. It was sold as a real tonic, a health drink, but the U.S. government decided otherwise in the late 1960s and made the company change the name to Cel-Ray Soda.

On the order of ginger ale, it really isn't as bizarre as it sounds. It's incredibly refreshing and thirst quenching and is, aside from beer, the perfect foil to Jewish delicatessen, which tends to be salty. In fact, the soda was sold exclusively in delis until the 1980s. Now, you can buy Cel-Ray in most New York supermarkets and some other city stores. Unfortunately, for lack of consumer interest, the company discontinued the diet version in 2005. Dr. Brown's (actually the American Beverage Company of Queens) also makes a popular cream soda that is vanilla flavored, and a black cherry. These both have been distributed nationally since the late 1970s. ✺

CHAPTER 5

❧ Dairy Main Courses ❧

Izzy is eating fish at his favorite dairy restaurant. The waiter comes by and asks, "Is everything okay?"
"Well," says Izzy, "I've eaten fresher fish."
"Not here you haven't," says the waiter.

—Old Jewish joke

Seymour is in a dairy restaurant on the Lower East Side talking to his food, a piece of fish. The waiter says, "Why are you talking to your food?"
Seymour says, "I'll tell you. Your menu says it's Boston scrod, from Cape Cod. Many years ago I lived on Cape Cod, so I asked the scrod, 'How are things up there on Cape Cod?' The fish says, 'To tell you the truth, I haven't been there in a long time myself.'"

—Another old Jewish joke

Because dietary laws require the separation of meat and dairy, which includes all milk-based products, Jews developed a genre of meal, a category of food store, and a type of restaurant devoted solely to dairy dishes and the food suitable to eat with dairy. Jewish dairy cuisine pretty much overlaps with lacto-ovo vegetarianism, except that fish might also be included in a so-called dairy meal. It is pareve. You could say it goes both ways. It can be eaten at a meat meal or as part of a dairy meal. But it was more a specialty of the dairy restaurants, and the stores that sell dairy, "appetizing stores," which sold smoked and pickled fish.

In truth, many kosher dairy establishments were called vegetarian to appeal to a market larger than only Jews. A famous kosher vegetarian-dairy restaurant in midtown Manhattan was called Farm. You get the picture.

There are almost no dairy restaurants left in the old sense, which is to say restaurants that served cheese-filled blintzes, vegetarian "cutlets" and "roasts," soups without

Russ & Daughters, the famous appetizing store in Manhattan

143

a chicken or meat broth base, noodle puddings with cheese, and desserts with real whipped cream. Today, the "dairy" restaurant serves pizza, falafel, Middle Eastern salads, and salads that mainstream restaurants serve, along with innovations such as vegetable lasagna and other pastas with meatless sauces, *penne alla vodka*—macaroni with tomato-cream sauce spiked with vodka—being among the most popular.

The three, old, great, and famous dairy restaurants of the Lower East Side were Ratner's, which closed in 2002, the Garden Cafeteria, which closed in 1996, and Rappaport's, which was on Second Avenue near the Yiddish theaters, and closed when the theaters closed or changed to movie houses and off-Broadway theaters in the early 1960s. There were plenty of dairy restaurants uptown, too. The garment center sported several. There is still one, Diamond Dairy Restaurant, on West 47th Street, in the so-called diamond district. It is, in fact, on the premises of one of the big jewelry exchanges, and is frequented by the most observant of the jewelers.

The Upper West Side, where many refugees from World War II settled, had several. Steinberg's, on Broadway and 81st Street, was one of the classiest. Its 1961 menu can be considered a catalog of Jewish dairy dishes. It featured the freshwater fish—pike, carp, and whitefish—favored by Eastern and Central Europeans, fish that you would not find in a nonkosher restaurant. It lists fried herring, served with a boiled potato and fried onions, a dish that is too salty for most contemporary tastes but manna from heaven for those of us who recall it from our youths. Here, "cutlets" were made with mushrooms, "steak" with eggplant. Vegetable chow mein "en casserole" gave the menu urbanity.

Dairy meals at home might have consisted of similar fare. It could be the same as the Jewish family breakfast, what is now called a New York brunch: smoked and pickled fish, cheeses, black bread, pumpernickel, Onion Buns (page 215), and Corn Bread (page 205), with butter and cream cheese to spread on them. Tuna salad or egg salad could be construed as the main course of a homey dairy meal. If blintzes were served, at least in our house where they were homemade most of the time, it was a festive dairy meal. A noodle kugel rich with sour cream and pot cheese could also make a dairy meal special.

In most of the Jewish homes I knew growing up in Brooklyn, however, if Mom announced dairy for dinner it meant she was busy all day—shopping, canasta, mah-jongg—and didn't have time to cook. For a dairy meal, you go to the appetizing store for fish, you go to the bakery for bread and cake, you open a can of tuna. It's not cooking; it's an assembly job.

Vegetable Cutlets

Some of us are old enough to remember with fond nostalgia the vegetable "cutlets" and "roasts" that were a specialty of Jewish dairy restaurants—Rappaport's, Garden Cafeteria, Ratner's. Take my word—today, you wouldn't want to eat them. At Ratner's, for instance, whose recipes are recorded in a cookbook written by Ratner cousin and reputable Los Angeles food writer Judith Gethers, the popular vegetable cutlets were made with all canned vegetables, even the carrots. There is some charm to the perfectly cubed carrots that come in a tin, but assuming most of us today would rather eat fresh vegetables, the following contemporized cutlets fill the bill.

Makes 8 cutlets, serves 4

4 tablespoons peanut, corn, canola, or extra-virgin olive oil, or pareve margarine

$1\frac{1}{4}$ cups finely diced red or yellow peppers or a mix of both

2 medium carrots, grated into short strands on the coarse side of a box grater (about $1\frac{1}{4}$ cups)

$1\frac{1}{4}$ cups tightly packed chopped fresh spinach

2 cups mashed potatoes (3 medium potatoes, peeled, boiled, and riced)

6 tablespoons grated raw onion

3 eggs

$1\frac{1}{2}$ to 2 teaspoons salt

$\frac{1}{2}$ teaspoon freshly ground black or white pepper

$1\frac{1}{4}$ cups matzo meal

Sour cream or yogurt, plain or blended with horseradish, for accompaniment (optional)

Ratner's Vegetarian Brown Gravy (page 146), for accompaniment (optional)

Homemade or purchased tomato sauce, for accompaniment (optional)

To prepare the batter, in a skillet, warm 2 tablespoons of the oil over medium heat, then sauté the peppers until barely tender, about 5 minutes. With a slotted spoon, transfer to a large bowl.

Add the carrots, spinach, potatoes, and onion to the peppers, along with the eggs, salt, pepper, and matzo meal; mix well. Let stand at room temperature for 30 minutes.

To make the cutlets, using about $\frac{1}{3}$ cup per cutlet, form the mixture into neat, $\frac{3}{4}$-inch-thick, hamburger-like patties. You should have 8.

In a medium skillet, heat the remaining 2 tablespoons oil over medium heat. Fry the patties, turning several times, until well browned on both sides.

Serve immediately with the toppings of your choice: sour cream, Ratner's Vegetarian Brown Gravy, or a favorite tomato sauce.

The cutlets will keep in the refrigerator for 1 day, tightly wrapped in plastic. Reheat on a baking sheet in a 375°F oven for about 20 minutes, straight from the refrigerator. Do not freeze, cooked or uncooked; freezing ruins the texture.

Ratner's Vegetarian Brown Gravy

In *The World-Famous Ratner's Meatless Cookbook*, by Judith Gethers, this is called "Vegetable Cutlet Gravy." It has more uses beyond vegetable cutlets. As I remember, Ratner's used it on many dishes. In any case, it is excellent as the base for Mushrooms and Egg Barley (page 87), and would be delicious on any pasta, mashed potatoes, boiled rice, or kasha. Even if you have no interest in vegetarian food, its delicious wild mushroom flavor is a good complement to broiled or roasted meat or chicken. I even use it to sauce sweetbreads (page 36).

The original recipe calls for using "mushroom water" as a base, which is made by boiling white mushrooms. I've tried it. It has very little flavor, which must be why Ratner's added a flavor booster in the form of something called "mushroom powder," an inexpensive commercial substitute for whole pieces of wild mushroom. At home, a sauce like this would have been made with the dried wild mushrooms one could buy in the supermarket packed into small, round, plastic boxes. These used to be Lithuanian-Polish black mushrooms, and Jewish cooks used them for Mushroom-Barley Soup (page 49), too. Unfortunately, today these boxes are filled with bland cultivated mushrooms from China. If you can't find Eastern European boletus, use dried Italian porcini or French cèpe. They are essentially the same. If anything, they are perhaps even more delicious.

Makes about 1 quart

1 ounce dried boletus-type mushrooms
3 cups very hot tap water
4 tablespoons butter
1 medium onion, cut into $^1/_2$-inch dice
  (about 1 cup)
1 medium carrot, cut into $^1/_4$-inch dice
  (about $^1/_2$ cup)
1 cup diced celery

1 small green pepper, cut into $^1/_4$-inch
  dice (about $1^1/_4$ cups or less)
1 large clove garlic, minced
$^1/_2$ cup all-purpose flour
1 teaspoon sweet Hungarian paprika
$^1/_2$ cup tomato puree
1 teaspoon salt
$^1/_4$ teaspoon freshly ground black pepper

To reconstitute the dried mushrooms, put them in a bowl, cover with the water, and let stand for 25 minutes. Drain the mushrooms, reserving the soaking water. Very finely chop the mushrooms. Set aside.

In a 3-quart saucepan, heat the butter over medium heat and sauté the onion, carrot, celery, green pepper, and garlic, stirring frequently, until tender, about 10 minutes. Add the reconstituted dried mushrooms and sauté an additional 3 minutes.

Sprinkle the flour and paprika over the vegetables and stir well to combine. Continue cooking over medium heat for 2 to 3 minutes, stirring often, until a film of flour is on the bottom of the pan.

Add the reserved mushroom soaking water and stir constantly to avoid lumps. Bring to a boil over medium heat and stir in the tomato puree, salt, and pepper. Simmer gently, partially covered, for 20 minutes. If a perfectly smooth sauce is desired, strain the solids out before serving.

Taste and correct the salt and pepper, if necessary.

Serve hot. The sauce can be stored in the refrigerator, in a tightly closed container, for several days. For longer storage, freeze for up to 3 months.

Blintzes

From the 1920s through the 1950s, blintzes were so mainstream in New York City that restaurant menus listed them next to such *trayf* items as grilled ham steak with pineapple rings. They shared menu and kitchen space with corned beef and cabbage, even chow mein. Then blintzes went on hiatus in nonkosher restaurants until the 1970s when new, non-Jewish Polish and Ukrainian immigrants, settling mainly on the Lower East Side (then being transformed into the East Village by hippies and drug addicts), opened cheap restaurants haunted by their down-and-out neighbors. Blintzes, pierogen, and soups became the main attraction of what New Yorkers called "Polish coffee shops."

Although frozen blintzes were introduced into New York supermarkets as early as the 1950s, many home cooks counted blintzes as a specialty, my maternal grandmother included. Elsie made a two-day ritual out of their preparation.

On the first day, she would put every leaf in the dining room table, cover it with tablecloths, then spend hours doing nothing but making the crêpes (*blen*, to cite a Yiddish word rarely used these days) in an old steel pan, just like a French cook. Each crêpe was turned out of the pan onto a clean dish towel. Eventually the towels were folded in such a way as to keep the crêpes from sticking together while they were stored in the refrigerator awaiting the second stage and second day of producing hundreds of blintzes.

The next day, Elsie would make the fillings. She didn't go in for sweet fruit fillings. She made only mashed potatoes seasoned with salt, pepper, and onions browned in butter, the same as knish filling (page 93) and a filling of salt-and-pepper-seasoned pot cheese blended with sour cream. After carefully rolling the fillings into the crêpes, making neat, tucked-in packages, a job I was often enlisted to help with, the blintzes were fried in butter, then eaten topped with sour cream. As she made so many blintzes at a time, many were stashed in the freezer and many were given away to family and neighbors.

I never realized how really easy it is to make blintzes because my grandmother made it into such a grand cooking project. I found out only late in her life that the reason she did it in such large quantity and only once a year (for the Jewish

---

Blintzes with orange marmalade

holiday of Shavuot, in the spring, when eating dairy is customary) was because of her very long nails and perfect manicure. Her nails were so long that they could make holes in the translucently thin pancakes, and she was only willing to take her manicure down once a year.

Makes 10 blintzes, serving 2 to 4

Crêpes
1 cup all-purpose flour
1 cup milk
$^1/_2$ cup cold water
$^1/_4$ teaspoon salt
2 eggs
2 tablespoons butter, melted

Potato Filling
Potato (Knish) Filling (page 93)

Cheese Filling
8 ounces farmer cheese (low-moisture fresh cheese that usually comes in 8-ounce vacuum packages)
$^1/_4$ cup sour cream
Salt and freshly ground black or white pepper to taste or 2 tablespoons confectioners' sugar

4 tablespoons butter, for frying
Sour cream, for garnish

Prepare by setting out clean dish towels, or a tablecloth, on you kitchen work surface.

To make the crêpes, combine the flour, milk, water, salt, eggs, and butter in the jar of a blender. Whirl for a few seconds to mix well. Stop the blender, scrape down the sides with a rubber spatula, then whirl again for about 30 seconds. The batter should be very smooth and the consistency of very heavy cream. You'll know whether it is right when you make the first crêpes. For a thinner crêpe, add 1 to 2 tablespoons more water.

To cook the crêpes, heat a 6- or 7-inch nonstick skillet over medium heat until quite hot. Holding the pan off the heat with one hand, pour in about 3 tablespoons of batter with the other (I use a $^1/_4$-cup measure—4 tablespoons—to judge the amount, which will vary slightly depending on the diameter of your pan).

Immediately begin rotating the pan to spread the batter into a pancake. This requires only a thin film of batter. Place the pan back on medium heat and cook for about 1 minute. The bottom will be lightly colored.

Using your fingers and with the aid of a spatula, fork, or the tip of a table knife, carefully lift the crêpe and flip it over. Cook another 15 seconds. Turn out onto a clean kitchen towel. The second side should not color—a spot or two is fine.

If preparing the crêpes ahead, once they are fully cooled, you can stack them, but put wax paper between each to ensure they do not stick together. Leave at

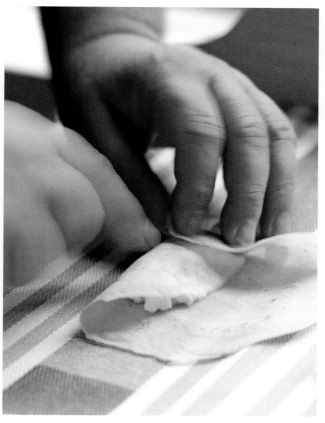

room temperature and fill within the day, or refrigerate, tightly wrapped in plastic, until ready to fill, or for up to 4 days. Freeze them for no longer than 3 months, at which time it is possible you will have to trim off the dried and brittle edges.

To make the potato filling, follow the directions in the recipe.

To make the cheese filling, in a small bowl, with a fork, blend the farmer cheese and sour cream together with salt and pepper to taste. If desired, instead of making the filling savory, make it sweet by blending in confectioners' sugar.

To assemble the blintzes, place a few spoonfuls of filling just below the center of 1 crêpe. Fold the bottom of the crêpe upward to enclose the filling. Fold in the sides over the end. Roll up the crêpe to completely enclose. Place seam side down on a platter. Repeat with the remaining crêpes and fillings.

To fry the blintzes, in a skillet large enough to hold at least half the blintzes, heat 2 tablespoons of the butter over medium heat. (If you want to fry all the blintzes together, use a 12-inch skillet and all the butter at once.) When sizzling, arrange the crêpes in the pan seam-side down. Fry until nicely browned. Carefully turn the blintzes over and fry on the second side. Transfer to a platter. Repeat with the remaining blintzes and butter.

Serve immediately with a dollop of sour cream on each.

Formed, but not fried, blintzes can be kept in the refrigerator, tightly covered, for up to 2 days. To freeze, place them on a parchment-lined baking sheet until they are frozen solid, then pack into plastic bags or containers. They should keep well enough for 3 months.

Noodles and Cottage Cheese or Pot Cheese

This is one of my favorite emergency meals. I always have cottage cheese in the refrigerator and noodles in the pantry. It is "what to cook when you think there's nothing in the house to eat," which happens to be the title of a book I wrote. Genuine, creamy, large-curd pot cheese, which is hard to find these days even in New York's kosher neighborhoods, would make it an even bigger treat.

There is nothing to it: boil the noodles (I prefer wide ones, but will use any size in a pinch) and top with cottage cheese, tossing the two together as you eat. If you are feeling indulgent, add butter to the noodles before adding the cottage cheese. The hot noodles will melt the butter. The cottage cheese, straight from the refrigerator, cools the noodles too much to allow the butter to melt.

Having been raised as a savory-loving Litvak, I season with salt and pepper, plenty of pepper. If you have a Galitzianer sweet tooth, however, sprinkle the noodles and cheese with sugar.

Sour Cream and You Name It

A favorite dairy meal of my mother was a bowl of sour cream with whatever. My father and I preferred it with boiled potatoes, butter, salt, and pepper. My sister went for sour cream with sliced bananas and a sprinkling of sugar. When in season, my mother usually liked strawberries, blueberries, or cantaloupe. She also liked, as I do now as an adult, sour cream (or yogurt) with chopped scallions, radishes, green pepper, cucumber, and tomato. Some people called this farmer's caviar, a delightful concept, although I haven't heard that name in many years.

This was definitely more a summer than winter meal. It was also one of the rare meals when she gave us a choice, when we could all eat something different.

Sour cream and potatoes was also the dish she served my sister and me at the very end of an illness, when we no longer had a fever, which the old adage advised one to starve. After a few days of tea and toast, the potatoes and sour cream became an allowable calorie splurge-cum-restorative to my always weight-conscious mother. ✎

Lox Fliegles and Potatoes

Lox trimmings used to be given away to special customers of the appetizing stores (others paid very little). Even today, with lox costing $18 a pound, and good smoked salmon as much as $24 a pound, trimmings are priced at as little as $5 a pound.

Although called *fliegles*, which means wings, the trimmings are actually the fins and tails of the salmon. They have plenty of flavor but very little meat, so they are useful for making a kind of potato soup or a less liquid dish of potatoes and onions, depending on your inclination and nostalgic memory.

My friend Shelly Fireman, who owns the two Brooklyn Diners in Manhattan (across the street from Carnegie Hall, and off Times Square on West 43rd Street), among other restaurants, reminded me of this dish. In fact, I have a very elegant version of it in *Soup Suppers,* another one of my cookbooks. It was a cold, pureed version, a take on vichyssoise, a recipe I got from the chef in a cutting-edge New York restaurant of the 1980s.

Shelly remembers the version he ate in his youth on the Grand Concourse—the Fifth Avenue of the Bronx—as a chunky, thickish dish. I like it more as a soup; plenty of broth with chunks of potato. You can also make it with water and a tiny bit of cream for enrichment, or all milk, which results in a very rich broth. Take your pick. In any case, you only need a half pound of trimmings to prepare a savory soup to serve four, so even today, as luxurious as it tastes, this is a very inexpensive dish to make.

Serves 4

2 tablespoons butter

1 medium onion, chopped

1 pound all-purpose potatoes,
  cut into 1/2-inch cubes

1/2 pound lox or smoked salmon
  "wings" and/or other trimmings

2 to 4 cups water or milk

1/4 to 1/2 cup heavy cream
  (if using water)

Salt and freshly ground pepper
  to taste

In a medium saucepan over medium heat, melt the butter and sauté the onion until tender but not colored, about 5 minutes. Add the potatoes and stir them in the butter for a minute or so. Add the lox wings and trimmings and the water or milk, using the lesser amount of liquid for a thick dish, the greater amount for a soup. Bring to a simmer, then adjust the heat so the liquid simmers gently for 40 minutes. The potatoes should be very tender and the broth should have a distinct taste of the salmon.

Remove the lox trimmings and strip off all the meat, breaking it into bite-sized pieces if necessary. Discard the bones, fins, and fat. Add the meat back to the pot. Add the cream, if using; the lesser amount for a thick dish, the greater for soup. Add salt and pepper as needed.

Serve immediately, or keep refrigerated, tightly covered, for up to one day. Reheat gently before serving.

Appetizing

In the world of kosher foods, "appetizing" is the opposite of delicatessen. Jewish delicatessens specialize in meats and the side dishes and prepared foods that are allowed to be eaten at kosher meat meals. Appetizing stores specialize in dairy products and the various and many pickled and smoked fish that the kosher laws allow to be eaten with dairy.

Although the word "appetizing" may still be printed on store awnings in Brooklyn or Manhattan, and in Jewish areas of the New York suburbs, it is not a word uttered as much today as it used to be. Even in the observant sections of the city, where family incomes are high enough to afford many luxuries, the array of "appetizing" is more limited than it used to be. Whereas bagels used to be sold in appetizing stores, a drastically reduced line of "appetizing" is now sold in bagel bakeries.

Niki Russ Federman and Josh Tupper of Russ & Daughters

The now internationally famous Zabar's, on the Upper West Side, started out as a simple appetizing store and still prides itself on the highest standard of lox, smoked salmon, pickled fish, and more. Barney Greengrass ("The Sturgeon King") and Murray's, both also on the Upper West Side of Manhattan, are two family-owned appetizing stores with an old-time feel and old-time quality. Perhaps the best appetizing store left in New York, however, is Russ & Daughters on Houston Street on the Lower East Side, now managed by a fourth generation of the Russ family.

Just as *delicatessen* refers to the store and the products it sells, the word *appetizing* refers to both the merchandise and the store that sells it. You can say, for instance,

"I'm going to the appetizing store to get a quarter-pound of lox." Or you can say, "We ate appetizing for dinner."

"Appetizing" even includes salty black lumpfish caviar, a standard at bar mitzvahs and Jewish weddings for generations, but the mainstays are bright-orange lox and its paler, less salty, smoked-salmon relative, "nova" ("novi" in local parlance) that no longer necessarily comes from Nova Scotia. Pickled cubes of lox float in brine with spices and sliced onions (page 163). There are thick slabs of kippered (hot-smoked) salmon, which is also called "baked" salmon. Large, golden, smoked whitefish glisten in glass-fronted cases next to tiny chubs, which look like miniature whitefish, but are another fish entirely. Smoked sturgeon is another staple, but controversial: some rabbis insist that sturgeon is not kosher because it doesn't have scales. My favorite fish is sable, a fatty, white-fleshed fish treated with a paprika coating, always carved as carefully as the precious smoked salmon and lox.

Last, but hardly least, there are numerous stainless-steel trays of herring—from salty purple matjes to pickled blue-gray whole herrings and fillets in "wine sauce" or sour cream sauce, both with sliced pickled onions. Of course, there is no wine in the wine sauce. It's merely the brine in which the herring was pickled.

New York City has always loved herring. The founding Dutch loved herring. The English loved herring. The Germans who came to New York City beginning in the 1840s loved herring, too. In early nineteenth-century New York, the stores called "groceries" sold booze more than household items, but they always had barrels full of herring. When Eastern Europeans began emigrating to New York City in the 1880s, there was plenty of herring already here.

Although you could buy Swiss cheese, American-style loaf Munster, and plain old yellow and orange American cheese, all sliced to order by the appetizing counter-man, the real lure was the fresh cheeses, traditional Eastern European–style cheeses. They carried dry, compact loaves of farmer cheese; seriously creamy cream cheese sold plain or with chopped vegetables (page 164) or chopped scallions (page 165); and pot cheese, a large-curd cottage cheese, often with a fresh cream enrichment. Today, the flavored cream cheeses and farmer cheese have assimilated into the supermarket dairy case, and bagel stores that sell smoked fish sell their Swiss and American cheese in plastic supermarket packaging. Appetizing stores also sold, in big hunks cut from a huge block, what they called "tub butter," actually whey butter made from the fat extracted from the liquid left over from cheese production.

A good appetizing store also made its own herring and whitefish salads, which are really spreads. The herring is ground and mixed with apple or chopped egg (page 6). Whitefish Salad (page 166) is no more than the shredded, ground, or mashed fish mixed with mayonnaise and sometimes raw onion or celery or both. Potato salad, mayonnaise-based coleslaw, and elbow macaroni salad can also be appetizing store items, but they are all-American and sold at delis, too.

There is, however, a uniquely New York appetizing salad called "Greek salad." This is nothing more than a cabbage slaw dressed with oil and vinegar; in essence the delicatessen's health salad (page 19) with the addition of black olives and bits of herring. Only the olives make it even remotely Greek, even when the olives are pitted black ones from California.

The appetizing store also carried breads that traditionally go with dairy foods. Heaped in bins behind the high refrigerated fish and salad cases were freshly baked bagels and bialys; crusty, airy, poppy-seeded Vienna (also called Kaiser) rolls; Corn Bread (page 205), which is really a kind of sour rye; brown pumpernickel; and black bread. They were all baked locally, but not on the premises.

In the sweets department, you could count on the appetizing store to carry the best dried fruits and nuts, chocolate-covered fruit jellies, and chocolate-enrobed graham crackers. Halvah (see page 165), in several flavor variations, was a staple item.

Until the 1970s, if you were Jewish in New York, all or some appetizing, depending on your degree of affluence and your family's interest in food, would likely appear on your table on Sunday morning. At the very least, you would have bagels with lox and cream cheese (see page 158). Add to that the platters of sliced tomatoes, cucumbers, and raw onion that accompanied the pickled herring and platters of smoked fish and cheeses, and this meal became known as a New York brunch.

Then, several things happened. American family life changed. Children were allowed to pursue their own activities apart from their parents and not join in for a Sunday morning family meal. The rate of intermarriage increased and, in general, Jewish assimilation progressed.

While the economically booming post–World War II era lasted, however, many families certainly indulged their appetites and budgets. "Appetizing" was a way for the newly affluent to show off their success. Smoked and pickled fish were and still are expensive. Looking back, I see there was some jockeying for status in the community in the way "appetizing" was ordered in those times. The appetizing stores would be crowded on a Sunday morning, mainly with men, not women. While in line, the men would talk sports, or cars, or about their children, their businesses, or their last vacation, often with the Sunday papers under their arms, waiting to place their orders. Everyone on line behind you or around you could hear what you ordered. It was like announcing your private predilections, as well as revealing your cash flow. ("Oh, the Goldbergs eat only plain lox. They probably can't afford nova.")

Even though you were not leading your business on Sunday morning, you could still express your masculine power by directing the fulfillment of your order. To cite a common example, smoked salmon was never sliced thin enough. "No, thinner, thinner," customers would urge the man behind the counter who had spent the better part of his life slicing smoked fish. Or you'd hear someone say, "I'll take a half-pound of herring, but make sure you weigh the fish before you put in the onions," showing your obvious distrust of the merchant, your savvy in the marketplace. Is it any wonder that appetizing countermen had the reputation of being grumpy?

Yom Kippur is the highest volume day for "appetizing" these days. Yom Kippur is a fast day, but when the fast is over at nightfall, Jews take the expression "break fast" seriously. Although it may be dark outside, many of us start our first meal in more than twenty-four hours with cereal. Some start with fruit juice or with melon. Some have to have herring to start, and platters of "appetizing" to follow, all symbols of fertility and prosperity. ✎

Bagels and Lox

When did the bagel meet cream cheese and lox? Today they seem like an obvious trio, a food combination that must have existed in the Old Country, somewhere in Poland or Russia.

When you think about it, though, it's not possible. Cream cheese as we know it is an American invention. The most famous brand is Philadelphia, but it was created in rural New York in 1872. Cream cheese may well be vaguely related to a fresh cheese made by dairymen in the shtetls of Eastern Europe, but it doesn't appear that anyone in nineteenth-century Poland was schmearing it on bagels. For one thing, the bagel was not designed to hold a spread, or to make a sandwich, for that matter. It has a hole in the middle.

Now, lox is salt-cured (not smoked) salmon, and the salt-curing process was certainly known by poor Jews who preserved fish by pickling them, but salmon was not one of those fish.

According to most sources, salt-cured salmon—true lox—became popular on the East Coast after the transcontinental railroad connected it to the West Coast in 1869. The Pacific Ocean was teaming with salmon and they were sent east in barrels, layered with salt, which drew out their moisture and formed a brine that could keep them edible for the duration of the trip—and longer. As good a foil as cream cheese is to the salty fish, lox probably caught on with the poor Jews of the Lower East Side significantly before they had cream cheese. Preserved fish had been a mainstay in the Old Country. In New York, the Jews lived in tenements with minimal cooking facilities. A ready-to-eat product like lox was akin to a convenience food.

Even as recently as the early twentieth century, and even though food is often a subject of Yiddish writing, you won't find mention of the bagels, cream cheese, and lox combination in Jewish literature, either. In my parent's youth during the Depression and war years, one ate pumpernickel or Corn Bread (page 205) with smoked fish and dairy.

So when did the bagel-lox-cream cheese dream team first appear? I asked Mark Federman, third-generation owner of Russ & Daughters, one of the last great appetizing stores left in the City. He, in turn, called his mother, Anne Russ Federman, and his aunt, Hattie Russ Gold, the two surviving of the three Russ daughters.

"They don't have any recollection of bagels and cream cheese with lox before 1940," said Federman. In fact, he added, the Russ sisters don't remember selling bagels at all until the 1940s.

Questioning numerous members of my parents generation, who would now be hovering over eighty (I even scouted Florida retirement communities), I found no one who remembers eating bagels with lox and cream cheese in their youth, but a few people remembered an Al Jolson song from the 1930s called "Bagels and Yox."

This all supports a theory that it was Al Jolson and other entertainers, in about 1933, that put the cream cheese on the bagel during a two-hour radio show sponsored by James Lewis Kraft. Instructions from Kraft were to weave mention of his products into the show, just as Arthur Godfrey and Jack Benny did on their radio programs. In short, his orders were to include the words *cream cheese* as often as possible, in as many jokes as possible.

"It would have just been like Jolson to use the words 'cream cheese' as a springboard into some quick joke about lox and bagels," says Herbert Goldman in *Jolson: The Legend Comes to Life*. "That may have been the start of the new Jewish trilogy of bagels, lox, and cream cheese, sort of a Jewish answer to the old Sunday triumvirate of bacon, eggs, and pancakes."

Lox, Eggs, and Onions

Smart-aleck New Yorkers who enjoyed speaking lingo that tourists couldn't understand used to call lox, eggs, and onions "a Leo." By me, it is still lox, eggs, and onions, and one of the most sublime creations of the Yiddish kitchen. Well, maybe you had to grow up eating it, and to have an emotional attachment to it.

It's hard to find it well made these days, although it is as easy (or as hard) to make as scrambled eggs. The café above the Fairway Market on Columbus Avenue and 74th Street, run by Mitchell London, one of former Mayor Ed Koch's famous personal chefs, does an incredible job. Barney Greengrass, the old-time appetizing store on Amsterdam and 89th Street, does it okay. Sarge's Delicatessen on Third Avenue and 36th Street does a superior job. All use Nova Scotia smoked salmon instead of salt-cured lox.

Lox, eggs, and onions was the only thing my father, Larry, could cook, other than Broadcast corned beef hash and Campbell's tomato soup, both out of cans. He was precise and meticulous about it, too, as he was about everything. After soaking the lox in milk for 30 minutes to leach out some of the salt, he'd cut the lox into perfect squares, fluff the eggs with an egg beater (as he and I learned from his mother), and, with lots of bubbling butter in the pan, very slowly drag the eggs around the pan to form large curds. I still make scrambled eggs this way, although with less butter. And I still soak salty lox in milk to leach out some of its salt. "Why not use smoked salmon?" I have been asked. Because it's not at all the same taste. I like it, but it's not the same.

For some unfathomable reason, some people like this as a flat pancake-style omelet, essentially a frittata. Cook it that way if you must. Or, to serve it as an appetizer with drinks, make it as an omelet and then cut it into small squares. To me, this is breakfast-brunch food, to enjoy with a buttered bagel, bialy, or seeded roll, or maybe supper. On the other hand, I would find it a treat at dinnertime, too. The large range of the number of eggs to be used reflects this—use fewer for breakfast, more perhaps for other meals.

Serves 4

¹/₄ pound sliced lox
1 or 2 tablespoons milk
3 or 4 tablespoons butter

2 medium onions, cut into
    ¹/₄-inch dice (about 2 cups)
8 to 12 eggs
Freshly ground black pepper

Cut the lox slices into ¹/₄- to ¹/₂-inch squares. Place the pieces in a small, shallow bowl, and cover with milk. Set aside to soak for 30 minutes.

In a 10-inch nonstick skillet, heat 3 tablespoons of the butter to bubbling over medium-high heat. Add the diced onions and fry, stirring frequently, until they are wilted, about 5 minutes. Meanwhile, break the eggs into a mixing bowl. When the onions are cooked, scrape them into the eggs. Drain the lox, discarding the milk, and add the lox to the egg mixture. Stir to mix well.

Add the remaining 1 tablespoon butter, if desired, to the same nonstick pan used to cook the onions. Pour the egg mixture into the skillet and place over medium heat. Let the eggs set a few seconds. As the eggs cook, push them around the pan with a wooden spoon or fork so as not to scratch the nonstick surface. First push them from the edge to the center, so you end up with large curds of scrambled eggs. I then shut off the heat and turn the curds over for a second. Cook to taste, either dry or slightly moist.

Serve immediately.

Pickled Lox

As commonplace as brined salmon (lox) has become, pickled lox remains a delicacy. It is expensive and, perhaps, just for rarefied tastes. It is always eaten in small quantity, and best, I think, with pumpernickel or other dark bread slathered with sweet butter. Lox loses much of its saltiness with this pickling treatment, but it needs the salt to start. Do not even attempt to prepare this with relatively low-salt smoked salmon. Pickled lox, like pickled herring, is usually served with the onions that have pickled along with it.

The fish is fabulous without any sauce, but some people also like it with a cream sauce blended from sour cream and buttermilk, like the one served with pickled herring. The lox and the onions need to sit in their brines for 2 to 3 days before they are ready to eat.

Serves 10 or more, along with other "appetizing"

Pickled Lox
2 pounds lox, in one piece about
   12 inches long by 6 inches
   wide at its widest point,
   skin on
2¹/₂ cups water
1 cup distilled white vinegar
¹/₂ cup sugar
1 rounded tablespoon mixed
   pickling spices

Pickled Onions
1¹/₄ cups water
¹/₂ cup distilled white vinegar
¹/₄ cup sugar
2 medium onions, finely sliced
   (about 2 cups)

Cream Sauce (optional)
1 cup sour cream
¹/₄ cup buttermilk
1 or 2 tablespoons of the
   pickling juices from the lox

To pickle the lox, cut the salmon crosswise into 2-inch-wide pieces (leave the skin on). Place them in a large nonreactive bowl.

Combine the water, vinegar, and sugar in another bowl; stir until the sugar dissolves.

Pour the pickling liquid over the lox pieces. Add the pickling spices. Let the mixture stand, covered with plastic wrap, at room temperature for about 12 hours. Then refrigerate for 2 to 3 days, until pickled to taste.

To pickle the onions, combine the water, vinegar, and sugar in a large bowl; stir until the sugar dissolves. Add the onions. Cover with plastic wrap and refrigerate for 3 days.

To make the sauce, blend together the sour cream, buttermilk, and just enough pickling juice from the salmon to flavor it lightly and make it runny.

Before serving, you may want to remove the skin from the salmon, but this is best done by each diner at the table. You may also want to cut the salmon into smaller chunks.

To serve, drain the salmon and serve cold, in a bowl, dressed with the cream mixture, and with the onions stirred in or scattered on top.

The salmon and onions will keep in the refrigerator for several days, tightly wrapped and kept separately. Do not freeze.

Vegetable Cream Cheese

 ————————————————————

This is not a recipe written in stone. The proportions are agreeable to me. If you like, add more or less, leave out one of the vegetables, or substitute red pepper for green. Like that. Instead of heavy cream, if your palate likes a sour edge, you can use a few tablespoons of sour cream or buttermilk to thin the cheese.

Enough for 6 to 8 schmears

1 (8-ounce) package cream cheese
2 tablespoons very finely minced
   green pepper
2 tablespoons very finely
   grated carrot

1 tablespoon very finely chopped
   scallion, both white and green parts
   (1 small scallion)
1 tablespoon very finely minced celery
1/4 cup heavy cream

Combine the ingredients in a bowl and, with an electric mixer, blend together well, until fluffy.

Store, covered, in the refrigerator for no more than 2 or 3 days.

Scallion Cream Cheese

You don't have to be Jewish, just a New Yorker, to call out "bagel with a schmear," still the city's most popular breakfast. To schmear is "to spread." You can schmear butter, but, when in a bagel bakery, it is usually understood that you mean for the bagel to be schmeared with cream cheese. And any place but a coffee cart on the street sells, at the very least, plain cream cheese, scallion cream cheese, vegetable cream cheese, and cream cheese studded with smoked salmon, not to mention tofu-based imitation cream cheeses and low-fat cream cheese. It makes me cringe, but I have also seen dried cranberry cream cheese and sundried tomato cream cheese.

Enough for 6 to 8 hefty schmears

1 (8-ounce) package cream cheese
1/2 cup finely chopped scallions,
　　including some green parts
　　(about 4 small scallions)
1/4 cup heavy cream

Combine the ingredients in a bowl and, with an electric mixer, blend together well, until fluffy.

Store, covered, in the refrigerator for no more than 2 or 3 days.

Halvah

Halvah is a Middle Eastern sweet made of ground sesame seeds whipped with egg whites and either honey or sugar. It can be studded with pistachios or marbled with chocolate. It can be coated in chocolate or not, although chocolate inside or out is strictly an American embellishment. How a Middle Eastern food was introduced into Poland, Latvia, and Lithuania, then to New York via immigrants from those countries, can only be speculated upon. In her book *The Bialy Eaters*, however, Mimi Sheraton notes that a special treat in Bialystok, the home city of bialys (in the Old Country they were called *Bialystok kuchen*), used to be a halvah on bialy sandwich.

Whitefish Salad

This is a latecomer to the appetizing repertoire. In the old days, who would have squandered expensive whitefish, a true delicacy, by mushing it up with mayonnaise to make a spread for a bagel? Even if someone long ago was so extravagant, whitefish salad has become popular only in the last twenty-five years. Nowadays, better and lesser versions (mostly lesser) are sold in every bagel shop. For a better salad, one you can serve proudly on a plate with radish roses, whole scallions, sliced cucumber, and cherry tomatoes, don't mush the ingredients together, but gently toss them, to maintain big flakes of fish.

Serves 6 to 8

1 (1½- to 2-pound) whole
    smoked whitefish
1 cup finely minced celery
2 heaping tablespoons coarsely
    chopped fresh parsley

1 cup mayonnaise
Juice of ½ lemon
Freshly ground black pepper
Bagels, bialys, pumpernickel, or
    black bread, for accompaniment

To prepare the fish, strip the meat off the whitefish in as big pieces as possible, being careful to discard all bones. Discard the head and fins. Put the whitefish pieces in a large bowl.

Add the celery, parsley, mayonnaise, lemon juice, and pepper (no salt will be necessary). With a table fork, gently toss and mix the ingredients together, trying not to break up the whitefish too much. It is best in flakes.

Serve chilled, with bagels, bialys, pumpernickel, or black bread. Keep in the refrigerator, tightly wrapped, for no more than 3 days.

At Russ & Daughters, from top left clockwise: smoked whitefish; slicing Nova smoked salmon; one of many cream cheese flavors; pickled lox

RUSS & DAUGHTERS
SCALLION
CREAM CHEESE
3 99 HALF LB

CHAPTER 6

❧ Passover ❧

All of Jewish history boils down to this: They tried to kill us. We won. Let's eat.

—Old Jewish saying

The dishes were soaked to be made "clean" for Passover.... When the dishes came out of the tub, the carp went in. If you watched carefully, you might be able to get into the bath before the fish. The carp was bought live so he would be fresh for the gefilte fish. We couldn't afford real pets, either, so whenever there was a fish in the tub, we gave it a name and played games with it. When my mother killed it, one of the kids was sure to yell, "How can you eat anything that has a first name?"

—Alan King, *Is Salami and Eggs Better Than Sex?*

Officially, Passover is the eight-day spring holiday that commemorates and celebrates the Jewish Exodus from Egypt led by Moses. You know, "Let my people go!" However, it is even more than that. It is the moment when the Jewish people became a distinct nation. Wandering together in the desert for forty years is an obviously bonding experience. Passover is meant to remind us how G-d liberated us from slavery and took us, as a nation, to Mt. Sinai, and how G-d continues to be involved in our individual and collective lives.

The Passover Haggadah, which recounts and comments on all the events and miracles of the liberation from Egypt, is read on the first two nights of Passover. This family and friends ritual, which takes place around the dining table, is called a seder. To help us relive and reflect on our liberation from slavery, the seder includes symbolic foods, all but one of which—the roasted shank bone—are pointed out and eaten during the readings.

Traditionally, it is the youngest member of the family, often followed by the rest of the children, who begins the reading by reciting The Four Questions, which

My grandfather's kiddush cup

all start with the phrase, "Why is this night different from all other nights?" It takes the whole Haggadah reading to answer these four questions, which usually takes a couple of hours, or even the entire night. But in short, the answer is because we were slaves in Egypt and we must remember our travails there, as well as the Exodus, and we must all relive it as if we are part of it.

In accordance, we eat matzo, unleavened bread (see page 172), and everything we eat on and with, and cook in and with, must be special for Passover, lest a trace of leavened or fermented food is present on our everyday things. Everything that is not special for Passover is called *chometz* and is forbidden for the eight days. This is actually an even stronger injunction than the normal kosher laws, because if a tiny bit of nonkosher food is accidentally mixed with kosher food, the result can still be kosher. But even if the tiniest amount of *chometz* is accidentally mixed with Passover food, all of it becomes *chometz*.

Following this rule, if you don't have china reserved only for Passover, you must, after cleaning it meticulously and not using it for twenty-four hours, immerse it in boiling water for twenty-four hours, or soak glass dishes for as long as three days, changing the water every 24 hours.

Whatever you use to eat on and with, you also have to clean the house thoroughly, including collecting and burning every last crumb of food that is forbidden to eat during the eight-day holiday. (Could this be the origin of spring cleaning?) To that end, on the night before Passover begins, there is a ritual search for *chometz*. And any foods that you cannot eat or use during Passover must be sold. That would include canned goods, frozen foods, and certainly any product that contains wheat, most obviously bread, crackers, pretzels, cookies, and cake, but also products with hidden wheat, such as soy sauce.

Both the search and the sale were symbolic in the Conservative Jewish community of my childhood. For the search, my grandfather planted some crumbs in an already cleaned kitchen cabinet, then dusted them out with a feather and burned them. For the

My mother's Lenox china Passover plate

sale, he was given one dollar by a non-Jewish neighbor. Then he tied the doors shut on all the cabinets that contained *chometz*.

The really big project was taking all the regular dishes and pots down to the basement and carrying all the Passover dishes and pots back up. This was my job, and I hated it. We didn't have to soak glasses or anything in the bathtub, as I heard less affluent families did, because we had everything different for Passover. And we didn't have carp swimming in the bathtub. My grandmother went to an old, reliable fish market where she could pick out the live fish from a big cement tank. I can still see her climbing the step up to the tank in her spiked heels, and with her long, well-manicured index finger, pointing to the specimen she wanted, then having the fish scaled and filleted on the spot. Of course, she kept the fish's head, tail, and bones to make the broth that would later jell around her fish patties.

In our house, there were also many dishes we ate during the holiday that we didn't eat the rest of the year, not that you weren't allowed to. Today, I find nothing more comforting than making Matzo Brei (page 177) on a frigid January evening when there's nothing else in the house to eat and I don't want to expose myself to the weather to go out and shop or go out to eat.

It wasn't just matzo brei that we indulged in on Passover. We ate matzo meal pancakes. We had matzo farfel kugel. We had Knaidlach (page 43). In strict Orthodox tradition, however, one is not allowed to moisten matzo during the eight days of Passover. It is only when the holiday has ended, or on the last day, and you have excess matzo products in the house, that these dishes become possible.

The injunction against flour resulted in few baked goods being made during Passover. We all looked forward to my grandmother's walnut sponge cake (page 182), and, in later years, my mother's recipe for Passover Mandelbread (page 185). Mostly, however, we ate Dried Fruit Compote (page 222) and Wine-Poached Pears (page 221). For a treat, there was chocolate-covered matzo, a specialty of Barton's Candy, which was a Jewish-owned, Brooklyn-based company that made special Passover confections, and my grandmother's homemade matzo farfel candy with honey and ginger, Ingberlach (page 189).

Today, anything flourless can pass as a Passover dessert or sweet, so seder tables are often laden with iced chocolate cakes and other fancy fabrications. In appearance, they may put Elsie's sponge cakes to shame, but they never taste as good as they look.

Matzo

Although matzo is called "the bread of affliction," it is also the bread of liberation, as Passover is called the holiday of redemption. It is the unleavened bread that the Jews needed to bake in haste when they left Egypt. As it is written in Exodus, "They baked the dough that they took out of Egypt into unleavened cakes, for they could

Making matzo at Streit's, the last of New York's matzo factories

not be leavened, because they were driven from Egypt and could not delay, nor had they made provisions for themselves."

This is where the prohibition against fermentation, leavening, comes from, and the rules about it are so strict on Passover that even if one drop of water touches flour and remains there for longer than eighteen minutes without it being baked, that product cannot be eaten during Passover.

If you ask a religious person for an explanation of the eighteen-minute rule, you are likely to be told that it is the time needed for wild yeasts to begin fermenting the flour. No yeast is ever added to the dough, but even yeasts that live in our environment must not begin leavening it. To ensure this, the wheat is reaped on a dry day, and not one too hot, and if, in any way, substances deemed "foreign" by the wheat watcher are reaped as well, that crop cannot be used.

It is probably no coincidence, however, that the number eighteen (*chai*, in Hebrew), has superstitious meaning because the word also means "life," as in *l'chaim*, the toast "To life!" or *m'chaia*, which means "life-giving" and is used as an expression of relief. For instance when you walk into an air-conditioned room in the middle of August, you might say, "Oy, a *m'chaia*.").

Most commercial matzo is baked within seven minutes of being mixed with water, but the mixing equipment must be steam-washed between batches to ensure that no fermentation occurs.

Not all matzo is for Passover. Only matzo made specifically for Passover can be used for the eight days, and it will be prominently labeled. *Shmurah* matzo is the most special Passover matzo. *Shmurah* means "guarded" and the highest level of *shmurah* matzo is made with flour that is, indeed, guarded from the moment it is reaped until it comes out of the oven, to be sure it never comes in contact with water or other liquids. This kind of *shmurah* matzo is usually handmade, but is also made by machine. There is also *shmurah* matzo whose flour is guarded only from the time of grinding. ✆

Matzo Meal Latkes

This is such a humble recipe that it rarely appears in cookbooks. Whenever I have found it in published sources, it is gussied up in some way—apples are added, sugar and spice is added, grated lemon peel. You get the picture. It does appear on the back of some matzo meal boxes, however, although on the Manischewitz box that I have in my kitchen right now, the eggs are separated and the beaten egg whites are folded into the batter at the end. If you want a sweet pancake, be warned that a batter with sugar will brown more quickly than one without. Sugar caramelizes.

We had a tradition in my family when I was a little boy, until my grandfather died when I was sixteen. Because my father always had to work until the last minute on the first night of Passover, and we would not be eating the festive seder meal until very late, in the afternoon my grandfather brought him matzo meal pancakes to tide him over. Meanwhile, back at home, we were sitting at a card table in the kitchen, the dining table having already been set for the seder, eating those same pancakes hot from the skillet. I always liked them with sour cream, which I still do, but we weren't allowed to eat dairy so close to seder time. I made do with salt and homemade applesauce. My younger sister and cousins preferred them sprinkled with sugar. Preserves and jams are a good topping, too.

The following formula is very adjustable. It produces a very light, puffy, egg-y pancake. If you would like pancakes with more substance, increase the matzo meal. As the batter stands it gets a little thicker, too. Fry a trial pancake, then adjust the batter to taste.

Makes 8 to 10 pancakes

3 eggs
³/₄ cup cold water
1 teaspoon salt
¹/₂ cup matzo meal
2 tablespoons sugar (optional)

Grapeseed or other acceptable Passover oil, Schmaltz (page 9), or butter, for frying
Sour cream, sugar, preserves, jam, or applesauce, for accompaniment

To prepare the batter, in a bowl, beat together the eggs, water, salt, matzo meal, and sugar. Let stand for 5 minutes. The mixture should be thick, but pourable.

In a skillet, add just enough oil to barely coat the pan bottom and heat over medium-high heat.

To make the pancakes, using a scant $^1/_4$ cup batter for each pancake, and drop the batter into the hot oil. It should start sizzling immediately. Fry until lightly browned, then flip the pancake over and fry on the second side. Repeat with the remaining batter, adding water to the batter if it gets too thick, and adding more oil to the pan, if needed.

Serve hot with a favorite accompaniment.

Egg White Variation

For very fluffy pancakes, separate the eggs, mix the yolks with the batter, then beat the whites to stiff peaks and fold them in.

Savory Variation

To the batter above (omit the sugar), add 1 medium onion, grated on the finest side of a box grater or pureed in a food mill. These are particularly good as a side dish to roast chicken or a meat dish with gravy.

Matzo Farfel Kugel

This is nothing more (or less) than a moist bread stuffing. If you add Bell's Poultry Seasoning, an American touch that is mainly powdered sage, it will taste like Thanksgiving, and, indeed, should be used to stuff chicken, turkey, or the pocket of a breast of veal. My mother always added mushrooms to her matzo kugel. I use a combination of white cultivated mushrooms for their substance and, for flavor, Italian porcini, which are in fact in the same boletus family as the fragrant mushrooms from Eastern Europe.

Serves 8 to 12

4 cups coarsely chopped onions, fried until medium brown (page 7)

1 cup ¼-inch diced celery

4 cups matzo farfel

8 cups boiling water

6 eggs

1½ teaspoons salt

½ to 1 teaspoon freshly ground black pepper

½ cup Chicken Soup (page 40)

4 tablespoons Schmaltz (page 9), melted, or grapeseed or other acceptable Passover oil

Prepare the onions according to the recipe. After the onions have turned golden, add the celery and sauté until the celery wilts but is still a little crunchy.

To prepare the batter, place the matzo farfel in a colander set in your sink. Very slowly, in a thin stream, stopping every few seconds, pour the boiling water over the farfel. The farfel should become limp, but not sodden.

In a very large bowl, beat the eggs with the salt, pepper, and the chicken soup. Stir in the onion mixture, then the moistened farfel. To taste for seasoning, fry a spoonful in a nonstick pan.

Preheat the oven to 375°F. Put 3 tablespoons of the schmaltz in an 8-inch square glass baking pan. Place in the oven for 5 minutes. Remove from the oven and pour in the farfel mixture. Drizzle the remaining 1 tablespoon schmaltz over the top.

Bake for 1 hour, until well browned. Let cool for at least 15 minutes before cutting and serving. It is also good at room temperature, and reheats beautifully in a 350°F oven. Some cooks actually prefer it reheated, when the crust develops even more crispness. Then again, there are eaters who only like the inside pieces. A functional Jewish family might be defined as one in which everyone gets the piece he or she likes.

Mushroom Variation

To the mixture, add 8 ounces of white mushrooms, thinly sliced or coarsely chopped (your choice), plus ½ ounce of dried Italian porcini reconstituted in ½ cup of the hottest possible tap water for 20 minutes. Drain the porcini and reserve the soaking liquid. Sauté both types of mushrooms in the same pan as the onions, and substitute the mushroom soaking liquid for the chicken soup. You will need to use a casserole or baking dish with more volume than an 8-inch square, as above. A 9-inch square or similar capacity pan is perfect.

Matzo Brei

Fried Matzo

Matzo brei is so popular in New York City that we have had citywide, sensationally media-covered matzo brei contests to see which person or restaurant makes it the best. It is basically a dish of dampened, broken matzo mixed with eggs and fried. However, every ingredient, every method and technique, is open to debate by New York Jews and Gentiles alike, who all think their method, or, in any case, the kind of matzo brei they grew up eating at home or in the homes of Jewish friends, is the best.

I say my matzo brei beats all.

Serves 2

3 matzo boards
8 cups boiling water
4 or 5 eggs
$1/4$ to $1/2$ teaspoon salt

2 tablespoons butter, Schmaltz (page 9) or grapeseed oil (which is kosher for Passover, not peanut, corn, or canola)
Freshly ground black pepper, for seasoning
Preserves, jam, or sour cream, for accompaniment

Into a colander set in your sink, break the matzo into more or less 1-inch pieces.

Very, very slowly, pour the boiling water over the matzo, wetting it down well, then let it stand for a few minutes to drain well and to plump up.

In a bowl, beat the eggs together with the salt. Add the wet matzo and mix well.

In a 10-inch skillet, melt the butter over medium-high heat. When sizzling, add the egg-matzo mixture. Immediately decrease the heat to medium-low. (Slow-cooking the eggs gives them a more custard-like consistency.)

When the bottom of the mixture starts to set, break it up by dragging it around the pan, from the outside edge to the center. Once the bottom is cooked, turn the mixture gently with a spatula. Cook for 3 to 4 minutes all together, until the matzo brei cooks evenly and is as moist (or as dry) as you like.

Serve hot, with some freshly ground pepper and with preserves, jam, or sour cream.

Shmurah *matzo (see page 172)*

Cottage-Cheese Chremslach

The word *chremslach* is applied to any number of very different, usually fried, matzo meal pancakes, including the plainest-possible recipe on page 173. There are also recipes called *chremsle*, *vremzle*, or *chremslach* that are croquettes with almonds and raisins. These cheese pancakes are wonderful for a midweek Passover dairy breakfast, lunch, or dinner. I like them topped with sour cream, but if you have a sweet tooth, try applesauce or orange marmalade or other preserves, or a sprinkling of sugar, or top them with sour cream and strawberries macerated with some sugar so they exude their juices and form a sauce.

Makes about 18

4 eggs
1 cup 4-percent cottage cheese
3/4 cup milk (whole or low-fat)
3/4 to 1 teaspoon salt
1 tablespoon sugar (optional)

1 cup matzo meal
Grapeseed or other acceptable
  Passover oil, oil (or oil and
  2 tablespoons butter for flavor),
  for frying

In a bowl, with a fork, beat together the eggs, cottage cheese, milk, salt, and sugar. Stir in the matzo meal. Set aside for 10 minutes.

In a 10- to 12-inch skillet, over medium heat, heat enough oil to cover the bottom by a scant 1/8 inch. When the oil is hot, pour a scant 1/4 cup of the batter into the skillet. It should form a pancake about 4 inches in diameter. If it is too thick to spread this much, add a little more milk. The pancake should sizzle immediately. Fry until the first side is golden brown, 60 to 90 seconds, depending on how hot the oil is. Turn the pancake. The second side takes less time, about 30 seconds.

Drain the pancakes on paper towels or brown paper and serve while still very hot.

Variation

For a puffier pancake, separate the eggs, beat the yolks with the milk, then beat the whites until they form peaks and fold into the batter.

Passover Pareve Apple Cake

When it was given to me, this recipe originally specified flour, not matzo cake meal. I didn't think it was very good, but I made it a few times anyway, as my family and friends liked it. Obsessing over how to improve the recipe to make it more to my own liking, it dawned on me that someone had converted a perfectly good Passover cake into an everyday cake and that if I converted it back it would be much better. I love it now, and everyone I have served it to raves about it. One day I didn't have quite enough ground cinnamon, however, and I blended together a substitute with the teaspoon of cinnamon I had, plus ground nutmeg, mace, and ginger to fill out the tablespoon measure. That was yet another improvement.

Makes one 8-inch-square cake

Topping
$^1/_2$ cup coarsely chopped walnuts or pecans
$^3/_4$ cup sugar
1 tablespoon ground cinnamon or a combination of ground cinnamon, nutmeg, mace, and ginger

Cake
3 eggs
$^3/_4$ cup sugar
$^1/_3$ cup vegetable oil
$^3/_4$ cup matzo cake meal
5 medium apples, peeled, cored, halved, and cut into $^1/_4$-inch-thick slices (about 5 cups), preferably Golden Delicious, Crispin (Mutzu), or other apples that keep their shape when cooked
$^1/_3$ cup raisins (optional)

Position an oven rack in the center of the oven. Preheat the oven to 350°F. Lightly oil an 8-inch-square glass baking dish.

To prepare the topping, mix together the walnuts, sugar, and cinnamon in a small bowl; set aside.

To prepare the cake batter, in a bowl, with a hand-held electric mixer, beat the eggs on medium speed until well mixed. Beat in the sugar, about 2 tablespoons at a time, beating until the mixture is thick and foamy. Beat in the oil, adding it in a steady stream. Scrape down the bowl with a rubber spatula. With the spatula, stir in the matzo cake meal, blending well.

Pour half of the batter mixture into the prepared pan. Sprinkle about half the topping mixture evenly over the batter. Top with half the apples and all the raisins. Scrape the remaining half of the batter over the apples, spreading it out to cover the apples. Arrange the remaining apples on top of the batter. Sprinkle evenly with the remaining topping mixture.

Bake for 1 hour and 15 minutes, or until the sides of the cake pull away very slightly from the baking dish and the topping has begun to caramelize. (A cake tester is not reliable. It will not come out clean due to the moist richness of this cake.) Let sit in the baking dish for several hours until completely cool before cutting into serving portions. This cake is yet another Yiddish food that improves with age. Keep the cake in its dish, covered tightly with plastic, and the next day the topping will have become a moist, candylike coating.

My Family's Passover Walnut Cake

Elsie's best baked items, her walnut sponge cake and orange sponge cake, are totally typical of the cakes we used to have for Passover. They are very delicate. While they were in the oven or cooling, heaven forbid you slammed a door or walked too heavy-footed. Sometimes they fell anyway. We didn't care. We loved the flavor. Since I learned how to make this walnut cake from her, however, I learned from my baking guru, Carole Walter, author of several award-winning cookbooks and one of the country's most respected baking teachers, that taking some sugar from the batter and beating it into the egg whites stabilizes the cake. I still have not dared to use a machine to grind the nuts. Like my grandmother, I use a hand-held, rotary nut grinder to ensure that they come out powdery and not pasty.

Makes one 10-inch tube cake

9 eggs, separated
1 cup sugar
2 tablespoons matzo cake meal

1 teaspoon vanilla extract (see note)
$1/8$ teaspoon salt
2 cups shelled walnuts, finely ground

Position an oven rack in the center of the oven. Preheat the oven to 350°F.

To make the batter, in the bowl of a stand mixer fitted with the paddle, beat the egg yolks on medium speed until well blended. Beat in all but 2 tablespoons of the sugar, 2 tablespoons at a time, beating well after each addition. The yolks should be thick and foamy. Still on medium speed, beat in the cake meal, vanilla, and salt.

Scrape the batter into a large bowl and, with a rubber spatula, stir in the ground walnuts.

Meticulously wash and dry the mixer bowl. Using the whisk attachment, beat the egg whites on medium speed until they hold soft peaks. Beat in the remaining 2 tablespoons of sugar a little at a time. Beat the whites until stiff.

Using a rubber spatula, carefully fold the beaten whites into the batter. Turn the batter into an ungreased 10-inch angel food pan with a removable bottom. Very gently, smooth the top with a rubber spatula, if necessary.

Bake for 45 to 50 minutes, or until the cake shrinks away slightly from the sides of the pan. Remove the pan from the oven and turn the pan upside down. If it does not have feet to rest on, slip it over the neck of a bottle to cool completely.

Loosen the cooled cake from the sides of the pan with a sharp, thin-bladed knife. Remove the tube from the pan. You may attempt to cut the cake away from the tube, but I generally leave it on until the first slice is taken out, when it becomes easier to remove without ruining the look of the cake.

This cake stays moist for several days at room temperature, covered well with aluminum foil. It's likely it will be eaten sooner, however.

Note:

Kosher-for-Passover vanilla extract may not be available. To make some yourself, place a vanilla bean in kosher-for-Passover vodka for about 1 week. The vodka will now be flavored.

Passover Mandelbread

This is also from my mother's recipes files, in her own handwriting. I don't really know where she got it, but I suspect it was from a *New York Post* Passover section. The newspaper, when it was owned by Dorothy Schiff from 1939 to 1976, was the favored paper of liberal-minded, middle-class Jews, and every Passover the paper had a huge special recipe section. Other New York City and suburban papers followed suit; there was so much Passover advertising available that it was irresistible to package the ads in a special section. But the *Post*'s was always the biggest and best. I have several in my library, although I can't find this recipe in them.

Frankly, this mandelbread is not as satisfying as the mandelbread one makes with flour (page 229). It is particularly firm and crumbly, even though it is baked only once, not twice like regular mandelbread. But it is very welcome as a Passover treat, when observers often feel deprived of baked goods.

Makes two 15 by 4-inch loaves

2³/₄ cups matzo cake meal
¹/₂ teaspoon salt
³/₄ cup potato starch
1 teaspoon ground cinnamon
2 cups sugar
¹/₂ cup (1 stick) pareve margarine

6 eggs
6 ounces semisweet or bittersweet chocolate, broken into pieces (these days it is possible to find Passover chocolate chips)
1 cup nuts (any kind), coarsely chopped

Position an oven rack in the center of the oven. Line a baking sheet with parchment paper. Preheat the oven to 350°F.

To prepare the batter, in a small bowl, combine the cake meal, salt, potato starch, and cinnamon. Mix well. Set aside.

In the bowl of a stand mixer with the paddle attachment, cream together the sugar and margarine on medium speed until light and fluffy. Beat in the eggs one at a time, beating well after each addition. Reduce the speed to low and add the blended dry ingredients. By hand, stir in the chocolate and nuts. Divide the dough in half and, on the baking sheet, form each into a long loaf about 2 inches wide.

Bake for 45 to 50 minutes, until firm. It will not be browned very much. Remove to a rack and let sit on the baking sheet until completely cool. When thoroughly cool, use a serrated knife to cut the loaves into ¹/₄-inch-thick slices.

Matzo Buttercrunch

This recipe was created by Marcy Goldman of Montreal and was published in her book *A Treasury of Jewish Holiday Baking*. She had disseminated it long before that, however, on her website, www.BetterBaking.com. Now I see it published (unfortunately not credited) in New York City newspapers and national magazines, and passed around by New Yorkers who claim it as their own. Taking credit for this confection where it is not due is understandable. The recipe is fabulous, although over the years, I have added more chocolate to Marcy's recipe, and I have changed the directions slightly. Marcy's inspiration was a standard old American recipe that uses soda crackers to make a similar candy, but without the chocolate and nuts.

The recipe is sublime when made with butter, but then it would not be possible to serve it at the usually meat-based seder meal. It still tastes pretty wonderful when made with unsalted pareve Passover margarine.

Makes one 12- by 15-inch sheet

4 to 6 unsalted matzo boards

1 cup unsalted butter or unsalted pareve margarine

1 cup firmly packed Passover brown sugar

12 ounces semisweet Passover chocolate chips, or semisweet chocolate, coarsely chopped

Preheat the oven to 375°F. Line a baking sheet completely with aluminum foil. Lay parchment paper on top of the foil. This is very important, as the mixture becomes sticky during baking.

Line the bottom of the pan evenly with the matzo boards, cutting extra pieces of matzo, as required, to fit any uncovered spaces.

In a 3-quart, heavy saucepan, combine the butter and brown sugar and cook over medium heat, stirring constantly, until the mixture comes to a boil. Continue boiling 3 more minutes, stirring constantly. Remove from the heat and immediately pour over the matzo.

Place the matzo candy in the oven and immediately reduce the heat to 350°F. Bake for 15 minutes, checking after 10 minutes to make sure the mixture is not burning. Remove from the oven and immediately sprinkle the matzo with chopped chocolate. Let stand 5 minutes, then, with an offset spatula, spread the melted chocolate evenly over the matzo.

While still warm, cut the candy into squares or odd shapes. I just break it into pieces. Chill in the refrigerator until set. Covered tightly with plastic, it should keep for several weeks in the refrigerator. Bring back to room temperature to serve.

Variations

- Use white chocolate (which is dairy), coarsely chopped (or both white and dark chocolates).

- Sprinkle chopped toasted nuts—almonds, hazelnuts, walnuts, or pecans—over the chocolate.

- If you prefer granulated sugar, or if you can't find kosher for Passover brown sugar, follow these directions for a no-bake version: Arrange the matzo on the lined baking sheet as described in the recipe. Place 2 cups granulated sugar and 2 tablespoons water in a heavy-bottomed saucepan. Heat on medium-low until the sugar dissolves. Continue cooking until the mixture turns medium amber in color. Pour over the matzo. Sprinkle with chocolate and spread as directed.

Ingberlach

Matzo Farfel Ginger Candy

I found this recipe written in my mother's careful penmanship in her recipe files after she died. She didn't make this very often, but she should have. It is a delicious candy and much easier to make than its first cousin, *teiglach*, which is based on deep-fried (or sometimes baked) little bits of dough, which can be made with either flour (for Rosh Hashanah) or with matzo cake meal (for Passover). *Teiglach*, by the way, is nearly identical to Neapolitan *struffoli*, which is a Christmas treat. The only difference is that *struffoli* are laced with candied fruits, while *teiglach* and *ingberlach* are laced with walnuts or hazelnuts. Ginger (*ingber* in Yiddish) is the seasoning. Honey, citrus juice, nuts, and ginger—sounds very contemporary, although it is ages old.

Makes about 48 1-inch squares

1 egg, lightly beaten
2 cups matzo farfel
2 cups honey
1/2 cup sugar

1/2 cup orange juice or freshly squeezed lemon juice
1 teaspoon ground ginger
1 cup coarsely chopped walnuts
Sweet Passover wine, for sprinkling

Position an oven rack in the center of the oven. Preheat the oven to 350°F.

In a bowl, pour the egg over the farfel and mix well. Spread the farfel on a baking sheet and dry it out in the oven until the farfel is no longer sticky and is lightly browned, about 10 minutes. Remove from the oven and set aside.

Meanwhile, combine the honey, sugar, orange juice, and ginger in a saucepan. Bring to a boil over medium heat. When the sugar has dissolved, add the farfel and walnuts. Cook until sticky, about 10 minutes.

Wet a wooden board lightly with sweet Passover wine, then pour on the hot farfel mixture. Spread evenly with the back of a wooden spoon. Set aside to cool completely, then cut into bite-size squares. Arrange the squares on a platter. Keep at room temperature, covered with foil, not plastic, for up to several weeks, even longer if it doesn't get eaten right away.

Rozanne's Charosis

There are innumerable ways of making *charosis*. Every family has its own recipe. It is a required component of the ceremonial seder plate, and it is eaten during the reading of the Haggadah, to symbolize the mortar used by the Jews for the many Egyptian building projects they were forced to construct during their enslavement in Egypt. But *charosis* is so delicious that it is usually eaten with gusto.

Traditional Eastern European *charosis* is usually made with apples, nuts, cinnamon, and sweet wine, in varying proportions. In Sephardic tradition, the fruit is usually a dried one, such as raisins, dates, or figs. The following recipe was created by my friend, the chef and food writer Rozanne Gold, for a seder we recently celebrated together, and it combines the two cultures in a sensational way. In my family, as in hers, walnuts were the nuts, but lacking those in her pantry she turned to pecans. This formula tasted so good, and Rozanne made so much, that we ate it all week as a snack spread on matzo.

Makes about 4 cups

1¹/₂ cups pecans

5 medium apples, peeled, cored, and cut into large chunks (about 6 cups)

8 ounces pitted dates (about 2 cups)

¹/₃ cup sweet Concord wine or other sweet Passover wine

Place the pecans in a skillet over medium heat. Toast the nuts, tossing them occasionally, until their aroma comes up from the pan, about 5 minutes. Allow to cool.

In the bowl of a food processor fitted with the steel blade, chop the nuts, apples, and dates together until finely ground, with pieces no bigger than a grain of rice, but not a paste. Scrape the mixture into a mixing bowl and stir in the wine.

Keep tightly covered in the refrigerator until ready to serve, or for up to 1 week.

Rachel's Charosis

Since she was a little girl, Rachel, my niece, has been asked to make the *charosis*. It was always so much better than my grandmother's, even though we always thought she was making it just like Mamma, the name we called my grandmother. But when she gave me this recipe, she said, "This is all to taste … I just keep tasting it and, you know me, I always lean toward the sweet side. I know that honey is not traditional, but our family has always enjoyed it. I used to not tell anyone that I put the honey in, like it was my secret ingredient, but now I don't see any reason not to tell." Now I know why we ate my grandmother's *charosis* merely out of ritualistic necessity, and we eat Rachel's for pleasure.

Makes about 4 cups

4 medium McIntosh apples, peeled, cored, and cut into chunks (about 5 cups)

1¼ cups walnut halves

¾ tablespoon ground cinnamon, plus more to taste

2 tablespoons honey, plus more to taste

3 to 5 tablespoons sweet Concord wine or other sweet Passover wine

Place the apples and walnuts in the bowl of a food processor. Pulse until the bits of apple and nuts are no bigger than a grain of rice, or slightly smaller—definitely not a paste. Transfer the mixture to a mixing bowl.

Add the cinnamon, honey, and 3 tablespoons of the wine. Mix well, adding more cinnamon and/or honey until you have a taste you like. You don't usually need to add more wine, but if the consistency is a little dry, you can.

CHAPTER 7

⸙ Breads ⸙

In the Jewish religion, bread is not only the staff of life but also symbolic of all food. The first blessing said at a meal is to thank G-d for bread. This blessing, in fact, is so inclusive that it actually exempts one from saying additional blessings over the other foods eaten at that meal. In that sense, bread is a symbol for all food. In my family, as in most Jewish families, there is always bread on the table; which bread depends on the menu and the occasion.

Every Jewish neighborhood in New York still has several bakeries that bake bread, and that's the way it used to be in every neighborhood. Behind the cases of cakes, cookies, Danish, and other sweets (see chapter 8), there are racks of bread from one end of the shop to the other. "Sliced?" the counter woman—always a woman—asks, and if the answer is affirmative she puts it in a slicing machine with mechanical jaws that close down on the loaf and turn it into neat slices.

Of course, for every Shabbos there is challah, the rich, often sweet egg bread that is usually braided for the Sabbath, but can also be baked in a rectangular loaf for everyday consumption. The braids appear in the bakeries on Thursday, in preparation for Shabbos, and they are hardly ever sliced because as part of the bread ritual the challah is cut by hand by the head of the family.

Moist, fragrant, caraway-studded New York Jewish rye, a very hard commodity to come by these days, has become internationally famous. It's originally German, which is why it is the bread of the Jewish delicatessen, a German concept.

New York City's dark black bread, or pumpernickel, which my grandfather, the curmudgeonly Jewish waiter, claimed was made from sawdust and other floor sweepings, was the bread one used to eat with smoked fish and herring before bagels became popular in the 1930s. It's another German bread. My grandfather may have been right about the dubious content of dark bread then, but nowadays

---

Challah ready for Shabbos at Isaac's Bakery, Avenue J, Brooklyn

193

A caraway-seeded rye on the slicing machine

that brown color is just as suspicious. It can come from colorants like coffee, certainly not from coarse, dark rye and barley flour, as it used to.

So-called Corn Bread (page 205), which is really a sour rye, damp and a little funky, is sold by the pound, not the loaf, as are other breads. And it is heavy, and used to be heavier.

Almost all the breads and rolls come seeded or unseeded, the seeds being caraway, poppy, or nigella (*chernitzlach* in Yiddish).

What in other places are called Vienna rolls, or Kaiser rolls, or weck, are called simply "hard rolls" in Jewish bakeries, sprinkled with poppy seeds or not. These are still New York's most popular breakfast and sandwich rolls, although you would hardly call them "hard" these days. In the old days, they had crisp crusts with insides that were as much air as dough, perfect for filling up with garlicky salami. Today they are sold on every coffee cart, and in every deli-grocery, spread with butter. A great breakfast treat from a New York deli-grocery (not a Jewish deli) with a griddle is scrambled or fried eggs on a buttered roll.

Bagels and bialys were not and still are not sold in bakeries, with the exception of an item called an egg bagel. Egg bagels are more like challah dough baked in a ring than a real boiled and baked bagel, which normal bakeries were not equipped to make.

Challah

Challah is one of the most important Jewish foods. A yeast bread enriched with eggs and oil, it is similar to French brioche, and it is the special loaf for the Sabbath and for many other important meals and occasions.

For the Sabbath, Orthodox families usually prepare two loaves, a reminder of the double portion of manna received each Friday during the forty years wandering in the desert. Each of these loaves are braided with six ropes of dough coming to tapered ends. These two loaves then represent twelve loaves, recalling a miracle that took place in both the sanctuary carried in the desert and in the ancient Temple in Jerusalem. (Don't ask. It's very complicated.)

At weddings and bar and bat mitzvah receptions, before anyone takes a bite of food, a ceremonious bread cutting and blessing is conducted with a giant challah, big enough for everyone at the reception to have a piece. On Rosh Hashanah, the Jewish New Year, the bread is shaped in a round coil to symbolize eternal life, or the soul's ascension, depending on whom you ask. There are actually many folkloric forms of challah, each with a spiritual story to back up its shape. For everyday meals, you can also buy challah baked into a rectangular loaf, like sandwich bread.

Challah has become so assimilated in New York City that it is carried in every supermarket. Restaurants make French toast with it. Diners, which are usually owned by Greeks, acknowledge the New York Jewish tastes of their customers, even if they are not Jewish, by always putting challah in their bread baskets.

Challah is also one of the many ethnic foods that have gone through the immigrant experience. As if it weren't already rich and special enough in its original egg, sugar, and oil-enriched form, commercial bakers now make it with so much sugar and fat that it might as well be cake. Typically very yellow commercial loaves are even artificially colored to give the impression that they are loaded with eggs. You know how many eggs it would take to make a loaf of bread that yellow? There are also honey-laced challahs and those studded with raisins, especially for Rosh Hashanah, when we eat sweet foods to ensure a sweet New Year. Chocolate-laced and chocolate-chip challah are new phenomena.

Traditionally, challah was baked only once a week, on Friday, for that evening's Sabbath dinner and the next day's lunch. (It is also baked for some other

special holy days.) Many kosher bakeries still sell challah only on Thursdays and Fridays, and many observant Jewish homemakers still bake their own challah for the Sabbath, which can be quite a project, as Orthodox families are large and the customary two loaves need to be very large. (An interesting sidelight on this custom is that the largest dough-mixing machines made for home use are sold mostly, in this country, to Orthodox Jewish households.) With today's health consciousness, challah is often made with whole wheat flour, too.

The baking of challah is also an important ritual in a Jewish home. Before it is baked, a piece is always "taken" and incinerated in the oven as a symbolic offering, basically representing the portion that was given to the high priest in the ancient Temple. In some Hasidic homes, challah has even become a course unto itself, a first course served with an array of dips, spreads, and salads—not merely chopped liver, but, say, things like Italian-style artichoke pesto, or baba ghanoush, the Middle Eastern eggplant spread. Then it's on to a fish dish, then chicken soup.

Because it is rich with eggs and oil, challah keeps well for several days at room temperature. Then again, it is so delicious it rarely lasts that long. If it does, try Challah French Toast (page 200). You may never go back to white bread.

Challah can also be frozen, and won't suffer too much if kept less than 3 months. This recipe includes four shaping variations: for braids, a coil, and loaves. Variations for onion buns and onion rolls made with challah dough can be found under Pletzel (page 215).

Thanks to George Greenstein for sharing his clear directions on making the 6-strand challah braid.

Makes 1 large loaf

1 package (2¹/₄ teaspoons)
   active dry yeast
1 cup warm water (no more than 110°F)
¹/₃ cup sugar
4¹/₂ to 5 cups bread flour, or
   5¹/₂ to 6 cups bleached
   all-purpose flour
3 eggs

¹/₄ cup peanut, corn, or canola oil
2 teaspoons salt

Egg Wash
1 egg
1 teaspoon sugar

In the bowl of a stand mixer fitted with the dough hook, combine the yeast and the water on low speed. Mix for a minute or so to dissolve the yeast.

Add the sugar. Mix again for a few seconds, then add about ¹/₂ cup of the flour. Mix again.

Add the eggs. Increase the speed slightly and mix again. Once the eggs are well incorporated, add 1 more cup of flour. On medium-low speed, work in the flour, then add the oil and salt.

Turn off the machine and add 3 cups of the remaining flour (a total of $4^1/_2$ cups). At medium speed, continue to work the flour into the dough, shutting the machine off once or twice to scrape down the sides of the bowl.

Let the machine knead the dough for 15 minutes, again turning the mixer off every few minutes to scrape down the bowl, if necessary, and to let the motor rest (with such a dense dough, the motor can overheat if it runs continuously). After a few minutes, the dough should start to come away from the sides of the bowl, although, with all-purpose flour, it may stick slightly to the bottom. If necessary, add more flour, a tablespoon at a time, stopping the motor each time you do so. In the end, the dough should be firm, smooth, and elastic, and only slightly sticky.

Put the dough into a large oiled bowl, turning to completely coat it with oil. Cover with plastic wrap and let rise until tripled in volume, $1^1/_2$ to 2 hours.

Punch down the dough. To make a 6-strand braid, form it into a long, flat loaf. Cut it into 6 crosswise pieces. Form each piece into an oval loaf and keep the pieces on a lightly floured board, covered with a clean dish towel, then let rise 30 minutes longer.

Roll each piece into a strand about 12 inches long, thick in the center and tapered to a point on each end. Line up the strands and pinch the ends together (Figure 1). Bring strand #6 from the right end over strand #1 and up to the left (Figure 2). Bring strand #1 from the left up to the top right (Figure 3).

You now have a four-legged, two-armed creature with the arms crossed over each other. Keeping the legs spread apart in pairs, bring the left arm (as you face it) down into the center between the legs (Figure 4). Bring the outer right leg over and up to form a new top left arm (Figure 5). Bring the top right arm down between the legs (Figure 6).

Repeat the pattern: the left outer leg comes up to form the new right arm, and the left arm comes down to the center; the right leg comes up to form the new left arm, and the right arm comes down to the center. Finish by pinching the ends tightly closed (Figure 7).

Always keep hold of the last strand you moved so that you remember your location in the pattern. When moving strands, grasp the arms by the ends where hands would be. Grasp the legs where feet would be. Keep the legs spread in pairs

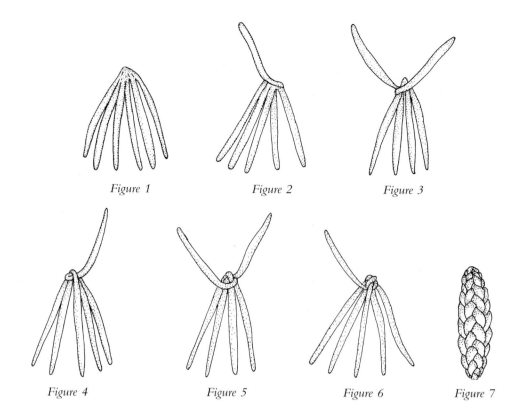

Figure 1   Figure 2   Figure 3

Figure 4   Figure 5   Figure 6   Figure 7

so that the arms can easily be brought down to the center. If you make an error and become confused, stop, open the braid, and begin again. When you're done, turn the bread upside down. The design should be perfectly symmetrical—if it's not, undo the braid and begin again.

Alternatively, to make 1 round loaf: form the dough into 1 long rope and coil the rope into a round loaf. Cover with a clean dish towel and let the dough rise another 30 minutes.

Alternatively, to make standard loaves: divide the dough into thirds and pack each third into an oiled 9- by 5-inch loaf pan. Cover the pans with clean dish towels and let the dough rise 30 minutes longer, until it is over the top of the pan.

Position an oven rack in the center of the oven. Preheat the oven to 350°F.

Make an egg wash by beating the egg and sugar together. Brush onto the surface of the dough, making sure to glaze the crevices between strands.

Bake for 35 to 40 minutes. To test for doneness, tap the bottom of the loaf with your fingers. It should sound hollow. Transfer to a rack to cool thoroughly before slicing and serving.

Challah French Toast

French toast made from challah first shows up on New York menus in the 1940s. But two places in Brooklyn were famous for it in the 1950s and 1960s. They were Wolfie's, which was a family-style restaurant and soda fountain on Nostrand Avenue near Brooklyn College (apparently no relation to the now defunct and more famous Wolfie's in Miami Beach, although they were the same kind of restaurant), and Cookie's, a group of restaurants similar to Wolfie's, all of which were situated next to the Brighton Beach subway line's various East 16th Street stations.

At Cookie's and Wolfie's, they served big, crisp-edged wedges of deep-fried, egg-saturated challah with a paper soufflé cup of cherry preserves. I suppose you could put maple syrup on them if you wanted, although I preferred nothing more than whipped butter to melt into the already rich, custardy interior.

Truth be told, French toast is vastly more delicious when fried in butter, as I do here, not deep-fried in oil. You can cut the challah into wedge-shaped chunks if you are nostalgic for it, but it is just as delicious in thick slices.

Serves 4

$^1/_2$ of a 2-pound challah, at least several days old (you can use any shape, but a rectangular loaf is easiest to cut)

5 eggs

$^1/_2$ cup milk

$^1/_2$ teaspoon salt

3 tablespoons butter

Cherry preserves or maple syrup, for accompaniment

To make wedges, use a serrated knife to slice the crust off the bread. With the same knife, cut the bread into wedge-shaped pieces that are $1^1/_2$ to 2 inches thick and 2 to 3 inches deep. You should be able to cut 12 pieces. Arrange the bread wedges in a 9-inch-square baking pan or one of similar size.

Or cut the challah, with crust, into $^3/_4$-inch-thick slices. Arrange these slices in a 13- by 9-inch baking dish.

To make the egg bath, in a bowl, with a fork or whisk, beat the eggs, milk, and salt until well blended.

Pour the egg mixture over the bread, then immediately turn the bread pieces so they are well coated in liquid. Let stand until all the egg has been absorbed, turning the bread a few more times, for at least 15 minutes, perhaps longer. (Once the bread has been well and evenly soaked, you can cover the dish with plastic wrap and keep it refrigerated for up to 1 day.)

To cook the bread, heat a 10- to 12-inch skillet over medium heat. Add half the butter. When melted and bubbling, fry half the challah pieces, turning once, until well browned all over. This takes only about 1 minute. Transfer the pieces to a platter once cooked. Add the remaining butter and fry the rest of the challah.

Serve immediately with cherry preserves or maple syrup.

Bagels

"Bagel Famine Threatens in City/Labor Dispute Puts Hole in Supply"
—*New York Times* headline, announcing bagel bakers' strike in 1951

Bagels were called "cement doughnuts" years ago. Given today's huge, puffy rings, that sobriquet may be hard to understand. The genuine article was small, dense, and chewy. It had a chewy crust, but the inside was soft and fragrant for about an hour after it came from the oven. Give it two hours and it needed to be reheated, revived. Give it a day and you had to split it and toast it to make it edible, by which process it also gained an entirely new character. A toasted bagel is a very different thing from a fresh bagel, and if you had one that was fresh it would have been weird to toast it. Those were the days when the sign "Hot Bagels" had real meaning and importance.

Bagels are to New York what croissants are to France, even to the point that they have been debased by commercialization. Just like the flaky French crescent-shaped morning bread, bagels are everywhere today, though hardly a one is worth the name if you are an old-timer with a taste memory. Even in New York. There was a time, in fact, more or less the 1960s and 1970s, when New York's bagel bakers (along with many other New Yorkers escaping the city's changing character) "emigrated" to other American cities. They went to Baltimore, to Philadelphia, to Toledo. And wherever they went, those cities got the benefit of their skills, while in New York a Jewish bagel baker became a rare bird.

Bagels are Polish, spelled *beigel* on the street carts of Kraków, where they are spiked on a dowel and sold as snack food. Bagels originally hail from Galicia

(which makes sense, given that so many New York Jews are Galitzianer), a region that is today divided between Poland and Ukraine but was, at the time the first Eastern Jewish immigrants arrived in New York City, part of the Austrian Empire.

According to one legend, the bagel was created in 1683 by a Jewish baker in Vienna, Austria, who wanted to thank the king of Poland for protecting his country from Turkish invasion. He made a roll in the shape of a riding stirrup (*bügel* in German means "a bracelet" or "ring"), commemorating the king's skill as a horseman. Wouldn't that make bagels Austrian?

Contradicting that story is the fact that bagels are mentioned in Kraków, Poland, municipal records of 1610. Somehow bagels also traveled east to Russia. Poland! Russia! Before World War I they blended together. My maternal grandfather, who was born in 1904 near Minsk, Russia, and came to New York in 1917, remembered them being sold by peddlers who carried them on strings. Or so he told me.

Bagels must have arrived in New York fairly early in the Eastern European migration because in 1910 a bagel bakers union was founded. There were thirty-six bagel bakeries in New York by 1915, and a few more than 300 bagel bakers. The union was a "closed shop," as they say in labor union circles. Only the sons (or nephews) of bakers were allowed in the union and given jobs.

Making bagels is a two-step process. The flour, from very high-gluten wheat, is made into a dough with yeast and a bit of malt. The dough is shaped into a ring and briefly boiled. The boiling gives the bagels their dense texture, their distinctive chewy crust, and their surface sheen. Traditional bagels are baked only after they have been boiled.

This was all done by hand until the early 1960s, when Dan Thompson, a Canadian bagel baker, introduced the Thompson Bagel Machine, which both shapes and boils the bagels. The technology allowed a dramatic increase in production, with the machines capable of turning out as much as four times the capacity of a human bagel baker. This set the stage for the Americanization of the bagel.

In the old, old days, which is to say before the mechanization of bagel baking, bagels came in a limited palette of flavors: plain, or sprinkled with coarse salt, poppy seed, or sesame seed. Then, in more recent old days, before the nationalization of the bagel in the 1990s, garlic and onion were added on the crust. Pumpernickel became popular. These days, even in a reasonably traditional New York bagel bakery, you are apt to find cinnamon-raisin bagels, whole wheat bagels, honey-sweetened bagels, oat bran bagels, and perhaps the most popular, the "everything"

You don't have to be Jewish (or kosher): Philip Romanzi of The Bagel Hole in Park Slope, Brooklyn, makes some of the best bagels in the city. Absolutely traditional, they're hand-rolled and boiled before they're baked, and come out glossy, crusty, and not too big, and they are seasoned just right.

bagel. A good "everything" is encrusted with a blend of sesame and poppy seed, salt, and toasted garlic and onion. Out in the hinterlands, they make blueberry bagels, dried cranberry bagels, and chocolate chip bagels. In my native New York estimation, these are an abomination.

That out of my system, I think I can safely say from the vantage of late middle age and a lifelong association with bagels—discussing, debating, not to mention eating them—that the new bagel, when well produced, is not such a bad thing. It shouldn't be too big. It shouldn't be really puffy. It shouldn't be too sweet. And it should be somewhat chewy. On second thought, that's a hard bagel to find.

The Lender family of New Haven, Connecticut, was the first to mass-market bagels. They opened their bakery in 1927, but in 1962, using the Thompson machine, they started baking bagels and freezing them for national distribution. The real break-out period for bagels, however, was the 1990s. I remember clearly the news stories about how bagel neophytes in Chicago were cutting themselves and flooding the city's emergency rooms. Midwesterners had not yet developed the skill to cut through a bagel without cutting through their palms. (Think about it.)

In the mid-1990s, the Kellogg Company paid $45 million to buy Lender's Bagels from Kraft Foods. About the same time, Dunkin' Donuts introduced bagels in their donut shops, and chains of bagel shops opened all over the country. According to an article in the *New York Times*, quoting the American Bagel Association, bagel sales grew to $1.6 billion in 1995 from $429 million in 1993, and were expected to hit $2.3 billion in 1996.

The latest bagel abomination occurred only a few years ago. Thomas' introduced a boxed bagel sold in supermarkets on the same shelves as its wonderful English muffins. The company calls these puffy ring rolls "New York bagels." Right! ❧

Corn Bread

Why is sourdough rye bread called "corn bread"? My friend George Greenstein, author of *Secrets of a Jewish Baker*, and, for most of his life, the owner of a Jewish bakery on Long Island, explains that the word *corn* was used to denote any type of grain in Poland, Lithuania, Latvia, and Russia, from where this bread originally comes.

At its best, the bread is heavy, dense, damp, and sour. This description does not make it sound appealing, and I would have to agree that it is not to everyone's taste. That's probably why even when you do find it these days—and it is still baked by kosher bakeries in Orthodox Jewish neighborhoods, and at bakeries in suburbs with a large Jewish population—it is less heavy, dense, damp, and sour than it used to be. Corn bread is rarely as dankly delicious as it was even a decade ago.

The following recipe seems lengthy and complicated only because George's instructions are so precise. The effort will produce the corn bread of memory. I offer it for the hobbyist bakers who love projects like this, and for those who miss old-fashioned corn bread so desperately that they are willing to bake it.

King Arthur Flour sells the necessary first clear flour (also known as common flour) through its catalog and website (www.kingarthurflour.com). A possible substitute is 1 1/2 cups all-purpose flour and 1/3 cup cake or pastry flour, but George warns that if you make this substitution the bread won't taste quite as good. Rye flour is often labeled "white rye flour."

Makes 2 small loaves

1 1/2 packages active dry yeast
 (scant 1 1/2 tablespoons)
1 1/2 cups warm water (110°F)
1 1/2 cups Rye Sour Starter
 (recipe follows)
1 1/2 cups rye flour
2 cups first clear flour (see headnote)

1 1/2 tablespoons salt
Additional first clear flour, for
 dusting work top
Water, for brushing bread
Cornmeal or cornmeal and rye flour,
 for dusting the baking sheet
2 1/2 tablespoons caraway seed,
 or more (optional)

In a large bowl, dissolve the yeast in the warm water. Add the Rye Sour, rye flour, first clear flour, and salt. Stir with a wooden spoon until thoroughly incorporated.

Turn out the dough onto a work surface covered with first clear flour. Use a plastic bowl scraper or dough cutter in one hand to help knead what will be a very soft, wet dough.

Knead for 5 minutes by scraping, folding, pulling, and stretching. Pretend that you are pulling taffy. The dough should have some elasticity and resist being stretched. Keep the dough soft. If the dough does not feel lively or elastic, add first clear flour $^1/_4$ cup at a time, stretching and kneading with each addition. Continue for another 3 minutes. The wetter the dough, the better the bread. The amount of flour will vary depending upon how stiff you made the sour.

Transfer the dough to a clean, wet bowl. Keep a container of cold water nearby. Keeping your hands wet at all times, pat the dough down and cover with a film of water. Cover the bowl with plastic wrap and set aside. Allow the dough to rise until doubled in volume, 45 to 60 minutes.

Shaping

Prepare a baking sheet sprinkled with cornmeal or a mixture of cornmeal and rye flour, upon which the bread will be baked.

Wet a clean work surface or board generously with water. When ready, cover the top of the dough with the caraway seed.

Keeping your hands wet at all times, scoop out half of the dough and shape into a round by bringing the sides of the dough down to the middle and gathering it together until you have a ball of dough. (Like smoothing your hair back along the sides and gathering it together at the back.) Handle the dough gently so that it does not tear.

Place the dough on the wet work surface. Turn and push the sides downward underneath to further round up the bread. Work your hands underneath and gently lift the loaf, then set it down onto the prepared baking sheet. Smooth the dough down with a caressing, circular motion. Press down, flattening out the top; it will spring up in the oven. Repeat the rounding up process with the other half of the dough to make 2 loaves. Sprinkle extra caraway seeds on top of the loaves. Allow the dough to stand no longer than 10 minutes. It can be placed in the oven without any standing time. Do not proof.

Baking

Place an empty broiler pan on the oven floor and preheat at 375°F for 5 minutes.

Brush the loaves with the water. Place the baking sheet holding the bread on the middle shelf of the oven, or on tiles or an oven stone if you have them. Carefully add 6 to 8 ice cubes or 1 cup hot water to the hot broiler pan and shut the door. Protect your hands and face from the burst of steam.

Bake for exactly 5 minutes. Steam in the oven is not desirable after that time. In exactly 5 minutes, carefully remove the hot broiler pan with the remaining water. (Select a space in advance on which to set the hot pan. Observe caution with the hot water.)

Slide out the bread and, with a skewer or an ice pick, make 10 to 12 holes all around the crust of each loaf; return the bread to the oven. Reduce the heat to 350°F and continue baking for 10 minutes, then make holes once more and brush again with the water.

When the bread begins to brown, turn each loaf around to ensure even baking. Bake until the crust is hard and unyielding to gentle pressure. Timing will vary depending on the amount of moisture in the dough. It may take 1 hour or longer. The bread is done when tapping on the bottom with your fingertips emits a hollow sound and the top and sides are hard. If you are using tiles or an oven stone, transfer the bread from the baking sheet to the tiles and continue baking for an additional 10 to 15 minutes to make the loaves crustier.

Remove the bread from the oven, brush the top with more water, and let cool on a wire rack.

The bread will keep well for more than a week in a bread box. It also freezes very well.

Rye Sour Starter

Caraway seed can be ground in a coffee or spice grinder or with a mortar and pestle. In the bakery, they crush the seeds with a rolling pin. The crushed seeds disappear in the ferment and add a distinctive flavor to the sour. The minced onion helps hasten the fermentation and adds flavor.

$^1/_2$ cup rye flour	1 tablespoon crushed caraway seed
$^1/_8$ teaspoon active dry yeast (see Note)	(optional)
1 cup warm water (110°F)	1 teaspoon minced onion

Combine all the ingredients in a large bowl and mix until smooth. The mixture should have a thin, soupy consistency. Cover and allow to stand in a warm spot until bubbly and fermented. It can be left for up to 24 hours. **Note:** Save the rest of the yeast packet for the first dough.

Rye Sour, Developing and Fortifying

In making sour, use approximately $^3/_4$ to 1 cup flour to each $^1/_2$ cup water. (Notice that Stage One calls for a higher ratio. This is done to adjust for the initial consistency of the starter.) The object is to make a thick consistency as close as possible to that of a soft dough. It is not necessary to thicken to the point that the mixture becomes burdensome. If the mixture is too soupy, add more flour $^1/_4$ cup at a time. Mix until smooth.

Stage One (prepare 24 hours in advance)

$^1/_2$ cup water
$1^1/_2$ cups rye flour
1 recipe Sour Starter

In a large bowl or container, combine the water, $1^1/_4$ cups of the flour, and the starter; stir until smooth. The dough should pull slightly and may start to come away from the sides of the bowl. Wipe down the sides of the bowl with wet hands or a bowl scraper. Sprinkle the remaining $^1/_4$ cup flour over the entire surface of the sour. Let stand, covered with a cloth or clear plastic wrap, until doubled in size and the floured top appears cracked with fissures spread widely apart. This may take 4 to 8 hours. Avoid letting the sour collapse.

Stage Two

If a double recipe is desired, increase to 1 cup warm water and 2 cups rye flour.

$^1/_2$ cup warm water (110°F)
1 cup rye flour

To the Stage One sour, add the water and $^3/_4$ cup of the flour; mix until smooth. Wipe down the sides of the bowl. Sprinkle the remaining $^1/_4$ cup flour over the entire surface of the sour. Allow to rise in a warm area for 4 to 8 hours. Proceed with Stage Three.

As the sour begins to rise, you can refrigerate it at any stage for later use or overnight for mixing the following day. Refrigeration retards the growth of the sour, which continues to rise slowly.

Whenever time permits, it is best to make two stages the day before, refrigerating the second stage overnight and preparing the third stage the morning of baking. If the dough is to be mixed first thing in the morning, the third stage is prepared the evening before, so it can rise slowly all night and be ready in the morning.

Stage Three

$^1/_2$ cup water (see Note)
1 cup rye flour, or more

To the Stage Two sour add the water and the 1 cup flour. Mix until smooth. Additional flour can be added to attain a dough-like consistency. The sour, when fully risen in Stage Three, is ready for use in the dough. When the third stage is mixed, set aside $^1/_4$ to $^1/_2$ cup and refrigerate in a covered container with a light film of cold water floated over the top. The sour can be kept under refrigeration for months at a time. **Note:** Use warm water if the sour has been refrigerated.

It is best to stir down the starter every 3 to 4 days if unused. Periodically (every 10 to 12 days) dispose of half and refresh it by mixing in equal amounts of flour and water. If there is some discoloration on the top, it can safely be skimmed off and the sour used as normal. When going away for long periods of time, freeze a small amount of sour. When preparing a new starter from scratch, add the frozen sour to preserve the original culture.

To ensure the proper strength of the sour, in each stage you can only double the amount of starter you begin with. For example, if beginning with $^1/_4$ cup starter, you can add up to $^1/_2$ cup water plus flour to thicken. If Stage One contains

1 cup sour, Stage Two can be prepared with up to 2 cups water plus flour. If a large amount of sour is required, extra stages can be added.

Sometimes the process goes awry. Perhaps there was insufficient sour left to start the next batch, or the sour may have been forgotten and was left standing to get old or dry. There is a remedy. The bakers call it an *einfrisch*, meaning "to refresh." A small amount of sour is thinned down with water to a soupy consistency. Swishing ¼ cup water around in what remains clinging to the sides of the empty bowl can yield enough to restart the sour. Let this *einfrisch* stand, covered, at room temperature or in a warm spot until bubbly. If desperate, add a pinch of yeast. When ready, add enough flour to make a first stage, allow to rise, and proceed with two more stages.

Bialys

Originally called *Bialystok kuchen* (Bialystok cake) in Bialystok, their Polish city of origin, bialys are a flour-dusted, puffy ring of dough with an onion-filled indentation instead of a hole. Like a bagel, which is also Polish, they are one old

Yiddish item that has remained unchanged since traveling here from the Old Country. The best in New York City are produced by Kossar's Bialys on Grand Street on the Lower East Side, baked under the strictest of kosher supervision. Hasidim from Williamsburg travel to lower Manhattan after Shabbos ends on Saturday night and line up to buy their bialys for *melava-malka*, the traditional meal for after Shabbos. This meal is the prototype for the famous "New York City Sunday brunch." They are a great accompaniment, as are bagels, to the lox, cream cheese, herring, and smoked fish that Jews enjoy for family breakfasts.

Bialys from Kossar's and other bialy bakeries are also sold on the city's coffee carts, in bagel stores (which usually buy them from a specialty bakery), coffee shops, and diners. They are a breakfast bread, usually eaten with nothing more than butter. At any rate, most bialys have disappeared by lunchtime. And even if they haven't, because they are still baked without dough conditioners (unlike bagels), they become hard and stale by early afternoon. ✎

Potatonik

Polish Potato Bread

Potatonik is not Potato Kugel (page 76), but many people confuse the two. Although the word is obviously Yinglish—English Yiddish—potatonik is Polish. It is a yeast-raised potato *bread* baked in a flat pan. Potato kugel is not leavened with yeast, although some people today put baking powder in their kugel, not that it makes it any lighter. A few kosher bakeries in Brooklyn still make potatonik, notably Isaac's on Avenue J and the several Korn's retail stores, but only on Thursdays when observant Jews do their Sabbath shopping. Potatonik is becoming extinct, although it is way too delicious to forget.

Makes 3 loaves

Sponge
1¹/₂ packages active dry yeast
  (scant 1¹/₂ tablespoons)
1 cup warm water (110°F)
1¹/₂ cups bread or unbleached
  all-purpose flour

Dough
³/₄ pound white all-purpose potatoes,
  skins on, scrubbed well, and cut into
  large pieces
1 medium onion (6 ounces), quartered

1 small stale roll, or 2 slices stale white
  bread, torn or processed into crumbs
¹/₂ cup all-purpose flour
1¹/₂ teaspoons salt
Scant ¹/₂ teaspoon baking powder
¹/₄ teaspoon freshly ground black
  pepper
¹/₂ cup peanut, corn, or canola oil
2 eggs, lightly beaten
Vegetable shortening, for greasing pans

To make the sponge, in a large bowl, sprinkle the yeast over the warm water. Stir to dissolve. Add the flour and mix until smooth. Cover with a clean dish towel and set aside until it puffs up, 20 to 25 minutes.

To make the dough, place the potatoes in the bowl of a food processor fitted with the metal blade. Pulse until finely ground, as for Potato Kugel (page 76). Add the potatoes to the sponge and stir until blended.

Puree the onion in the same processor bowl. Add it to the sponge with the potatoes.

Add the stale roll crumbs, flour, salt, baking powder, and pepper. Mix until well incorporated. Add the oil and eggs and mix well again.

Divide the mixture between 3 well-greased 8- or 9-inch loaf pans. The batter will rise in the oven.

Preheat the oven to 350°F. Position an oven rack in the center of the oven.

Bake all 3 loaves at once, for about 1 hour, or until the crusts are brown and feel firm when gently pressed in the center.

Place on a rack to cool for 5 minutes, covered with a clean kitchen towel so the loaves steam.

Invert the loaves and tap the pan bottom to release the loaves onto the rack. Serve warm.

Potatonik can be refrigerated for several days or frozen for 1 to 2 weeks. Reheat at 325°F until warm. When reheating, bake for 35 to 45 minutes to develop a hard crust.

Tzibeleh Kuchen

Onion Cookies

 ———————————————————————————

You would have to be a New Yorker over fifty to remember these. Properly, they are *tzibeleh kuchen*, but some would call them *tzibeleh pletzel*. Pletzel (page 214), however, can also be a *crisp* board of dough covered with onions. These little treats, wonderful with Chopped Herring Salad (page 6), Chopped Liver (page 11), or a bowl of soup, never become crisp, no matter at what temperature you bake them, how long you bake them, or how thin you roll them. The moisture of the onions that makes them so appealing will eventually soften them up. They're at their best straight from the oven or, at least, reheated. They return to their prime by putting them on a baking sheet for 10 minutes in a preheated 350°F oven.

Makes 2¹/₂ to 3 dozen cookies

1 pound onions, ground or finely
   minced, drained
¹/₄ cup reserved onion juice or water
¹/₄ teaspoon sugar
¹/₂ cup vegetable oil
2 eggs

3 cups all-purpose flour
1 teaspoon baking powder
1¹/₂ tablespoons salt
¹/₂ cup poppy seed (optional)
1 egg lightly beaten with 1 tablespoon
   water, for egg wash

Preheat the oven to 400°F. Lightly grease a baking sheet or line one with parchment paper.

To prepare the dough, in a large bowl, mix together the onions, onion juice, sugar, oil, and eggs.

In another bowl, combine the flour, baking powder, salt, and poppy seed. Stir well to mix thoroughly.

Add the dry ingredients to the wet ingredients and mix, but only long enough to blend thoroughly. Overmixing will make the cookies tough.

Flour a work surface, preferably a floured cloth. Turn out the dough onto the surface and divide in half.

With your hands, form one dough half into an oblong. Roll out into a rectangle about ¹/₄ to ¹/₂ inch thick. With a rotating cutter (a pizza/pastry cutter) or a sharp blade dipped in flour, trim the edges to make them even, then divide the rectangle into 2- by 2-inch squares (or cut into diamonds or cut out circles with a round cookie cutter).

Brush a light coating of egg wash over the tops.

Slide a metal spatula under 6 to 8 pieces at a time and transfer them to the prepared baking sheet. Slide them off onto the sheet, arranging them about a finger width apart for even baking.

Bake for 15 to 20 minutes, or until barely brown on the edges. Cool on a wire rack while still on the pan. They are best when eaten the same day, but they keep well stored in a tightly closed container.

Pletzel

Onion Boards

In Yiddish, *pletzel* is a small town square, i.e., a plaza or piazza. This is probably where the name of the bread came from, for pletzel is a kind of flatbread, sometimes called "onion board" because it is covered with minced onions and sometimes poppy seed as well and is about the size of a baking sheet—in other words, a large expanse of dough that could, if you use your imagination, recall a plaza. One tears off pieces to eat it. Think of it as Jewish focaccia. In commercial bakeries, bialy dough is used to make pletzel, but we'll leave that to the professionals. At home, challah dough is the base for this wonderful treat. *Pletzlach*, by the way, is the plural of pletzel, and the word *zemmel*, although it is sometimes used to refer to pletzel, is really an onion roll.

Makes 4 boards

1 recipe Challah (page 195)
1 medium onion, very finely minced
1 tablespoon peanut, corn, or canola oil

3 tablespoons poppy seed (optional)
Kosher salt, for sprinkling

To make the dough, follow the recipe directions for Challah; after the first rise, when the dough has fully tripled in volume, $1^1/_2$ to 2 hours, punch it down.

Preheat the oven to 350°F. Position the oven racks with one in the lower third and one in the upper third of the oven. Lightly grease 2 large baking sheets.

Divide the dough in half. Set each half on a prepared baking sheet. Roll out each piece of dough as thinly as possible into an irregular rectangle that is no more than $^1/_4$ inch thick, or even thinner. The thinner you can get it, the better. It should cover the baking sheet.

With a fork, make holes all over the dough sheets.

Mix the onion and oil together. Spread half the onion and half the poppy seed on each of the dough sheets. Sprinkle with salt to taste, then press the onions, poppy seed, and salt into the dough with the palms of your hands, pressing with your fingers, too, to flatten any thicker sections.

Don't let the dough rise. Immediately bake for about 35 minutes, or until nicely browned and quite firm.

You shouldn't cut pletzel. Just tear off pieces.

Zemmel Variation

To make *zemmel*-type onion rolls, divide the dough into 12 to 16 pieces. Form each piece into a ball, then flatten into a round about 4 inches in diameter. Top with the onion, poppy seed, and salt. Arrange the rolls on baking sheets, cover with a clean dish towel, and let rise for 30 minutes. Bake as above.

Onion Bun Variation

You can also make onion buns by taking each piece of dough and shaping it into a rectangle. Place 1 tablespoon of onions on one end of the dough and roll the dough into thirds to enclose it. Let rise for 30 to 40 minutes and bake as above.

Zemmel rolls

CHAPTER 8

❖ Desserts and ❖ Sweet Baking

Traditional Yiddish desserts tend to be plain. Considering the prohibition on mixing dairy and meat, one couldn't, before the advent of nondairy cream products, end a festive meal, which was almost always a meat meal, with a wonderfully gloppy sweet. Not even a butter cookie. Nowadays, there is tofu-based ice cream, soy-based whipped cream, and bakeries that make butter-creamy and whipped-creamy extravaganzas that would defy the imagination.

There certainly were *balabusta* bakers among Ashkenazic Jews, but truth to tell, most home cooks didn't bake more than a specialty or two, rugelach and apple cake being the most common. There was always a good bakery nearby. Why bake when you can buy?

Indeed, New York City's neighborhood bakeries were mostly what everyone called "Jewish bakeries." They were the dominant type of bakery from the early 1920s, when first-generation immigrants created a housing boom in the boroughs, until the late 1970s, when the middle class flight to the suburbs was complete and the city was down on its heels.

The city's first big wave of immigration, beginning in the 1840s, was from Germanic countries, and included many Jews. That's why New York City, indeed all of America, has a strong German baking tradition. In the 1880s, Jews from Hungary started arriving with their sophisticated cake and pastry repertoire—strudel!—as well as bread bakers from Poland, Lithuania, and Russia. They all helped line the shelves of bakeries in the five boroughs with an incredible mix of handcrafted baked goods.

Cinnamon Danish horns

Danish pastry used to be a daily mainstay in every bakery, and is still a favorite. Why is it called Danish? In Denmark, it's called Vienna bread, revealing its actual heritage. It's a yeast dough that is treated like puff pastry, which is to say, butter is spread on a sheet of raised, rolled-out dough that is then repeatedly folded to form many layers. Shaped into crescents, horns, pockets, and boats, Danish are filled with cinnamon and raisins, the most basic flavor; with prune butter, apricot butter, and poppy seed paste (mohn); with chocolate; and, perhaps the most popular, with a type of fresh cheese called "baker's cheese," akin to farmer's cheese, sweetened, of course.

Danish, especially cheese Danish, can now be found on every coffee cart in town, and wrapped in plastic at the cash register of almost any convenience store/grocery/bodega/deli. Most of these are dreadful. It is hard to find good cheese Danish, properly buttery and well filled with moist cheese, but they still exist.

All the Danish flavors are also formed into mini Danish, which are easily confused with Rugelach (page 225), but there is also another dough, a crisp and crumbly dough that is called "frozen pastry," a term no longer used because if you say "frozen" today customers think the Danish was actually frozen. The word merely refers to the crispness of the dough. As far as I can tell, there is only one "frozen pastry" still made. It's approximately 6 inches long and is called a chocolate horn after its filling and shape. It is easily recognizable because it is always drizzled with chocolate and dusted with confectioners' sugar.

Babka (page 230), a simple yeast cake filled with a bit of cinnamon and nuts, was, years ago, the most popular of the many "coffee cakes" sold in the Jewish bakery. Like so many other foods, it has gone through what I think of as the immigrant experience. Instead of cake with a little filling, today it has so much filling, including chocolate, the most popular, of course, that it is more like a candy bar surrounded by cake.

Clockwise from top left: chocolate "frozen dough" horns; chocolate-filled rolled strips; a tray of cheese Danish; chocolate Danish

Wine-Poached Pears

I have vivid memories of these rosy-hued pears that my grandmother always served very well chilled on Passover and Rosh Hashanah, and occasionally at other times, too. They are incredibly refreshing at the end of a heavy meal, and they were the only thing she cooked with wine. Then, there was always the left-over syrup she put in the refrigerator. My father and I loved adding it to seltzer to make a drink even better than store-bought soda.

Elsie would make these in large quantity—we were always at least fifteen for a holiday meal—but because I think they are a delicious dessert for any day of the week, I've portioned it down to just six pears. Be sure to use a pot in which the pears fit closely. If the pot is too big, you will need to make way too much syrup.

Serves 6

1 cup sugar

1 cup water

1¹/₂ cups sweet red Passover wine, such as Malaga or Concord

1- to 2-inch-wide strips lemon zest (optional)

6 firm, ripe Bosc pears

To make the wine syrup, in a 3-quart saucepan (or the size that holds your pears snuggly on their sides but not pressed together), combine the sugar, water, wine, and lemon zest. Bring to a boil over high heat, stirring a few times to help dissolve the sugar.

Peel the pears, preferably with a swivel-bladed vegetable peeler, but leave the stems intact. There is no need to core the pears.

Place the peeled pears in the syrup. The syrup will not entirely cover the pears. Adjust the heat so the syrup simmers gently. Cook the pears, uncovered, for 45 minutes. Every 10 minutes or so, turn the pears so they cook and color evenly.

Remove from the heat and let the pears cool in the syrup in the pan, again turning them every 10 minutes or so for at least 30 minutes.

Chill well before serving. The pears are excellent as soon as they are chilled, but they will keep in the refrigerator, tightly covered, for several weeks. They will, in fact, improve with time, as they get more and more impregnated with the syrup.

Dried Fruit Compote

One reason that Jewish cooks have created a repertoire of fruit desserts is that the kosher laws forbid the mixing of meat and dairy products at the same meal. Before the advent of soy-based and tofu-based milk and cream substitutes that make possible gooey, fluffy, creamy pareve desserts, even nondairy ice cream, there wasn't much choice.

Jewish or not, Eastern Europeans have great respect and desire for fresh fruit. Perhaps it is because fruit used to be so exotic and expensive in their cold northern European home countries, with their very short growing seasons. Evidence: these days one of the best neighborhoods to shop for fruit in New York is Brighton Beach, in Brooklyn, dubbed "Little Odessa" because it is home to the Russian immigrants who came from the Soviet Union in the 1970s and 1980s.

The word *compote* is used for both fresh fruit salads and stewed fresh and dried fruit. This is my grandmother's recipe. All winter she would have a jar of this in the refrigerator. It is an elixir as is, but if you want to gild the lily, and it ends a dairy meal, or you eat it as a snack, add a few spoonfuls of heavy cream to each cup, or eat it with ice cream.

Serves at least 8

2 pounds mixed dried fruit, or
  1 pound mixed dried fruit and
  1 pound of either dried apricots
  or pitted prunes

1 lemon, one slice reserved and
  the remainder juiced
1 cup sugar

Put the dried fruit into a large bowl or the nonreactive saucepan (for instance, enameled cast iron or stainless steel) that you will cook them in. Cover with cold water. Add a thick slice of the lemon, reserving the rest for later. Cover with plastic wrap or the pot lid and let stand at room temperature for 8 hours.

If soaked in a bowl, transfer the fruit, lemon slice, and soaking water to a nonreactive saucepan. Add more cold water, as necessary, to cover the fruit. Add the sugar and the juice of the rest of the lemon. Over medium heat, bring to a simmer. Simmer gently, uncovered, for 15 minutes. The fruits will be tender and plump.

Taste for lemon juice. It's unlikely you will need more sugar. The final acid-sugar balance should taste "winey," as my grandmother would say.

Rugelach

In the kosher bakeries of New York City—we're mainly talking Brooklyn here—there are three kinds of rugelach being sold these days. There is the cream cheese and butter pastry type that used to be made only at home. To their credit, the bakeries have maintained the haphazard, *balabatish* look of these. There are yeast rugelach, a Danish-pastry style with a layered dough, similar to the old days but now shaped into larger crescents that are more precisely coiled. The third type is made with what used to be called "frozen dough," a form of puff pastry, fatty and crunchy.

Like babka, rugelach is another ethnic food that has gone through the "immigrant experience," during which Old Country foods get richer and bigger. These days in metro New York City, you can find rugelach the size of Danish at stores the likes of Dean & DeLuca. And chocolate, not traditional walnut and cinnamon—maybe with a dab of apricot preserves—is the most popular flavor.

Not so long ago, rugelach were dainty crescents, one of the more elegant Yiddish sweets. Indeed, the word *ruggle* means "royal." *Ach* makes it plural.

Kipfel, a dainty Hungarian pastry, are, in general, the same as rugelach. Sometimes, instead of being formed into crescents, they are made by folding a round of filled pastry into a half-moon. Or they can be made with two rounds of dough, filled and pinched together into a full round, like the ravioli-shaped pastries made in Italy. Most recipes I find for kipfel use sour cream dough, and it is more likely that the sour cream pastry, and not the cream cheese version that has become standard, is the original.

Philadelphia cream cheese is international now, and so are rugelach. I will never forget eating a wonderful little pastry in Solopaca, a wine market town in the province of Benevento, north of Naples—in any case, an out-of-the way place. When I asked how these pastries were made, the bakery clerk said it was a secret. When pressed, she said cheese was the secret. Cheese? Of course, it dawned on me, Philadelphia! We were eating rugelach on a hill town in southern Italy.

The Standard Pastry recipe here is the one most frequently published and used, although some versions add an egg yolk or perhaps a spoonful or two of sour cream in addition to the cream cheese. However, I find the second, Sour Cream Pastry, a slightly more tender and appealing version. Tom Halik of Just

Rugelach and Hamantaschen (page 237)

Rugulach (as with many Yiddish words, there are many English spellings), a Brooklyn-based baker who sells his very delicious and popular pastries at various New York City Greenmarkets (our farmers' markets) and through mail order, uses a version of the Standard Pastry, but he rolls it out very thin, and instead of making small crescents, he uses an easier and more contemporary way of forming rugelach, shaping a strudel-like roll and cutting it into approximately 1-inch-wide slices. Directions for both doughs and shapes follow.

Makes 4 dozen

Standard Pastry
1 cup (2 sticks) unsalted butter,
   at room temperature
1 (8-ounce) package cream cheese,
   at room temperature
2 cups bleached all-purpose flour
$1/4$ teaspoon salt

Sour Cream Pastry
$1/2$ cup (1 stick) unsalted butter,
   at room temperature
4 ounces cream cheese, at room
   temperature
$1/2$ cup sour cream
1 egg
$2^{3}/4$ cups bleached all-purpose flour
$1/4$ teaspoon salt

Apricot-Walnut Filling
$2/3$ cup apricot preserves
1 cup finely chopped walnuts
$1/2$ cup sugar mixed with 1 tablespoon
   ground cinnamon
$1/2$ cup raisins

1 egg, beaten, for egg wash
1 tablespoon sugar mixed with
   $1/8$ teaspoon ground cinnamon,
   for sprinkling

To make the Standard Pastry, in a stand mixer fitted with the paddle, cream together the butter and cream cheese on medium speed. Stop beating, add the flour and salt all at once, then continue to beat on low speed until the dough holds together around the paddle.

To make the Sour Cream Pastry, in a stand mixer fitted with the paddle, cream together the butter and cream cheese on medium speed. Add the sour cream and egg to the creamed butter mixture and continue beating on medium speed until the mixture is smooth. Stop beating, add the flour and salt all at once, then continue to beat on low speed until the dough holds together around the paddle.

If making crescent pastries, divide the dough evenly into 4 balls. Wrap each ball in plastic wrap. If making into loaves to slice, divide the dough evenly into fourths, and shape each piece into a log about 2 inches in diameter, using a piece of wax paper to help form the sticky dough, then wrap it in plastic.

Chill the dough for at least 4 hours. The dough can be held in the refrigerator for up to a week, or in the freezer for up to several months.

When ready to bake, let the dough come to cool room temperature before rolling it out. It should be pliable but not soft.

Position a rack in the center of the oven. Preheat the oven to 350°F.

To make the crescents, on a lightly floured board, roll out 1 dough ball into an approximately 9-inch circle. To make rugelach slices, roll out 1 log of dough into an approximately 6- by 12-inch rectangle.

To make the filling, warm the apricot preserves (in the microwave or by submersing the jar in a hot water bath—both good techniques for this step). Brush about 2 tablespoons of preserves over each dough circle or rectangle, brushing to the edges. Evenly sprinkle each piece of dough with about 2 tablespoons of nuts, then 1 tablespoon of cinnamon sugar, then 2 tablespoons of raisins.

To make crescents, cut each circle into 8 wedges. Roll each wedge from the outside into the point. As each crescent is formed, place it on an ungreased baking sheet. If making strudel-style pastries, roll up the rectangle from a long side. Either way, don't make the rolls tight.

Brush the rolled-up doughs with beaten egg and sprinkle with an additional 1 tablespoon cinnamon sugar. (Some sugar will inevitably end up on the board. Don't worry about it.) Slice the strudel-style pastries into ¾- to 1-inch pieces. Transfer the pieces to an ungreased baking sheet. Repeat with the remaining balls of dough.

Bake for 25 minutes, until well browned. As soon as the rugelach come from the oven, transfer with a metal spatula to a serving plate. Cool completely before serving. They are actually better the day after they are baked. The rugelach may be stored in an airtight container for a little over 1 week.

Making rugelach at Gertel's (no longer retail on the Lower East Side, but wholesale in Brooklyn)

Mandlebrodt (Mandelbread)

Isn't it ironic? It used to be that biscotti were explained as Italian mandelbread. These days, mandelbread is explained as Jewish biscotti.

The following recipe produces the kind of crisp, dry cookie that is perfect for dunking in coffee, tea, or milk. Italians dunk their biscotti in sweet wine, which is a pretty good way to go, too.

Makes about 4 dozen slices

4 cups bleached all-purpose flour, possibly a little more
1 tablespoon baking powder
1 teaspoon salt
4 eggs
1 1/3 cups sugar

3/4 cup vegetable oil
1/2 teaspoon almond extract
1 teaspoon vanilla extract
1 tablespoon grated orange zest
2 cups coarsely chopped almonds

Position an oven rack in the center of the oven. Preheat the oven to 350°F.

Line 2 baking sheets with parchment paper, securing the corners down with a dab of butter. (Only one baking sheet is used for the initial baking. Both are used for the final baking.)

In a large bowl, add the flour, baking powder, and salt; stir well to blend.

In the bowl of a stand mixer fitted with the whisk, beat the eggs on medium speed until well blended.

Increase the speed to high, then beat in the sugar 2 tablespoons at a time. Continue to beat until the mixture is thick and foamy, 4 to 5 minutes.

Add the oil, the almond and vanilla extracts, and orange zest to the eggs. Beat again briefly to blend.

Replace the whisk attachment with the paddle. On the lowest speed, beat in the flour mixture and the almonds. Beat just until the dough holds together. It should be soft, but not too sticky. If necessary, beat in a few more tablespoons of flour.

On a lightly floured surface, divide the dough into 2 pieces and, with dampened hands, form each half into a log about 12 inches long by 3 inches wide. With the aid of a bench scraper or wide spatula, transfer the rolls to one of the lined baking sheets, spacing them at least 4 inches apart. The loaves will grow as they bake to about 5 by 14 inches.

Bake for 45 minutes, until golden.

Remove from the oven (don't turn it off) and let the logs cool for 5 to 10 minutes. While the logs are still warm, using a serrated knife, cut them into ¹/₂-inch-thick slices. Arrange the slices, cut side down, on the 2 cookie sheets.

Place the sliced mandelbread back in the oven for 5 minutes longer. Remove from the oven. Turn the slices over. Bake the second side for 5 minutes. (If the slices are a little thicker, they will need a few more minutes on each side.)

Cool the slices on a rack. When cooled, store in an airtight container.

Chocolate Babka

Babka is a derivative of the word meaning old lady or "grandma" in Polish—baba. (Incidentally, the Neapolitan cake called baba is said to have been derived from a Polish cake.) It's said that this yeast cake is called babka because, in its original form, it was stout and round, just like grandmothers used to be before they went to aerobics classes and practiced yoga.

At Gertel's Bakery, a kosher bakery on the Lower East Side that was one of the last holdouts from the neighborhood's Jewish immigrant era until it closed as this book was going to press, they used to bake it round and stout. Theirs was a giant, streusel-topped cake from which pieces were cut and sold by the pound. However, for as long as I can remember, neighborhood bakeries have sold babka in rectangular loaves, each cake housed in pleated paper.

It wasn't so long ago that you could buy an authentically austere babka in New York. It was a simple cake, a dryish cake, a "coffee cake" in the true sense that it was best eaten with a lubricating cup of coffee or "a glass tea," as Yiddish speakers used to say, and still do. Not a glass *of* tea, by the way, just "a glass tea," held in a glass holder called a zarf, or by the rim with thumb and forefinger when the tea was really too hot to hold. It's very Middle Eastern, actually.

But today's babka is a prime example of the transformation that foods often go through after they arrive on our shores. They get either bigger or richer or both. They are foods that have gone through the immigrant experience.

These days, no longer is it enough for babka to be baked from a rich yeast dough swirled with a little bit of cinnamon-sugar and chopped nuts. Today, babkas are practically candy. The cake merely functions as a structure to house generous lacings of chocolate and almond paste. This recipe is the chocolate babka of your dreams. I got it from Audrey Cohen of New Jersey, who won a local chocolate dessert contest with it. Recipes like it, however, have been around for many years.

Makes 2 loaves

Dough
3 cups all-purpose flour
Pinch of salt
A generous $^3/_4$ cup sugar
1 cup (2 sticks), butter, cut into
   tablespoon-size pieces
$^1/_2$ cup whole milk
1 package (about $2^1/_4$ teaspoons)
   active dry yeast

3 eggs, separated
1 teaspoon ground cinnamon,
   plus more for sprinkling (optional)

Filling
2 cups (12 ounces) semisweet
   chocolate chips
1 cup walnuts (optional)

To make the dough, in the bowl of food processor fitted with the metal blade, combine the flour, salt, and 3 heaping tablespoons of the sugar. Pulse to blend.

Add the pieces of butter to the flour mixture and pulse until crumbly.

In a small saucepan, heat the milk over low heat until warm, not hot, to the touch (no more than 110°F). Stir in 1 level tablespoon of the sugar and the yeast. Allow to stand for 7 minutes, until bubbly and risen.

Add the egg yolks and yeast mixture to the flour mixture. Pulse several times, scraping down the bowl once or twice, until a ball is formed. Remove the dough and place it in a large bowl. Cover with a clean towel and refrigerate overnight.

Grease two $8^1/_2$- by $4^1/_2$-inch loaf pans.

Flour a work surface and a rolling pin.

To assemble the babkas, in a stand mixer fitted with the whisk, beat the egg whites until soft peaks form. One tablespoon at a time, add the remaining $^1/_2$ cup sugar, then the 1 teaspoon cinnamon. Beat until the whites form firm peaks.

Divide the dough in half. Keep one half refrigerated while working with the other.

For each half, knead the dough a few times. Roll out on a floured surface to an approximately 22- by 18-inch rectangle. It will be thin.

Spread the rectangle of dough with half the beaten egg whites to within 1 inch of the edges. Sprinkle evenly with half the chocolate, half the walnuts, and lightly with more cinnamon.

Turn in about 1 inch of the short edges of the dough rectangle, then carefully roll up jelly roll–style. If the dough is sticking slightly, use a bench scraper (pastry scraper) to ease it off the work surface.

Cut each roll into 8 sections. For each babka, place 8 cut sections in 1 loaf pan, cut sides up and down, packing them so the uncut sides touch.

Cover each with a clean towel and let rise at room temperature for about 2 hours. The dough should come up higher than the sides of the pans.

Position an oven rack in the center of the oven. Preheat the oven to 350°F. Bake the loaves for 35 to 40 minutes, until light brown.

Cool the babkas in the pans for about 5 minutes, then invert them onto serving plates. Serve top side up or bottom side up, whichever looks better to you. Slice with a serrated blade, or break apart into natural segments.

Orange Sponge Cake

Sponge cake is the airy, bouncy cake that haunted Sabbath kiddushes, the light repast offered after Saturday morning services. I say haunted because it was usually not very good, an artificially flavored, often rubbery sheet cake bought from a second-rate bakery. But since it was often the only food other than challah, even more rubbery honey cake, and painfully plain kichel, you ate it. A glass of wine or shot of schnapps helped it go down.

A well-composed sponge cake is, however, a complete delight. This recipe is adapted from one by Judi Dick, who provided the recipes in *A Taste of Nostalgia*, coauthored with Rabbi Abraham J. Twerski, M.D., who provided the enlightening stories and cultural and religious insights into the foods of Ashkenazic Jews.

The recipe is from Judi's mother, but, she confesses, she never made it until she started working on the book. She didn't like separating eggs. She didn't like having two bowls to wash. Now she regrets having dropped it from her repertoire for so many years because, as she says, it "is really scrumptious." I totally agree.

Makes one 10-inch tube cake

8 eggs, separated
1¼ cups sugar
1 cup orange juice (without pulp)
1 teaspoon vanilla extract

1½ cups sifted bleached
  all-purpose flour
1 teaspoon salt

Position an oven rack in the center of the oven. Preheat the oven to 350°F.

In the bowl of a stand mixer fitted with the whisk, beat the egg yolks on medium speed until well blended. Beat in 1 cup of the sugar, a few tablespoons at a time, until the mixture is thick and foamy.

On low speed, beat in the orange juice and vanilla. Still on low speed, blend in the flour and salt. With a rubber spatula, scrape this mixture into a large bowl. Meticulously clean and dry the mixer bowl and whisk. Beat the egg whites with the mixer on low speed until foamy, then, on medium speed, beat in the remaining ¼ cup sugar, 1 tablespoon at a time. Increase the speed to high and continue to beat until the whites hold stiff peaks.

Carefully fold about half the egg whites into the yolk–flour base. When the mixture is nearly uniform in color, fold in the remaining whites.

Pour the batter into an ungreased 10-inch tube pan with a removable bottom. Do not smooth the top.

Bake for 45 to 50 minutes, or until the top is golden and the cake springs back when touched gently. (Warning: the top of the cake may split. It will taste delicious anyway.)

Cool the pan upside down if it has feet to rest on, or invert it and slip it over the neck of a bottle. Let cool completely. Do not cut the cake until it has totally cooled to room temperature.

Loosen the cooled cake from the sides of the pan with a sharp, thin-bladed knife. Lift it out by the tube, initially leaving the cake on the base. After the first few slices are taken, you should be able to free the cake from the tube and transfer it to a serving plate.

Pareve Apple-Walnut Cake

Cake exactly like this, chock full of apples and flavored with cinnamon and vanilla, is still sold in some Brooklyn kosher bakeries, usually baked in sheets and sold by the pound. If you ask the baker, he might tell you it is Austro-Hungarian. It was presented to me as German in origin when I was first given the recipe more than thirty years ago. It is a very moist cake that will keep for a week at room temperature, covered loosely with foil. If the outside dries out slightly, that's all the better. The crusty exterior is delicious. (If you cover the cake with plastic, or put it under a cake dome, the crust will soften.) An old-fashioned, aluminum tube pan with removable bottom promotes a good crust, and the cake will unmold with its crustiest side up. If you don't have such a pan, a bundt pan produces a more decorative shape, but the crusty top becomes the bottom when the cake is unmolded. It's your choice. Either type of pan is fine, as long as it holds 12 cups of batter.

Makes one 10-inch tube cake

Pareve margarine, for greasing
   the pan
3 cups bleached all-purpose flour
1 tablespoon baking powder
1 teaspoon salt
2 teaspoons ground cinnamon
2 cups plus 5 tablespoons
   granulated sugar

4 to 5 apples, peeled, cored, and
   cut into roughly 1-inch pieces
   (about 4 to 5 cups)
4 eggs
1 cup vegetable oil
1/4 cup orange or apple juice
1 tablespoon vanilla extract
1 cup coarsely chopped walnuts
Confectioners' sugar, for dusting
   (optional)

Grease a 12-cup (10-inch) tube pan or bundt pan with margarine.

Position a rack in the center of the oven. Preheat the oven to 375°F.

In a large bowl, combine the flour, baking powder, and salt. Stir to blend. Set aside.

In another bowl, combine the cinnamon and 5 tablespoons of the granulated sugar; stir to blend. Mix in the apple pieces. Set aside.

In the bowl of stand mixer fitted with the paddle, beat the eggs and the remaining 2 cups sugar together on medium speed until the mixture is light yellow and thick, about 1 minute. Slowly pour in the oil and continue beating another few seconds. Beat in the orange juice and vanilla.

Stop the machine. Add the flour mixture all at once. Stir on the lowest speed just until the flour is thoroughly blended in. Do not overmix. By hand, stir in the apples and walnuts. Pour the batter evenly into the prepared pan.

Bake for 1¹/₂ hours. It should be well browned and separating from the sides of the pan.

Place the cake on a rack and let it cool in the pan for 15 to 20 minutes. Turn the cake out onto the rack and cool to room temperature before slicing. You may want to dust the top of the cake with confectioners' sugar. Use a knife with a serrated blade for slicing.

Hamantaschen

It is said that Haman, the villain in the biblical story of Esther that is retold every spring and is the basis for the joyous festival of Purim, wore a three-cornered hat, or wore a robe with three-cornered pockets. That's why these Purim treats are made in a triangular shape, either for the hat or the pockets, but more likely the pockets because *taschen* means pockets in German, the basic language of Yiddish.

That is mythic folklore, of course. It makes more sense to say that they are called hamantaschen because they were originally filled only with mohn, poppy seed; hence poppy seed pockets. Coincidentally, mohntaschen sounds like hamantachen, so they became hamantachen. Then again, in the Jewish faith there is no such thing as coincidence. Everything is by divine providence. It's all beside the point, actually. These are such beloved pastries that they are now made all year long.

In short, and to oversimplify the story of Purim, Esther was the Jewish queen of Persia, the wife of King Ahasuerus. But the king didn't know that this great beauty and charming woman was Jewish. In fact, to keep her heritage a secret at court, she became a vegetarian, the simplest way for her to follow Jewish dietary laws. This is one reason that the most traditional hamantaschen are filled with poppy seeds, which were one of Esther's favored foods. Now, Mordechai, Esther's uncle, was the leader of the Jews in Persia and he refused, as the Jewish religion dictates, to bow before Haman, the king's prime minister. To get rid of the disrespectful Jewish Mordechai, Haman convinced the king that the Jews were a threat to his kingdom and should be eradicated. However, when Esther told the king that she herself was Jewish, he reversed his decision and instead of hanging all Jews, he hung Haman. The Jews rejoiced.

Hamantaschen have become the signature food of Purim, the number one favorite treat. The dough for this recipe is from Carole Walter's award-winning *Great Cookies.* I couldn't improve on it. The traditional fillings are lekvar (prune paste), mohn (poppy seed), and apricot paste. All of these can be purchased in cans or jars. You can also use apricot preserves, marmalade, or other jam or preserves. As we live in an age of chocoholism, and I have had many requests for chocolate hamantaschen, I offer a chocolate filling here.

Makes about 36

Dough
3 cups bleached all-purpose flour
1 cup sugar
2 teaspoons baking powder
1/4 teaspoon salt
10 tablespoons (1 stick plus 2 tablespoons) cold, unsalted butter or pareve margarine, cut into 1/2-inch cubes
2 eggs
2 egg yolks
1 teaspoon vanilla extract

Chocolate Filling
6 ounces semisweet chocolate
1/2 cup (1 stick) butter
1/4 teaspoon salt
1 teaspoon vanilla extract
1 cup sugar
2 eggs, lightly beaten
1/4 cup bleached all-purpose flour
1/4 to 1/2 cup finely chopped walnuts (optional)

2 large egg whites, lightly beaten with 2 teaspoons of sugar for the egg wash

To make the dough, in the bowl of a food processor fitted with the metal blade, place the flour, sugar, baking powder, and salt. Pulse several times to combine.

Add the butter and pulse several more times, then process for a few seconds to form mealy crumbs.

In a small bowl, beat together the eggs, egg yolks, and vanilla.

Pour this egg mixture into the processor and pulse several times to mix it in, then process for about 10 seconds. With a rubber spatula, stir the mixture up from the bottom, then process again until the dough begins to clump together, about another 10 seconds.

Turn out onto a lightly floured surface and, with floured hands, press the dough together, divide in half, and form into 2 disks. Wrap each disk with plastic wrap and refrigerate for at least 1 hour, or up to 3 days. (The dough may be frozen for up to 4 months.)

To prepare the filling, in a small saucepan, over low heat, melt the chocolate and butter together, stirring until perfectly smooth. Add the salt, vanilla, sugar, eggs, flour, and walnuts, and stir until well blended.

Any unused portion of the filling can be frozen for up to 4 months, or it can be baked into brownies in a 325°F oven for about 35 minutes.

If baking all the hamantaschen at once, on two baking sheets, position the racks in the lower and upper thirds of the oven. If making only one sheet at a time, the rack should be in the center of the oven. Preheat the oven to 350°F.

Dab the corners of the baking sheets with butter and line them with parchment paper.

If the dough is coming straight from the refrigerator, let it warm slightly at room temperature (for about 20 minutes) so it can be rolled out. On a lightly floured board, roll the dough to a thickness of about $^3/_{16}$ inch. Using a 3-inch–round cookie cutter, cut circles of dough and place them on the prepared sheets.

When all of the dough has been cut, place about 2 teaspoons of filling in the center of each circle. Brush the perimeter of the circle with the egg wash. Using a dough scraper, lift the dough to partially cover the filling, spacing it at one-third intervals, like a tri-cornered hat. Brush the tops of the formed cookies with the egg wash.

Bake for 15 to 18 minutes, or until the cookies are golden brown. If baking more than one sheet at a time, to ensure even browning, rotate the sheets top to bottom and front to back toward the end of the baking time.

Remove from the oven and let rest on the baking sheets for 2 or 3 minutes. Loosen the cookies with a thin metal spatula and transfer to wire cooling racks.

Store the cookies in an airtight container, layered between strips of wax paper, for up to 5 days. These cookies may be frozen.

Note:

When re-rolling the scraps, do not gather them in your hand. Stack the scraps on a 12-inch-long piece of plastic wrap, bring the four sides to the middle, and using the plastic wrap as an aid, press the pieces of dough together, forming a small rectangle. Refrigerate before re-rolling.

New York Cheesecake

New York cheesecake, which is ironically always made with Philadelphia cream cheese, is a variant on the Eastern European cheesecakes that were made in the old country with fresh "curd cheeses," cheeses on the order of pot cheese and cottage cheese. Think Russian paskha, the Easter cheese dessert formed into a four-sided pyramid, and you've got an idea of the ancestry, although the original cheesecakes of Jewish Eastern Europe were probably much poorer and drier than the rich, festive paskha.

Cream cheese was the ingredient that turned a dry cake into a much beloved, iconic food of New York. According to Kraft Foods, which now produces Philadelphia cream cheese, the product was developed in 1872 by a New York dairyman who combined cream with milk to create an ultra-rich cheese. The new cheese was supposed to imitate French Neufchâtel. Then in 1880, a New York cheese distributor, A. L. Reynolds, first began distributing cream cheese wrapped in tinfoil wrappers, calling it "Philadelphia Brand."

But why Philadelphia? Says Kraft, the name "Philadelphia Brand" was adopted by Reynolds because, at that time, Philadelphia was known for its fine food products.

There was, in fact, a much earlier cream cheese from Philadelphia, pointing to the inspiration for the name. In Thomas F. De Voe's book *The Market Assistant*, an 1867 treatise on the markets of New York, Philadelphia, Boston, and Brooklyn, the author notes that there was a kind of cream cheese "sometimes found in our markets, but more particularly in those of Philadelphia."

He even describes its manufacture: "It is made from rich sour cream tied up in linen cloth to drain, then laid on a deep dish, still covered around, and turned every day, and sprinkled with salt for ten days or a fortnight, until it is ripe." This sour cream could not have been the cultured sour cream that we know, but a more natural product.

De Voe also says, "There is another article much used called Smearkase, a German name for churds [sic]. It is made into pies, cakes, spread on bread, and also eaten with pepper and salt. I ate some in Philadelphia made into cake, which I found was very good."

New York cheesecake as we know it, however, didn't appear until the twentieth century. It is possible that, as he claimed, Arnold Reuben of Reuben's delicatessen was the first to serve such a cake to the public. He also claimed his family developed the first recipe for a cream cheese cake. It is at best unlikely, though, because at about the same time that Reuben claimed his family invented cheesecake, Kraft ran a promotion for its cream cheese with a recipe called "Phila-delphia Supreme Cheesecake."

What no one could have seen coming was that cheesecake, because it was introduced at decidedly nonkosher Jewish delicatessens such as Reuben's and Lindy's, would become known as a Jewish creation. And certainly it could not have dawned on anyone that cream cheese—created in rural New York, akin to a German cheese from Philadelphia, and popularized by a non-Jewish company (Kraft)—would become the ultimate complement to Jewish bagels. But that's another story (see page 158). ✺

Junior's Cheesecake

 ———————————————————————

Truth be told, this recipe, from *Welcome to Junior's*, the restaurant's own cookbook, makes an even better cake than the one you can buy there (as great as that may be). That's understandable. Junior's now bakes cakes in vast quantities, sells them on QVC, and sends them all over the country. Given all that, it remains a superior cheesecake. Still, making one at a time with love is preferable.

Be sure to have the cream cheese at room temperature. It will beat up lighter and higher, yet still produce a fabulously rich and creamy cheesecake. The thin sponge cake layer at the bottom is a distinctive feature of Junior's cheesecake, but if you don't want to bother making it, you can prepare the cheesecake without it. However, place a round of parchment paper on the bottom of the pan to ease removal of the cake.

Makes one 9-inch cake

1 recipe Thin Sponge Cake Layer for
    Cheesecake (recipe follows)

Filling
4 (8-ounce) packages cream cheese
$1^2/_3$ cups sugar
$^1/_4$ cup cornstarch
1 tablespoon vanilla extract
2 extra-large eggs
$^3/_4$ cup heavy cream

Make the the sponge cake as directed. When you remove the cake from the oven, leave the oven on. While the cake cools in the pan, make the cream cheese filling. Place one 8-ounce package of the cream cheese, $^1/_3$ cup of the sugar, and the cornstarch in a large bowl. Beat with an electric mixer on low, until creamy, about 3 minutes. Then beat in the remaining 3 packages cream cheese.

Increase the mixer speed to high and beat in the remaining $1^1/_3$ cups sugar. Then beat in the vanilla. Blend in the eggs, one at a time, beating the batter well after adding each one. Blend in the heavy cream. At this point, mix the filling only until completely blended. Be careful not to overmix the batter.

Gently spoon the cheese filling on top of the baked sponge cake layer. Place the springform pan in a large shallow pan containing hot water that comes about 1 inch up the sides of the pan. Bake the cheesecake until the center barely jiggles when you shake the pan, about 1 hour.

Cool the cake on a wire rack for 1 hour. Then, with the cake still in the pan, cover the cake with plastic wrap and refrigerate until it's completely cold, at least 4 hours or overnight.

Remove the sides of the springform pan. Slide the cake off the bottom of the pan onto a serving plate. Or if you wish, simply leave the cake on the removable bottom of the pan and place it on a serving plate. If any cake is left over, cover it with plastic wrap and store it in the refrigerator.

Thin Sponge Cake Layer for Cheesecake

Watch this cake carefully while it's baking. There's not much batter, so it needs only about 10 minutes of baking—just enough time for the cake to turn light golden and set on the top. The cake should not brown on top.

Makes one 9-inch sponge cake layer $^3/_4$ inch high, enough for 1 cheesecake

$^1/_2$ cup sifted cake flour
1 teaspoon baking powder
Pinch of salt
3 extra-large eggs, separated

$^1/_3$ cup plus 2 tablespoons sugar
1 teaspoon vanilla extract
3 tablespoons unsalted butter, melted
$^1/_4$ teaspoon cream of tartar

Position an oven rack in the center of the oven. Preheat the oven to 350°F. Generously butter a 9-inch springform pan.

Into a medium bowl, sift the cake flour, baking powder, and salt together. Set aside.

In a large bowl, beat the egg yolks with an electric mixer on high for 3 minutes. Then, with the mixer still running, gradually add the $^1/_3$ cup of sugar and continue beating until thick light-yellow ribbons form in the bowl, about 5 minutes more. Beat in the vanilla extract.

Sift the flour mixture over the batter and stir it in by hand until no more white flecks appear. Then blend in the butter.

In a clean bowl, using clean, dry beaters, beat the egg whites and cream of tartar together on high speed until frothy. Less than a tablespoon at a time, add the remaining 2 tablespoons of sugar and continue beating until stiff peaks form.

Stir about $^1/_3$ cup of the whites into the batter, then gently fold in the remaining whites (don't worry if a few white specks remain).

Gently spoon the batter into the pan.

Bake the cake just until the center of the cake springs back when lightly touched, only about 10 minutes (watch carefully!). Let the cake cool in the pan on a wire rack while you continue making the cheesecake filling. Do not remove the cake from the pan.

On the counter at Junior's, Brooklyn

Lindy's Cheesecake

This is the genuine article, the very cheesecake recipe over which Nathan Detroit made a bet with Sky Masterson in the Broadway musical *Guys and Dolls*, the one whose name even today is world renowned.

However, in its heyday, the 1930s, Lindy's cheesecake was not necessarily always the most famous in New York. Reuben's cheesecake was more famous, and many other restaurants featured "famous" cheesecakes. Lindy's recipe has come down to us, I think, because Leo Linderman, owner of Lindy's, understood the value of publicity and shared the recipe. One of those customers who asked for the recipe was Duncan Hines, who published it in 1955 in *Duncan Hines' Food Odyssey*. As the nation's first legitimate national restaurant critic, Hines had a huge following. He traveled from coast to coast, inspecting the hygiene in kitchens and eating and evaluating food and service.

"As I write this," he told readers of *Odyssey*, "gold is worth somewhere around $32 an ounce. Lindy's cheese cake at 45 cents a slice is somewhat less expensive, yet a good many people who've eaten at Lindy's famous Broadway restaurant consider it pure gold."

The crust in the following recipe, though authentic, is not necessary to make a wonderfully creamy cheesecake. And since it is difficult to assemble, I often make the cake without the crust, and to great success. Just fit a sheet of parchment paper on the bottom of the springform pan, so the cake can be removed.

Makes one 9-inch cake

Crust
2-inch piece of vanilla bean
1 cup all-purpose flour
1/4 cup sugar
1 teaspoon grated lemon zest
1 large egg yolk
1 stick (1/2 cup) unsalted butter,
   cut into bits
1/4 teaspoon salt

Filling
2 1/2 pounds cream cheese,
   at room temperature
1 3/4 cups sugar
3 tablespoons all-purpose flour
1 1/2 teaspoons grated orange zest
1 1/2 teaspoons grated lemon zest
1/2 teaspoon vanilla extract
5 large eggs
2 large egg yolks
1/4 cup heavy cream

Position an oven rack in the center of the oven. Preheat the oven to 400°F.

To make the crust, split the vanilla bean lengthwise and scrape the seeds into a bowl. Stir in the flour, the sugar, and the lemon zest. Add the egg yolk, the butter, and the salt and knead the mixture until it forms a dough. Flatten the dough into a round and chill it, wrapped in wax paper, for 1 hour.

Remove the sides of a 9-inch springform pan. Oil the bottom of the pan lightly, and press some of the dough onto it to form a $^1/_8$-inch-thick layer.

Bake the bottom crust in the middle of the oven for 10 to 12 minutes, or until it is golden. Remove from the oven, let cool 10 minutes, then chill it in the refrigerator.

Butter the sides of the pan, attach it to the bottom, and press the remaining dough up the sides, $^1/_8$ inch thick. Set aside.

To make the filling, in the bowl of a stand mixer fitted with the paddle (or in a large bowl, using a hand-held mixer), beat the cream cheese with the sugar, the flour, the orange and lemon zests, and the vanilla until the mixture is smooth.

Beat in the whole eggs and the egg yolks, 1 at a time, beating lightly after each addition.

When all the eggs have been incorporated, stir in the cream.

Increase the oven temperature to 550°F. Pour the filling into the prepared crust and bake the cheesecake in the middle of the oven for 12 minutes.

Decrease the heat to 200°F. Bake the cheesecake for 1 more hour.

Let the cheesecake cool in the pan on a rack. Still in the pan, chill it overnight.

Serve cool, but not well chilled. Remove the cake from the refrigerator about 1 hour before serving.

Lekach

Honey Cake

Honey cake is not so much loved as revered. Eating honey ensures a sweet New Year in Jewish tradition—one might easily say superstition—and honey cake is the embodiment of that Rosh Hashanah tradition. We also dip apple slices and challah into honey to ensure a sweet New Year. Honey cake also appears at the Sabbath morning kiddush, along with sponge cake, as an accompaniment to the kiddush wine or schnapps. As in strict religious observance, this kiddush meal should be the first meal of the day. And as Sabbath morning services don't usually conclude until close to noon, or after, everyone used to pounce on the honey cake in the days when it was the prime kiddush food. Today's Sabbath kiddush is generally a much more elaborate food affair. There is always some sponsor, often the family of a bar mitzvah boy, obliged to put out a nice spread.

This recipe is about as simple and as good as Ashkenazic honey cake gets. It is adapted from *The Molly Goldberg Cookbook*, published in 1955. Later recipes try to make honey cake into spice cake, but in this version you can clearly taste the honey, with only a hint of brandy to frame it. I use very good cognac. It makes a difference. This cake is also not as rubbery as many recipes. Perhaps the crunchy walnuts are a distraction, although almonds are the more usual nut in this cake. Loaves are often decorated with sliced almonds decoratively glazed onto the top.

A measuring tip for the honey: put some oil in a measuring cup. Roll it around to coat the inside of the cup. Pour in the honey. The oil will come to the surface and you will be able to measure the honey accurately, while the oiled cup allows the honey to pour out easily and completely.

Makes 1 small loaf

1 tablespoon vegetable oil
1/2 cup honey
1/4 cup hot, freshly brewed strong coffee
2 tablespoons good brandy
1 3/4 cups sifted bleached all-purpose flour

1/8 teaspoon salt
3/4 teaspoon baking powder
1/2 teaspoon baking soda
1 cup coarsely chopped nuts (hazelnuts, almonds, or walnuts)
2 eggs
1/2 cup sugar

Position an oven rack in the upper third of the oven. Preheat the oven to 325°F.

Oil a 3½- by 5½-inch loaf pan, then line it on the bottom and sides with either parchment paper, aluminum foil, or a paper loaf-pan liner.

In a small bowl, add the oil and honey (see headnote). Pour in the hot coffee and stir until the honey becomes more fluid, then stir in the brandy.

In another small bowl, stir together the flour, salt, baking powder, and baking soda. Stir in the nuts.

In the bowl of a stand mixer fitted with the whisk, beat the eggs until well blended. Add the sugar and beat until light in color, fluffy, and thick. Beat in the honey mixture.

With a spoon or spatula, stir in the dry ingredients by hand.

Pour the batter into the prepared pan. Bake for 55 minutes. Do not open the oven door.

Cool for 15 minutes in the pan. Using the parchment-paper lining to lift it, remove the cake from the pan and let cool completely. Peel off the paper before serving.

Golden Blossom Honey

Golden Blossom Honey has been the honey taste in New York Jewish cooking since 1921, when the company was founded by John G. Patton, a Gentile who had been in the bulk honey business in California. His son, John H., came up with the signature blend of white clover, orange blossom, and sage buckwheat honeys that continues to give the product its distinctively delicate taste. Golden Blossom, which is processed in New Jersey, quickly became the best-selling honey in the New York City metro region, reaching 60 percent of the market. The company is still owned by the Patton family, and it is still the most popular brand in the Northeast as well as southeast Florida, although today it has many competitors. ✇

The Candy Store and the Egg Cream

For at least sixty-something years, until the late 1960s, the corner "candy store" was the focal point of neighborhood life in New York. The sign outside may have said "Luncheonette," but lunch was the least of it. The candy store was where you bought the newspaper and cigarettes. It was where they hand-packed Breyers ice cream (from Philadelphia) into white cardboard containers like the ones Chinese food comes in (or used to come in). It was where you got an ice cream cone. The candy store was where you could get a grilled cheese sandwich, or a tuna sandwich—nothing more elaborate than a hamburger.

And, finally, it was where children bought penny candies like sugar buttons on paper, malted milk balls, chocolate nonpareils, and brightly colored syrup-filled wax bottles and lips. It was where everyone of every age stopped at the fountain to gossip over a Coke, an egg cream, or a cherry lime rickey, which is cherry and lime syrups mixed together with seltzer, not to mention munch on well-salted, crisp pretzel rods or soft bagel-like pretzels.

According to legend, the egg cream was invented sometime in the late nineteenth century at Louis Auster's candy store on the Lower East Side. Stanley Auster, the grandson of Louis, claims he is the last living person privy to his grandfather's original formula. So, naturally, I called him. It was more than a decade ago; I wanted him to talk about egg creams on my radio program.

"I can't talk about egg creams," Stanley insisted, "I'm having heart problems."

"Stanley," a woman's voice, presumably Mrs. Auster's, yelled in the background. "Talk on the radio about egg creams instead of yourself. Maybe you'll feel better."

Stanley Auster says that his grandfather created a special chocolate syrup and made his own carbon-dioxide-charged seltzer with a particularly vigorous bubble, and that he merchandized the egg cream into a local sensation. What it has since become is a symbol of The Good Old Days in New York. Still, Stanley says he won't even share the secret recipe with his daughter, "who couldn't care less." He will go to his grave with it.

"My grandfather died around 1955. He was 97. Very few people came to the funeral. He left the store when he was 85. He became quite feeble in his early nineties. A lot of people had moved away. The Jewish theaters started closing down. People weren't so interested in egg creams anymore. The Jewishness left the area. It just became an ordinary candy store after a while. That's why my uncle closed up the store on Second Avenue.

"The last batch of syrup was made by my uncle Mendy about 1974. Someone did me a favor where I was working. When I asked him how I could pay him back, he asked me if he could have some egg-cream syrup. I asked my uncle Mendy. It was difficult. He had to use a substitute cocoa and one other substitute. He made around eight quarts, and he gave me two. It was delicious, but not exactly the way it was. The soda didn't have enough pressure. But there was something else. The egg cream is not only a great drink, but it's associated with a certain camaraderie or folksiness among people. Just having an egg cream alone today is not the full flavor of it. It's having an egg cream with a group of people. It's having an egg cream with a pretzel. It's having an egg cream while talking about various things. Nobody ever sat down to have an egg cream. People usually drank it while standing and kibitzing, and those days are long gone."

The Gem Spa, on the corner of Second Avenue and St. Marks Place, is the last remaining original venue of egg creams. The store is now owned by Pakistanis, as most New York newsstands are today, but they still know how to mix a good egg cream. This was the last of the several Auster candy stores, and it is possible that the fountain that pumps the seltzer is original, although it does not make a soda any more carbonated than any other.

"'Two cents plain' was what people ordered when they wanted seltzer from a fountain. For three cents you got syrup, too," says Seymour Kaye, the last of the old school Lower East Side Jewish restaurateurs (see page 120). "When Auster moved from East Third Street and Avenue D to Second Avenue and St. Marks Place, he had to raise the price from a nickel to seven cents. The two cents extra kept the customers away. It was sort of the end of Auster's."

A well-made egg cream is an elixir beyond understanding to those who didn't grow up drinking them. It is made with only three ingredients: chocolate syrup, milk, and seltzer. As with all very simple recipes, those ingredients must be just so, and your technique extremely careful. The perfect egg cream has a head as white as the milk in it and a body of cocoa-colored soda. The visual difference mirrors both a taste difference and a textural contrast between the soda and its head.

Egg creams are best made, served, and appreciated in clear Coke glasses, the classic ones that curve up from a narrow, cylindrical base to a voluptuous upper basin. Some of New York's corner candy store soda fountains used to use paper cones that fit into stainless steel holders, but syrup sticks in the points of those, and it isn't nearly as pleasant to drink from paper as from glass. In the old days, at fancier fountains, they might, in fact, have used a Coke-type fountain glass placed in a zarf, which is a metal holder with a cuplike handle. At better fountains, milk shakes and malteds were often served in glasses like this, too.

It may be more fun making an egg cream with an old-fashioned seltzer siphon bottle (blue and green are very romantic), but using bottled supermarket seltzer may, in fact, give a better result because it has stronger carbonation—perhaps even as strong as the famously strong pressure at Louis Auster's candy store.

Fox's U-Bet chocolate syrup is the classic egg cream flavoring, but sometime in the 1950s, vanilla egg creams came along. Then there were coffee egg creams, then other flavors too inventive to mention. Many of us believe that the only true egg cream is a chocolate egg cream. Fox's U-Bet will give your egg cream a real New York flavor, but the drink is just as delicious made with other chocolate syrups. One of the best egg creams left in New York is made at the two Brooklyn Diners in Manhattan, one on 57th Sreet and Seventh Avenue, the other on 43rd Street and Broadway, in Times Square.

To make an egg cream:

Fill a 12-ounce glass with about ³/₄ inch of Fox's U-Bet chocolate syrup. Top the syrup with about 1 inch of very cold whole milk. Fill the glass about two thirds of the way with seltzer. Stir, but only at the bottom of the glass, to mix the chocolate with the milk and force a white head to surface. Fill the glass with more seltzer, being careful that the foam doesn't run over the side. You should have a fairly sweet chocolate soda with at least an inch of milk-white head. ✍

❧ A Glossary of ❧ Yiddish Food Terms

In this book, the most commonly recognized transliterated spellings have been used for Yiddish words. There are, however, many variations in Yiddish spellings. There are many dialects of Yiddish. YIVO, the Institute for Jewish Research, publishes a Yiddish dictionary, available on the Internet, but I have not adhered to their phonetic spellings. The dictionary was created about eighty years ago and was a compromise between many different Yiddish-speaking factions. As a result, and as it was developed so many years ago, many of the words are today unrecognizable to the casual Yiddish user.

Arbes (page 2) Seasoned chickpeas in Polish Yiddish dialects. Also called *nahit* in Russian Yiddish, from the Turkish *nohut*.

Bagel (page 201) A ring-shaped chewy roll, originally from Poland, that is both boiled and baked. Bagels used to be as tough and tasty as New York itself, but have gone a little bit soft.

Balabusta A consummate homemaker, who is mother, cook, housekeeper, wife, hostess, pretty much in that order of importance.

Bialy (page 210) A sort of flattish roll, dusty with flour, indented in the center, and topped with strands or minced pieces of onion. It's named after the town of Bialystok, Poland, where it was called *Bialystok kuchen* (Bialystok cake). The most famous bialy baker in New York City is Kossar's, on Grand Street. Bialys are sold alongside bagels in stores, but almost every coffee cart and coffee shop sells a reasonable facsimile. New Yorkers eat them cut in half with a schmear of butter or cream cheese. In general today, bialys more closely resemble what they were sixty years ago than do bagels.

Blintzes (page 149) Always in the plural because who could eat just one? Thin crêpes enclose either a sweet or a savory cheese filling or mashed potato flavored with fried onions as in knishes (page 90). Blintzes with fruit-and-cheese fillings (blueberry, strawberry, pineapple) are a latter-day novelty.

Borscht (pages 53, 57, and 59) A group of Russian vegetable soups, usually beet-based, but not always.

Brisket (page 105) A cut of meat from the belly of the animal, either a calf or a steer. Because it is a tough cut, it is either braised (pot roasted) or boiled. It is the cut that is cured to make corned beef.

Brust Breast meat. It can refer to flanken (*brust* flanken) or to brisket.

Bubulah A term of endearment ("How's my *bubulah*?"), it is also used for a large, single-serving matzo meal pancake or *chremsl* (page 178).

Burekes Beets, the basis for borscht.

Challah (page 195) Sabbath and holiday yeast bread, made with eggs and oil.

Chernitzlach Small black seeds (nigella seeds), slightly bitter, used mainly on rye bread.

Cholent (page 103) The long-cooked Sabbath day casserole, usually based on barley and beans, often with potatoes, and either beef or chicken.

Cholov Israel More or less the dairy equivalent of *glatt* kosher. It is a designation given to milk and milk products that are not only supervised, but also from cows that have been husbanded by and milked by Sabbath-observant Jews. This is a requirement of very observant Jews.

Chometz Foods forbidden during Passover, not only leavened breads and cakes, but also any grain-based foods, plus, in some observant communities, legumes and rice, as well as any food that has not been produced under supervision on premises with equipment prepared especially for Passover. *Chometzdik* is the adjectival form, as in "You can't eat in her kitchen on Passover. It's *chometzdik.*"

Chrain (page 35) The fiery root vegetable, horseradish. It is practically an essential condiment with gefilte fish, grated and either naturally white or colored red with beet juice, but it is also a regular accompaniment to boiled brisket or flanken. On Passover, it is the "bitter herb" on the Passover plate of symbolic foods, and it is eaten as part of the Haggadah ritual, as well as enjoyed during the festive meal.

Chremsl, Chremslach (page 178) Many different Passover pancakes and fritters made with matzo meal go by this name.

Deckle Literally "top" or "cover" in German and Yiddish, the word is used for the crescent-shaped piece of coarse-grained but flavorful meat on top of the rib; it's called "top of the rib" in American markets and in restaurants wise enough to offer it for its own sake. There is also *brust* deckle, which is the top muscle of a brisket and often called "second cut" or "thick cut."

Einlauf A kind of soup noodle made by pouring batter into the simmering soup.

Eyer kichel Small baked rounds or squares of puffy egg dough, sugared or not. In poorer times, *eyer kichel* was the main offering of a Sabbath kiddush. It is still popular, but usually upstaged by more elaborate food. It is also eaten as a sweet treat, especially with a glass of tea. A staple of Jewish bakeries are Hungarian bow ties, a type of *eyer kichel* in which a strip of puffy egg dough is twisted into a bow-tie shape and baked with a heavy coating of coarse crystal sugar.

Farfel (pages 37 and 174) Tiny beads of egg pasta, often also called egg barley, or sometimes broken bits of matzo. Both types are used in soups and for other dishes.

Flanken (page 113) Literally, flank, and actually, short ribs cut across the bone instead of parallel to the bone. There are two kinds: plate flanken is what is usually sold in supermarkets, and is often cut from too far back in the hindquarter to be considered kosher. Cut from further up, it is called breast (*brust*) flanken, which is mostly what is available in kosher markets.

Fleishig Meat, encompassing foods of animal origin, including poultry, that, according to Jewish dietary laws, cannot be eaten at the same meal as dairy (*milchig*), or until three hours after a dairy meal. (The exact time actually varies from community to community.) The opposite is also prohibited: one cannot drink milk with meat (who would want to?), have a cheeseburger, or eat a dessert made with cream or butter after a steak.

Fliegle (page 154) Wing, as from a chicken, duck, goose, or other poultry. Also used as a word for lox or smoked salmon fins and trimmings.

Fluden A layered pastry with a filling of dried fruit and nuts.

Forshpeiz Appetizer, which on Yiddish tables could mean everything from chickpeas to chopped liver, cabbage salads to sweetbreads.

Fresser In Yiddish (and colloquial New York City usage), a *fresser* is someone who eats a lot or obviously enjoys his food, while *fress*, from the German, meaning "devour," can also mean "to overeat."

Gedempte fleish (page 109) Well-cooked meat, such as any braised or potted, but often meaning overcooked meat. A steak can be *gedempte* in a bad way. A brisket is *gedempte* in a good way.

Gefilte fish (page 31) Either loved or hated, these cakes of ground freshwater fish are practically a symbol of Yiddish cooking.

Glatt kosher A term that technically refers only to meat that is from animals whose innards have been carefully inspected after ritual slaughter and have been deemed perfect, without any blemish, sign of disease, or deformity. This is a condition required for observant Jews to partake of meat. However, in common parlance, *glatt* kosher has come to mean "super kosher." Another requirement, for instance, is that the store selling the kosher food be closed on the Sabbath. A Sabbath-observant store or person is called *shomer shabbos*.

Goldene yoichle (page 40) Literally, golden broth, which of course refers to chicken soup.

Griebenes (page 10) Chicken or goose skin cracklings, usually mixed with caramelized onions because it is the by-product of rendering chicken or goose fat with onion. Often used to flavor Chopped Liver (page 11), Potato Kugel (page 76), Matzo Farfel Kugel (page 174), or mashed potatoes. *Griebenes* are also often eaten for their own sake, as a delicacy typically reserved for the head of the family or a favored (or too thin) child.

Halvah (page 165) A Middle Eastern confection made of pureed sesame seeds, whipped with honey or sugar and egg whites. How it got to Poland is anyone's guess.

Hamantaschen (page 237) Triangular filled pastries or cookies prepared for Purim. Traditionally the filling is either prune butter (lekvar) or ground poppy seeds (mohn), with apricot and raspberry as latter-day creations, and chocolate very of the moment.

Hechsher The kashruth certification symbol. There are many different symbols used by the many different supervising groups, but the first group in the U.S. and the largest now is the Orthodox Union. Its *hechsher* is the letter *U* inside the letter *O*. It is referred to as the *OU*.

Helzel Yiddish for neck, but the dish called *helzel* is stuffed neck skin of a chicken (or turkey), which was filled like Kishka (page 88) and roasted with the Shabbos chicken. Also called *gorgle*.

Hochtmesser The curve-bladed, single-handled chopper that old-time Jewish cooks used to use in conjunction with a wooden chopping bowl. It is similar in shape to the Italian mezzaluna.

Holishkes (page 118) Stuffed cabbage, usually in a tomato-based sweet-and-sour sauce, sometimes with raisins or other dried fruit.

Ingberlach (page 189) From the Yiddish word *ingber* (ginger), this is candy flavored with ginger and honey, generally made for Passover and Rosh Hashanah.

Karnatzlach (page 125) A garlicky Romanian beef sausage (*mititei* in Romanian) made without a casing.

Kasha Buckwheat groats, which are sold whole, coarsely ground, medium ground, and finely ground. Kasha is used as a simple side dish to meat main courses, and also as a pilaf mixed with bow-tie egg pasta, Kasha Varnishkes (page 85). Kasha also fills knishes (page 90), and can be used as a vegetarian filling for stuffed cabbage.

Kasher To render kosher, such as salting meat and poultry, or searing liver.

Kashruth The Jewish dietary laws.

Kichel Cookie; the short form of *eyer kichel*, egg cookies.

Kiddush The benediction recited before eating. Also, "a kiddush" has come to mean the offer of a glass of wine or schnapps with a bite of bread or sponge cake (page 234), or in some communities a piece of kugel, directly after morning or evening prayers. In the old days, in less affluent times, a kiddush was hosted by the congregation to attract people to synagogue. The repast was usually meager. Since the 1950s, however, a family having a bar mitzvah or a wedding, or to honor some other happy occasion, such as the naming of a female child, would offer the kiddush. After World War II, and still in some wealthy and competitive communities, these have turned into ostentatious luncheon buffets. Even the Lubavitch Hasidim of Crown Heights, Brooklyn, have gotten into the act. An elaborate kiddush in that community could consist of hot cholent, with or without meat, and as many as three or four kinds of kugel, and Knaidlach (page 43), or dumplings, matzo balls being the most famous.

Kipfel A crescent-shaped Hungarian pastry related to rugelach.

Kishka (page 88) Literally, the word means "gut." (As in "The play was so tragic, it got him in the kishkas.") As a food reference, however, it is essentially a starch sausage: a large cow's intestine stuffed with a mixture of either chicken fat or suet, flour or matzo meal, and seasoning such as onion, carrot, garlic, and paprika. Another (more fancy) name is "stuffed derma" or "derma farci," and called such it was, until fairly recently, always served at Jewish wedding and bar mitzvah receptions.

Kemach yoshon Literally means "old flour" in Hebrew. The Old Testament, Leviticus 23, prescribes rules for harvesting and milling flour. To oversimplify, all the rules have been closely followed for *kemach yoshon*. In Israel, the very observant insist on it. The custom has reached New York, where bakeries advertise in their windows that their products are *kemach yoshon*. However, in the diaspora, there is still an argument that these ancient rules do not apply.

Knaidle (plural Knaidlach) (page 43) A dumpling, the most famous of which is the matzo ball, but there are others.

Knish (page 90) A wrapped pastry with fillings that are, traditionally, seasoned mashed potatoes, kasha, or liver. Today, knishes also have cheese fillings with fruit and vegetable fillings, such as broccoli. Perhaps a New York Jewish creation.

Knubble Garlic, a key ingredient in savory Knubble Borscht (page 59) and spicy knubblewurst, a beef sausage that is an old deli staple.

Kosher The Yiddish word (but adopted into American English) denoting foods that follow kashruth, Jewish dietary laws. In American slang, the phrase "not kosher" means something that is not lawful, or at least not entirely ethical or moral. The basic laws, all of which are outlined in the Old Testament (mainly Leviticus 14), are simple, although their observance and execution can be complicated by centuries of Talmudic interpretation as well as customs established in every different Jewish community.

Everyone would agree on these rules, although there are many more:

1. Meat and dairy ingredients must never mix. To this end, each requires separate kitchen utensils, pots, pans, equipment, and cooking surfaces, as well as dishes and eating utensils. Some foods, however, fall into neither category: eggs, fish, fruits, vegetables, grains, legumes, vegetable oils, and fats are all considered neutral, or pareve.

2. You can eat only animals with cloven hooves and that chew cud, and no animals or birds of prey. Animals must be killed in a "kosher" manner, which is to say a ritual humane slaughter—the throat is slit and death is instantaneous, under the supervision of a *mashgiach* (pronounced so the last syllable rhymes with Bach, the composer), a person

trained to make sure everything is done according to the rules.

3. Only certain cuts of red meat—from the forequarters—are allowed. The hindquarters, defined as behind the fifth rib, can be eaten only if the sciatic nerve is removed at the time of slaughter, a difficult operation that is today done only in Israel. Hind-quarters from kosher slaughters are sold as nonkosher meat.

4. In the case of prepared foods, *mashgiach* supervision is required to ensure that nothing forbidden, nothing not kosher (*trayf*), contaminates the food preparation area or the food itself. For instance, to use an exaggerated example, potato chips fried in vegetable oil (nothing *trayf* there) would not be kosher if they were produced without proper supervision in the same plant as fried pork rinds. Packaged kosher foods always have a symbol on them denoting which organization or specific *mashgiach* supervised the production. The symbol is called a *hechsher*. Kosher restaurants and take-out stores always have a sign in the window or near the entrance denoting which organization super-vises the kitchen.

5. Raw meat and poultry must be salted with coarse salt or soaked in salt water to rid them of blood before cooking. Liver must be seared by a flame—in a broiler, for instance. An electric broiler heating element is acceptable these days. These processes are referred to as koshering, and these days, the salting and soaking is mostly done by a butcher rather than in the home. The

coarse salt used for drawing juices out is called kosher salt.

6. Eggs must not be tainted by even a spot of blood, so each egg is individually examined before adding it to a recipe.

7. Vegetables must be washed thoroughly, or even soaked, to be sure they do not harbor insects.

Kreplach (page 47) Filled pasta dumplings usually eaten in chicken soup, and particularly favored for Rosh Hashanah, for the evening meal before Yom Kippur, and on Purim.

Kugel (pages 70, 73, 74, and 76) A baked pudding, which can be either sweet or savory, usually based on a starchy ingredient like noodles, potatoes, rice, or bread.

Lekach (page 247) Honey cake, made especially for Rosh Hashanah because it symbolizes the wish for a sweet New Year.

Lekvar Prune butter or paste, used mainly to fill Hamantaschen (page 237) on Purim and Danish pastry other times of the year.

Lox (page 158) Salt-cured salmon, the über partner to a bagel with a cream cheese schmear.

Lukshen Noodles, usually fine egg noodles, used mainly for soup or for kugel.

Lungen Cow's lung, which by law can no longer be sold for human consumption, but which used to be stewed and was considered a great delicacy. Sometimes it was paired in the same dish with *miltz* (spleen).

Mandelbrodt (mandelbread) (pages 185 and 229) These days, people are calling it Jewish biscotti, but biscotti used to be Italian mandelbrodt to Jews. In either case,

it is a dense loaf cake that is thinly sliced and usually baked twice to crisp it, like biscotti. Mandelbrodt means "almond bread." The original flavoring was almonds, but now in America, you'll find versions made with chocolate and many exotic flavors.

Mandlen Soup nuts, from *mandel*, the German word for almond, that usually float in broth. Egg dough is rolled into ropes, cut into small pieces and either fried or baked. They have an almond color and do, indeed, resemble nuts as they bob in soup. They are also the basis for a candy called *teiglach*, fried *mandlen* boiled in honey with ginger, much like Neapolitan *struffoli*.

Matzo (page 172) Crackerlike unleavened bread, required eating on Passover instead of leavened bread.

Mehren The Yiddish word *mehren* means both "carrots" and "increase." Carrots are a traditional food for Rosh Hashanah and other festive holidays, symbolizing the hope for a prosperous and fruitful New Year.

Milchig For the sake of kashruth, *milchig* is the opposite of *fleishig* (meat). In other words, it refers to products that contain dairy (milk products), such as milk itself, cream, butter, and cheese, or any foods that contain those ingredients, for instance cakes, pastries, puddings, or custards.

Miltz Cow's spleen, an old-time delicacy for the strong of heart (cow's heart also being a delicacy).

Mohn Poppy seed paste, usually sweetened with honey. Used as a filling for Hamantaschen (page 237) on Purim and as a filling for Danish pastry and other confections. Whole poppy seeds are used to top breads, rolls, and bagels.

Nosh Another Yiddish word now part of colloquial American English: it means both "snack" and "to snack." Examples: "I'm hungry, but all I need is a nosh." "I couldn't help noshing all day long." Snack foods as a category can be called *nosherei*. A serial snacker is a nosher. And so on.

Ongeshtopt Over-stuffed, often referring to a sandwich, but could be a fat person or a piece of upholstered furniture, too.

Pareve Denotes foods that are neutral, neither *fleishig* nor *milchig*. They can be eaten with either meat meals or dairy meals. Pareve foods include eggs, fish, vegetables, fruits, nuts, grains, and cereals. The word *pareve* will appear on all kosher products that meet the requirements.

Petrishke Parsley root, which looks like a tiny parsnip and tastes like a cross between parsley and celery. It is used almost exclusively to season chicken soup, and is available only in kosher shopping districts.

Pierogen Filled dumplings of Polish origin, similar to Kreplach (page 47). The singular is pierogi, but you can't eat just one. They are filled with either cheese or potato, and either boiled or fried. They were a specialty of the old dairy restaurants, where they were served with sour cream. The potato version could have been served as part of a meat meal, but for some reason they never were. Today, you need to go to a nonkosher Polish restaurant to find them, where they will also be stuffed with wilted cabbage or mushrooms or both. In New York and Chicago, as well as other cities with a Polish population, they are also sold both fresh and frozen in supermarkets.

Pletzel (page 214) Jewish focaccia. A flat bread, probably of Polish origin, usually topped with onions (*tzibeleh pletzel*), and sometimes with poppy seeds, too.

Potatonik (page 211) The word is Yinglish (Yiddish-English), the dish is a cross between potato bread and potato kugel (pudding). As it is yeast-raised, it's usually not prepared at home, but bought in a bakery. In Brooklyn, potatonik is baked only on Thursdays because that is the day observant Jews shop for Shabbos.

P'tcha (pitcha) (page 27) Calf's foot jelly, usually seasoned with much raw, chopped garlic.

Pulke Thigh, usually used for poultry, but also for humans. As in, "Boy, does that baby have fat pulkes!"

Pumpernickel A dark bread that used to be made with unbolted rye and therefore was dense and moist, but is now a shadow of its former self: its dark tone comes from colorants such as coffee or cocoa.

Pupik The word literally means belly button: "He was naked down to his *pupik*." Or, "Her blouse was so short, it exposed her *pupik*." But, in the case of poultry, it is a polite reference to the fatty tail also known as "the Pope's nose." It can also be the gizzard.

Retes Hungarian strudel.

Ritach (page 13) This large black radish is a seasonal Passover vegetable sometimes grated into chopped liver. As *ritach mit tzibeleh*, grated black radish with chopped or grated onions mixed with shmaltz, it's a condiment to serve alongside chopped liver or spread on bread.

Rugelach (page 225) A bakery favorite also beloved by home bakers, these small filled pastries are traditionally rolled and formed into crescents, but these days are often made in a log for slicing, like strudel.

Schalet A synonym for kugel, derived from the Polish Yiddish word *schaltinose*, meaning pancake.

Schav (page 64) A cold summer soup made with sorrel, often served with a boiled potato and chopped raw vegetables, such as cucumber, scallions, and radishes.

Schmear A Yiddish term that is understood to mean, even by Latinos in New York City, a thin slathering of something, usually cream cheese, as in "I'll have a bagel with a schmear." You could also have a schmear of butter or, indeed, of anything spreadable. Used figuratively, schmear can also mean to tip someone on the sly, as in "In order to get a table, you'll have to schmear the maitre d'." In other words, slather his hand with money.

Schnapps High-alcohol beverages, such as brandy, rye, Scotch, or blended whiskey, traditionally served at a kiddish, but also drunk simply for pleasure. At Purim, it is written, you should get so drunk that you can't tell the difference between the name Haman, the villain of the story, and Mordechai, the hero.

Schtikel A little piece, as in "a *schtikel* pickle" or "give me a *schtikel* of bread."

Shlishkas (page 81) Small potato dumplings, identical to Italian gnocchi, usually served with breadcrumbs fried in schmaltz or butter, but also with caramelized cabbage and/or pot cheese and sour cream, or as a dessert with breadcrumbs and sugar.

Shochet The man trained and authorized to perform kosher slaughter.

Slivovitz A fruit brandy, a spirit distilled from plums, that is a favorite of Ashkenazic Jews. It was and is a popular drink for Passover, when spirits distilled from grain, such as whiskey, are forbidden, but those from fruit are allowed.

Tam Pronounced "tom," it refers to a depth of flavor that can only be described as soulful.

Trayf Foods forbidden by the Jewish dietary laws. See *Kosher*.

Tzibeleh Yiddish for "onions," preferably cooked until dark brown and caramelized (Smothered Onions, page 7), but also sprinkled on breads and added raw to salads.

Tzimmes (page 97) Literally, "a fuss," but also the word applied to a casserole of mixed ingredients, often sweet potatoes with prunes and meat, but also carrots with honey and perhaps a piece of meat.

Vishniak A Polish alcoholic beverage made from cherries. Like slivovitz (see above), it is mostly popular at Passover, when grain-based spirits are forbidden.

Yoich Translates as "gravy," but it is most commonly used as the word for the jellied broth made from calf's feet in the dish called P'tcha (page 27) or the jellied broth resulting from making Gefilte Fish (page 31).

Zemmel Flat onion rolls (see page 215).

✣ Acknowledgments ✣

Cookbooks aren't written in isolation, like novels. The writer-cook needs eaters, tasters, kitchen assistance, dishwashers, pot scrubbers, encouragement, criticism…help. For this book in particular, I am very thankful for and grateful to two grandmothers and a grandfather who loved to cook and liked to enlist me as help in their kitchens. My maternal grandmother, Brooklyn-born Elsie Binder Sonkin, lived in the same two-family house in Brooklyn where I lived with my parents and sister, so she naturally was the biggest influence on me. And she was a superb Yiddishe cook. Proof is that our neighbors and friends always asked for her recipes and advice. My Manhattan-born paternal grandmother, Rose Cohen Schwartz, claimed she couldn't even boil an egg ("burl" an egg, in her heavy New York accent) until she married my also native New Yorker grandfather, Bernard (Barney) Schwartz, who had been a professional chef before they met, and in the food business one way or another after they married. But Rosie was also a wonderful cook, and she taught me many things. Among other things, Barney taught me knife skills and kitchen discipline at an age when I shouldn't have been touching a blade or lighting a stove. My maternal grandfather, Louis Sonkin, an electrical contractor, didn't cook at all, but, boy, could he criticize. I like to say I was born with a wooden spoon in my mouth. "Taste this Arthur. More salt? More pepper?" It's no wonder I became a food editor, restaurant critic, food writer, and cooking teacher.

Although my mother, Sydell, was a good cook, she didn't really like to do it. On the other hand, she had a great appreciation for food and the bonding rituals of the table. And she loved to go to restaurants. My father was food-obsessed. It is from him that I learned to be a food adventurer, to seek out new food experiences and to appreciate everything, from the lowest to the highest. Eating in a Chinatown kitchen with ducks hanging and dripping fat from the ceiling was Larry's idea of heaven, but he also liked to check out the new restaurants in Manhattan.

For the last thirty years, I have been consulting and commiserating on life and food nearly daily with Rozanne Gold. She is a chef, cookbook writer, and as good a friend as a man could ever want. Michael Whiteman, her husband and a leading restaurant consultant and restaurateur, has a taste memory for Yiddish food that goes just a little bit further back than mine. I consulted his palate on numerous occasions. I also have to thank my dear friend, and coincidentally my cousin, Erica Marcus, for her wisdom about people and life, publishing and food. She is the food feature writer for *Newsday* on Long Island, and a former cookbook editor. We figure we share more genes than do most second cousins. Andy Port, executive editor of the *New York Times Magazine*, is another lifeline, my lifelong friend as well as my "dial-an-editor." Max Gross, her son and my godson, the Hapless Jewish Writer, gives me *naches* (prideful joy) every day, and is one of my best tasters.

Carole Walter, one of our country's best baking teachers and an award-winning cookbook writer, is my advisor about all things baked and sweet. George Greenstein, a Jewish baker from way back, is my invaluable resource about all things yeasty. Ann (Annarosa) Amendolara Nurse is my "Barese mamma," as she calls herself. She is another cooking advisor. Her food is southern Italian, not Yiddish, but, being Brooklyn-born, she's eaten plenty of matzo balls in her long life.

John Capalbo, a friend of more than thirty years, has just begun to help me test recipes, but his hands are visible in this book, and his expertise as a baker was very helpful. My good friend Avi Keller, who is a member of the Chabad Lubovitch community in Brooklyn and is a professional *mashgiach*, helped make sure that my kashruth and other religious matters were all correct.

I am very fortunate to be surrounded by many people who care about me. Above all, my life partner of more than twenty-five years, Bob Harned, who keeps me grounded (well, he tries his best), plus he is an eagle-eye proofreader. My sister, Andrea, and her adult children, Rachel and Brian, are always beside me. This book is dedicated to them.

The team at Ten Speed Press made this the smoothest publishing experience I have ever had. I am indebted to Lorena Jones, Ten Speed's publisher, who was so enthusiastic about this project; to Clancy Drake, my editor, who made all systems run smoothly and without hysteria, and who is a total mensch, to use a word she now likes to use herself; to Nancy Austin, Ten Speed's design director, who supervised the photo shoot (in my apartment); and to Chloe Rawlins for her beautiful design. Thanks, too, to Ben Fink, for his superb photography, and Megan Fawn Schlow, the food stylist with whom I so enjoyed playing in the kitchen.

❧ Index ❧